# Traveling with Service Animals

# Traveling with Service Animals

## By Air, Road, Rail, and Ship across North America

Henry Kisor and Christine Goodier

**UNIVERSITY OF ILLINOIS PRESS**
Urbana, Chicago, and Springfield

© 2019 by the Board of Trustees
of the University of Illinois
All rights reserved
1 2 3 4 5 C P 5 4 3 2 1
∞ This book is printed on acid-free paper.

Library of Congress Control Number: 2019014752

*To Dogs for Better Lives*
*for bringing Raylene and Trooper into ours*
*and to all service dogs from coast to coast*

# Contents

# Preface: Why This Book?

Over the last few years, the numbers of trained service animals in the United States and Canada have exploded. No one knows exactly how many there are—estimates have ranged from as few as 10,000 to as many as 385,000—but the number is undoubtedly growing by leaps and bounds as people with disabilities increasingly discover the usefulness of service animals.

Guide dogs for people who are blind and visually impaired as well as hearing dogs for those who are deaf and hard of hearing have been around for decades. Newer assistance dogs (another term for service dogs) help those with mobility challenges by turning on lights, fetching items from the pantry, pulling wheelchairs, opening doors, and performing other everyday tasks.

Still other service dogs alert people with diabetes to abnormal sugar levels, respond to people with epilepsy during seizures, and prevent children with autism from harmful actions. PTSD dogs sense when veterans and others dealing with post-traumatic stress disorder are suffering and help them through psychiatric difficulties. Research is presently being done into whether service dogs can assist people living with Alzheimer's disease.

Henry Kisor's hearing dog, Trooper, on the quay at San Juan, Puerto Rico, after going ashore from the cruise ship behind him. (Photograph by Henry Kisor)

Service dogs come in all sizes. Chihuahuas make excellent hearing dogs. Great Danes help their handlers pull themselves up to a standing position and support them while walking.

Miniature horses (the other federally recognized service animal species in the United States) can do almost everything big dogs do, and live four times longer. Many people with allergies, religious aversions, or difficulty in coping with the death of beloved dogs prefer these animals.

There is almost no limit to what service animals can do, and new jobs for them are being discovered every day.

## Exactly What Is a Service or Assistance Dog?

Let's get one thing straight: According to the U.S. Department of Justice, a *service dog* is "any dog that is *individually trained* to do work or perform tasks for the benefit of an individual living with a disability, including

a physical, sensory, psychiatric, intellectual, or other mental disability"
(italics ours). The Canadian provinces have similar definitions.

Proper terminology for these animals is still evolving. Instead of the
umbrella term "service dog," the influential International Association of
Assistance Dog Partners as well as several other such groups are working
for the adoption of "assistance dog," further breaking that into "guide
dog" for the blind, "hearing dog" for the deaf, and "service dog" for all
other disabilities.

As a nod to widespread usage and to avoid confusion, however, this
book employs the generic "service dog" or "service animal." Those are
what the federal government still calls them, and those are what the
general public and the transportation industry presently understand.

These dogs are most often trained by nonprofit organizations, but
in the United States they also can be the products of independent
professional trainers or amateurs training their own dogs to perform
tasks to help with a disability. In some Canadian provinces, service
animals must be trained by approved schools in order to be government certified for access to public venues such as restaurants. Those
trained by their owners or private individuals are not always certified
for public access. (Alberta and British Columbia, however, have programs to allow dogs schooled by owners or private trainers to take a
qualification test.)

By both U.S. and Canadian provincial law, handlers have the right to
take their service dogs anywhere the public is allowed—hotels, motels,
campgrounds, museums, libraries, shops, grocery stores, restaurants,
hospitals, airplanes, trains, buses, and taxis, with very few exceptions,
such as operating rooms, restaurant kitchens, and swimming pools.

Those classified as emotional support or comfort dogs, therapy dogs,
or companion animals are *not* service dogs. Nor are untrained animals
fraudulently claimed as service dogs.

In the United States, a public entity is permitted to ask only two
questions: (1) Is that a service dog required to help with a disability?
(2) What task does the dog perform? A hotelier, cab driver, or restaurant
greeter cannot ask what the handler's disability is—that would be an

intrusion into health privacy. Nor can registration or training papers be demanded. No identification such as a certification card or service animal vest is necessary (although it's often a good idea, and chapter 1, "The Basics," explains why).

In some Canadian provinces, service dogs must wear identifying vests or harnesses, and in other provinces, their handlers must carry government ID cards. Public entities can ask for documentary proof of disability on the human's part and proof of the dog's training by an accredited school, and this varies from province to province.

This book is not a dog training manual but is designed to aid handlers with dogs already working with well-established obedience and assistance skills. Many U.S. citizens and Canadians with disabilities want to travel but are unsure how they can do so with their service animals. This book is for them, for their families and friends, for those contemplating acquiring service dogs, for their trainers—and for those in the travel industry who want to know how best to serve their canine customers.

Needless to say, this book and its anecdotes are also for dog lovers who like a tale well (cough) wagged.

Concerns for medical privacy are the reason we do not discuss the disabilities of the service dog handlers we quote in this book, nor do we use the full names of some of them or reveal where they live. For many if not most partners of service animals, their disabilities are a highly sensitive personal issue. As for us, our animals were trained by Dogs for Better Lives (formerly Dogs for the Deaf) in Central Point, Oregon, and you can draw your own conclusions about that.

Pack your bags, leash your pups, and let's go.

*Henry Kisor and Christine Goodier*

# Traveling with Service Animals

## Chapter 1

# The Basics

● **Henry:** Never be shy about traveling with a service dog.

While planning a cruise with a port call in Cartagena, Colombia, I emailed the National Aviary of Colombia to see if it would allow my hearing dog Trooper to visit on a guided tour from the ship. Ordinarily I'd avoid taking a dog to such a biologically sensitive venue, even though I'm an avid bird photographer. Comments on the Internet, however, suggested to me that the park featured several small protected enclosures with a path winding around them. It seemed that Trooper might be able to wait outside the enclosures with my wife, Debby, while I went in with a camera. The encouraging Spanish-accented response:

> We are happy that you are coming to visit us and we want to offer the best possible experience for you and your service dog. You will be the first person with service dog that visits us, and since dogs are predators to birds, the behavior of the birds will change. We have three immersion aviaries where the dog will have to stay outside. We will make sure one of our employees is with you at

*all times. If you can tell us what is your disability so we can plan
something to help you, that will be great.*

*We want to know your expectations, and what kind of experi-
ence you want to have during your visit so we can fulfill them to
the best of our ability.*

That certainly was friendly. Even friendlier was the reception
when Trooper, Debby, and I finally arrived. A tall young Colombian
veterinary student named Bernest Castro Arrieta was assigned as
our minder, to yank us out of trouble if trouble appeared. It turned
out that a single long path wound *through*, not around, the linked
"immersion aviaries" through which visitors could walk, but we were
not asked to stay outside.

Bernest was as solicitous of Trooper as he was of the birds. The
temperature was in the humid midnineties and the white gravel
path reflected the heat, so the young vet hopeful not only made sure
Trooper had plenty of water but also examined the pads of his paws
to make sure they were not burned.

As for the birds, they ignored Trooper, and Trooper ignored them ...
until the party arrived at an outdoor pen, protected from tourists by
metal webbing, where several huge emus ruled the roost. Upon spot-
ting Trooper in our party, the emus erupted in anger and followed,
honking all the way, as Bernest hustled us down the path and out of
sight.

Afterward many photographs of us were taken, some by the
delighted aviary staff, the latter presumably for publicity purposes.
The staff was not bothered by the emus' reaction to Trooper—those
birds can be cantankerous—but were more concerned about the
dog's well-being. (He didn't seem to mind.) The lesson: Even if a visit
somewhere may not at first sound like a good idea, investigate. You
might be surprised.

Traveling with your dog in the beginning of your partnership may
seem daunting, but there's a world of wonderful experience waiting as

long as you're unafraid to push the envelope—and are willing to plan ahead to do so.

Start by setting up small-scale practice sessions closer to home so you and the dog will be comfortably prepared when you pack your bags for a bucket-list adventure. Some dog partners take their animals on what sailors call "shakedown cruises" in airports and restaurants, aboard planes, trains, and ships, and in resorts and hotels to help their dogs become more travel-ready.

One such proactive handler is Dianne Urhausen, a Californian whose dog, Henri, was trained by Canine Companions for Independence, a nationwide organization headquartered in Santa Rosa, California. Urhausen exposed her partner early on to an assortment of real-world travel situations with a few short trips before their first cruise together through the Panama Canal.

"I wanted to make sure that flying would not be an issue, so we flew to Las Vegas to see how she did on a short two-hour flight from San Francisco," Urhausen said. "I also took her on a ferry ride to test her

Dianne Urhausen took her assistance dog, Henri, to Disneyland to see how she handled crowds and hotel stays. (Photo by Peter Urhausen)

sea legs and to Disneyland to see how she handled crowds and staying in a hotel for a few days."

Melanie, an Arizonan who has traveled extensively with her hearing dog, Paddington, a Labradoodle trained by Diamond Dogz of Arizona, also tested the waters before making long expeditions. "We started out with road trips from Phoenix to Chicago, and those all went well," she said. From that modest beginning, the team went on to make dozens of airline flights together for business or pleasure.

If you are nervous about leaving home for an extended period, it's reassuring to remember that travel includes many of the same challenges that you learned how to handle at the start of your partnership.

"Have a leash that attaches to you in some way to eliminate 'dropped leash' panic attacks," said Flo Kiewel, a Montanan who has traveled with her hearing dog by car, taxi, bus, train, and plane. "Yes, hearing dogs are very well trained, but they are still dogs and can be startled by a sudden loud noise or wander off while you doze," she said. Both her

Flo Kiewel and her hearing dog, AJ, have traveled together by car, taxi, bus, train, and plane. (Photo courtesy Flo Kiewel)

cocker spaniels, first Midnight and now AJ, were trained by International Hearing Dog of Henderson, Colorado.

Rock climbing carabiners clipped to belts and leashes are a good way to secure your dog if you need both hands for maneuvering your luggage or possessions.

Then there are curious fellow travelers, who may or may not be distracting. "Be prepared for lots of questions," said Jen from Connecticut, whose dog, Emmy, a yellow Labrador retriever, was trained by NEADS World Class Service Dogs in Princeton, Massachusetts. "People everywhere will want to know all about the dog."

Finally, don't forget that the trainer who has worked closely with you and your dog can be a rich source of suggestions if you have worries or questions about things you and your dog may encounter as you travel. Similarly, this book will help service dog handlers foresee almost anything that might occur while traveling on an airplane, a train, a cruise

Melanie and Paddington, here seen at the Museum of the Dog (then near St. Louis, Missouri, now in New York City), have traveled all over the United States and have made forty-five flights together. (Photo courtesy of Melanie)

Jen, who travels with her service dog, Emmy, warns other teams to be prepared for lots of questions. (Photo courtesy of Jen)

ship, during an auto or RV trip, on a bus ride, and even when using local public transportation.

## Keeping to a Schedule

Ideally, service dogs are supposed to be trained to eliminate on command. Some do and some don't. Knowing your dog's alimentary timetable, however, will help a great deal. If you're flying, taking the train, or riding a bus, it's almost imperative for the dog's comfort—and your convenience—that you look for ways to plan your days around the pooch's eating and eliminating schedules.

● **Henry:** I'm an early riser, so I take Trooper out for his morning pee at 6 a.m., feeding him immediately afterward. Between 8:30 and 9:30 a.m. we take a leisurely walk of several blocks around our neighborhood, during which he always poops.

At 3 p.m. we go out again for a few blocks, and I give him a chance to poop a second time if he wishes. Then he gets his supper at 3:30 p.m.

Between 8 and 8:30 p.m. we take the last pee walk of the day, a short one to the end of our block. Both of us are in our respective beds by 9 p.m.

During the first year of our partnership I tried to follow this schedule almost to the minute, and it paid dividends: Trooper soon came to learn that certain things were expected of him at certain times of the day. This is not "going on command," but it comes reasonably close, and I try to stick to this schedule when we are traveling.

## Using Relief Stations

For service dogs, major airports are supposed to provide indoor post-security relief stations—large wooden or plastic boxes filled with artificial grass—and some do, although many pet relief areas are still outside and must be used before going through security. Cruise ships typically provide three-foot-by-four-foot wooden enclosures filled with turf or mulch on a protected outside deck. (There are no such things in urban railroad stations except for the Union Depot in St. Paul, Minnesota.) If your dog hasn't met one of those artificial facilities before, there might be a few embarrassing moments until the idea sinks in. Training your dog well in advance of travel to use such boxes could be a good idea.

**Henry:** Two years ago, my wife, Debby, and I decided to celebrate our fiftieth wedding anniversary by taking a two-week Alaskan cruise. Would Trooper take to the shipboard potty easily? There isn't anywhere else for a dog to transact business afloat. We figured he needed a few weeks of training.

And so one June day I constructed a sixteen-square-foot pine box in the back yard of our summer cabin in the woods, filling it with garden mulch and old leaves. I intended to lead Trooper to it on leash and say "Go potty!" while holding a treat out of sight. Sooner or later, he'd get the idea.

There was one flaw in that plan. Scores of chipmunks abound in the yard. Trooper is an energetic terrier, and terriers have extraordinarily high prey drives. Every time I took him out, he wanted to nail a 'munk, not learn a task. Weeks went by. I started to dream about being put ashore on a desert island because he peed on the captain's leg.

I decided to take the dog on a short Caribbean voyage in early November, an experiment to see if my efforts would somehow bear fruit. If they didn't, well, then Debby and I would just do something else for our fiftieth anniversary.

After we boarded and our luggage was stowed in our cabin, Trooper and I set out to find the relief box. Forward on the promenade deck, the front desk said.

Then came the moment of truth, the instant that would determine our future.

Without hesitation Trooper approached the box, gave it a healthy sniff, then stepped in and quickly lifted a leg. Good boy! And he was a good boy for the rest of the voyage.

Many travelers employ similar training techniques before exposing their dogs to airport or cruise ship relief stations. "Since I knew that we would be traveling with a service dog," Dianne Urhausen said, "one of the first things we did was to build a five-by-five relief box in our backyard with artificial turf and gravel drainage. Henri uses the box every day, and so using a relief box on a cruise ship was no big deal for her."

Then there are absorbent "belly bands" and "pee pads" of varying sizes, the latter large plastic-backed slabs. They were originally intended for housebreaking puppies but have been found to come in handy for adult dogs on long nonstop trips, such as a thirteen-hour flight from Chicago to Tokyo, or voyages on small cruise ships where relief areas need to be inside staterooms. Adult dogs must be trained to use these pads, and the training can take a while. (Female dogs are easier to train because they squat to pee, while male dogs tend to whiz in all directions.)

# Packing for a Trip

"Traveling with a service dog takes me back to the days of traveling with my kids," Urhausen said. "We need nap time and regular mealtimes, and must be careful not to have her out in the hot weather too long. Not to mention the suitcase full of her things that I must bring."

When you travel, always take along a "go bag" full of enough food, treats, toys, a sleeping pad or blanket, water, and poop bags to tide your dog over delays. Common carriers are not responsible for feeding and watering a service dog—you are.

Chapter 4 of this book, "On the Road," goes into more detail about what to take on a long RV or auto trip.

**Henry:** When going by train or ship, I'll pack most of Trooper's food in our suitcases, but I always carry a small backpack with three or four days' worth of kibble and munchies, and a bottle of water just in case. The backpack also has room for a couple of collapsible plastic bowls, a spare leash, and a small fleece baby blanket for Trooper to sleep on. If we're taking a long-distance car trip, a few days' rations is enough—we can always find a pet shop or farm feed store in most small towns.

Trooper is a small dog at eighteen pounds, so his supplies for a couple of weeks' traveling don't take up much room. I've heard, however, of service dog people with Labs and shepherds shipping ahead large boxes of provender to hotels or resorts by UPS or FedEx. Sometimes they or their companions drag along separate trunks of dog supplies.

**Chris:** At seventy pounds, my hearing dog, Raylene, is a typical hungry Labrador requiring her own suitcase for food, bowls, toys, training treats, first aid kit, grooming kit, and other supplies. I usually pack a roll of paper towels to mop up after dripping jowls. Her dry kibble is a veterinary prescription brand, not easily replaced, so I bring it all, along with the pill and powdered supplements she'll need for twice-daily meals. Before leaving home, I measure Raylene's feed-ings (plus plenty of extras) into zip-up plastic bags and bring along a spoon and measuring cup to whip up tasty chow with the addition of warm water. Food for three days goes into my carry-on bag just in case our luggage goes astray. A roll-up travel mat with a shoulder strap completes the paraphernalia she'll need to travel in comfort. ●

## You Can Take Your Dog Almost Anywhere, But . . .

As pointed out in the preface, the Americans with Disabilities Act declares that you can take your service dog just about anywhere the general public is allowed in the United States. In Canada, provincial laws allow the same.

Should your dog *always* accompany you everywhere? Your canine partner's safety and well-being are of paramount importance, of course, and *you* are in charge. "I make decisions about when it's appropriate or not to take the dog with me," said Suzy Wilburn, a Floridian who travels frequently with her guide dog, Carson. "His maturity and training level are also factors when considering a big trip. When he was two years old, it would not have happened." Carson, a yellow Labrador, was trained by Southeastern Guide Dogs in Palmetto, Florida, where Wilburn is direc-tor of admissions and alumni support.

There are places where even service animals are not welcome—and for good reason. An example is public swimming pools. Your dog can accompany you to poolside facilities such as snack bars, lounges, or chairs but for sanitary reasons must not go into the water. (Some public pools do have end-of-season doggie swims.)

As noted at the start of this chapter, zoos and other collections of wild animals may not be good destinations for service dogs, because canines are biologically a predatory species whose presence may upset the residents. Inquire before visiting. Some zoos provide kennels for service dogs so that their partners can enter and view restricted exhibits.

"I make decisions about when it's appropriate or not to take the dog with me," says Suzy Wilburn, who always keeps Carson's maturity and training level in mind when deciding on a trip. (Photo by Southeastern Guide Dogs)

**Henry:** When Trooper and I entered Chicago's Lincoln Park Zoo, a passing groundskeeper told me to go over to the information desk at the lion house and check in. "Then nobody will bother you," he said.

At the desk Trooper and I were given a "Service Animal Map" of the zoo grounds showing two spots forbidden to service dogs—the primate house and the farm in the zoo—and were sent off with cheery smiles while the desk people radioed the staff that a service animal was on the property.

All went without incident except at the snow leopard's outdoor enclosure. The big cat spotted Trooper as we walked by and became agitated. It paced along the fence, staring at the dog, and snarled, much as those emus did at the National Aviary of Colombia. Needless to say, we hurried away quickly.

There are other places that might not be hospitable to service dogs. Some modern museums feature exhibits constructed with twenty-first-century showmanship whose ultra-realistic high-tech special effects might frighten service dogs unaccustomed to, for instance, the chaos of war. "Living museums" such as Revolutionary War replica forts often employ musket fire whose sharp reports may be painful to dogs' ears. Before going to such places, inquire about "trigger warning" conditions that might not be good for dogs or sensitive humans. It might be best to leave your animal outside with a spouse or friend while you go inside.

● **Henry:** When Trooper and I visited the Abraham Lincoln Presidential Library Museum in Springfield, Illinois, we attended a multimedia theatrical production of the president's life that contained an almost overwhelming re-creation of a Civil War artillery barrage. The cannon flashes, explosions, and tactile shaking of the theater seats made us feel as if we had been caught on the battleground at Gettysburg. Trooper was frightened badly and quivered in my lap. After the noise of battle drifted away I decided to stick it out … until the assassin's fatal pistol shot at Ford's Theatre, a thunderclap that stunned me and spooked Trooper again. Had I known about the experience, I'd never have taken him inside. ●

## Checking In at U.S. Hotels

Whatever your mode of transportation and whatever venue you visit, you are likely to spend one or more nights in a hotel or motel. By law, of course, U.S. and Canadian hostelries must obey the rules and allow your service dog to stay in your room and accompany you to the breakfast room, fitness center, and other places guests are allowed except, of course, in the swimming pool or hot tub.

Melanie speaks for just about all service dog teams when she tells about her experiences with Paddington. "When I book hotels, I generally inform them, 'I am traveling with my hearing service dog,' although I do not need to do that," she said. "A hotel clerk in Palm Springs, California, responded, 'Pets are not allowed.' I replied, 'He is not a pet. He is my hearing service dog.' The clerk went to the manager, then came back and asked for identification. I said ADA regulations do not require service dog teams to show identification or any other paperwork. The clerk again went to her manager, then returned and said we could check in.

"Another hotel, this one in Florida, also asked for paperwork before they agreed to let us check in," Melanie reported. "I usually don't get aggressive—I'm just assertive with the ADA regulations. In the beginning, my husband often jumped in, and I had him to calm down."

● **Henry:** At check-in, a U.S. desk clerk may ask you to pay a pet fee or sign a formal "Service Dog Agreement" promising not to leave the dog alone in your room, to pick up waste, to pay for any damage the dog causes, etc. Such fees and agreements are illegal and should be gently rejected, perhaps with a request that a supervisor be called in.

When I am presented with such a document, I simply observe calmly that according to federal disability rules, the document is both gratuitous and discriminatory. It singles me out as a person with a disability and implies I cannot be trusted to control my animal responsibly, and that causes me distress. Besides, the normal contract between a guest and a hotel already provides for reimbursement for damage.

The underlying argument is simple. A service animal is not a pet but essentially a four-footed medical aid. A hotel wouldn't ask a guest with an oxygen tank to sign an agreement of liability. Nor should it when the guest brings a service dog. ●

## It's a Good Idea to Call Ahead

One lesson we've drawn from all our travels that can be applied across almost all modes of transportation (and overnight stays) is this: Call ahead to the airline, railroad, cruise company, bus line, hotel, or campground and let them know you are bringing a service dog. In Canada that's a must.

Diane Munro, who travels with her hearing dog, Valley, recommends giving venues advance notice that you will be bringing a service animal. (Photo courtesy of Diane Munro)

"Always give the company you're booking with advance notice that you are bringing a service animal and let them know what accommodations you need," said Diane Munro, who lives in Michigan and travels with her hearing dog, Valley, a Labrador trained by Dogs for Better Lives. "This will hopefully avoid any negative treatment on the day of travel."

Suzy Wilburn also advocates planning ahead. "We coach our graduates about taking cruises," she said. She recommends that they keep things positive and approach the cruise lines with a cooperative attitude of "Let me inform you of what's happening so we can work together."

Whatever the mode of travel, a notation about your service animal will be made on the daily customer log or transportation manifest, and the staff or crews will be ready for you, sometimes even giving you better service because they know you have a disability—and a means to deal with it, often relieving them of the responsibility.

● **Chris:** When it comes to notifying American hotels in advance, not all service dog handlers agree, fearing the hotel might assign the team an undesirable room. I have never noticed any difference in room quality. Advising the hotel in advance is not a legal requirement, so it's your option. You can always ask that the room be changed if it's not satisfactory. ●

Be patient when you book hotel rooms, airline flights, or train or bus tickets in Canada or the United States. Many inexperienced lower-level ticket and customer service agents may never have handled bookings from service dog teams, and out of honest ignorance may ask questions and, in the United States, demand documentation not permitted by the

Chris Goodier and hearing dog Raylene walked across Canada's border to Niagara Falls during an RV road trip. (Photo by Robert Goodier)

ADA. Often these agents are based offshore, have no knowledge about U.S. and Canadian service dog law, and sometimes will haughtily tell you that "pets are not allowed." In these cases, just ask for a supervisor. A calm and reasonable demeanor often will win over the ignorant or skeptical.

## Canada Travel

In Canada, provincial laws also give service dog teams the right to stay in hotels, but some provinces also give hotels the right to ask for documentary proof that your dog is a service dog (such as a certificate from an approved training organization) and that you are a person with a disability (a membership card from a disability organization or a note from your doctor). Often hotel reservation people won't demand anything, but paperwork might educate an uninformed desk clerk when you check in.

Sometimes the papers demanded may sound unrealistic to U.S. citizens. Some Canadian transportation entities, for instance, may ask for a letter from your doctor attesting that you are *unable to travel* without

Jean M.'s toy Pomeranian, Cha-Cha, waiting to board VIA Rail's *Canadian* at Toronto Union Station. (Photo by Henry Kisor)

a service dog, especially if you want a human assistance companion as well. Of course, not all service dogs are responsible for our lives—many are intended to make them safer and easier. If, however, U.S. citizens traveling in Canada ask for a supervisor, they'll very likely meet success if they proffer a copy of an ID card from their dog's training establishment.

Jean M. of Ontario had her service dog Cha-Cha—an impossibly cute four-pound toy Pomeranian—trained privately, but tested and certified by the government-approved Thames Centre Service Dogs. Cha-Cha wears a vest from that organization with "Service Dog" on one side and "*Chien d'Assistance*" on the other. She alerts her partner by either barking three times in measured cadence, stepping on her toes, or drumming her back feet on Jean's chest.

Tom M., Jean's husband, says Canadian service dog teams face the same problems as Americans do, including official cluelessness and occasional challenges in public venues, in the province of Quebec in particular. In his experience, service dogs do not appear to be widely recognized in Quebec society, with the notable exception of guide dogs for the blind. (Quebec does have access laws for all service dogs.)

"When traveling in Quebec," Tom said, "we have noticed that the term 'MIRA' seems to be used as a popular general term for a service dog. MIRA is an organization in Quebec that trains service dogs. [The nonprofit also has a U.S. counterpart.] Cha-Cha has been challenged by people in public spaces and public services in Quebec with the statement, 'She's not MIRA.' So as we call a vacuum bottle a Thermos, a bandage a Band-Aid, and facial tissue Kleenex, service dogs are often called 'MIRA' in Quebec."

(The name, by the way, has its origins as the nickname of a female Labrador named Mirabelle, who was one of the first two guide dogs trained by Éric St-Pierre, a Québécois who named his foundation in her honor. Only later did M. St-Pierre realize that "Mira" is an imperative of the Spanish verb "look"—and "la mira" is the noun for "sight.")

A young Québécoise named Najawarie concurs with Jean and Tom. Her service dog, Moon Moon, is an *Altdeutscher Schäferhund* (Old

German Shepherd Dog in English), a long-haired version of the German shepherd, and was trained in France by Psy'chien, a psychiatric service dog organization.

"Even bus drivers and public transportation workers often expect a person with a service dog to be blind or the dog to wear a red MIRA vest," she said. "If you are not blind and your dog's vest isn't red, be prepared for an occasional access challenge when you want to take public transportation.

"Staying polite and explaining things usually works well," Najawarie said. Most of the time I'll say, 'It's a service dog, and training associations and disability organizations can use different colors.' Do carry identification to prove that your dog has been professionally trained and that you belong to a disability organization." It may be helpful for U.S. citizens to obtain a letter from a physician attesting to their disabilities.

## Mexico Travel

As for the third North American country, Mexico is not particularly friendly to service dogs, at least officially. It recently passed a number of disability rights laws, but their implementation has been slow and spotty. Except in Mexico City, there is no law governing service dogs at all, let alone their access rights. They are treated as pets, and taking them over the U.S. border to Mexico requires care with the paperwork as outlined below.

Many Mexican hotels, resorts, restaurants, and tour bus companies that cater to Americans and Canadians *may* welcome service dogs. Always call ahead and ask, just to forestall disappointment on checking in.

## Essential Documents for Travel in North America

Carry a copy of your dog's rabies vaccination certificate wherever you go, even if it's just to the next state or province. Many airlines require proof of rabies inoculation. Service dogs must always follow state and local health regulations. In the United States, a good source of information is the U.S. Department of Agriculture's Animal and Plant Health Inspection Service (APHIS), responsible for protecting animal health and welfare as well as the international export of live animals, including pets such as dogs and cats, for the United States. Its website is https://www.aphis.usda.gov/aphis/pet-travel, and this book refers to it frequently.

The corresponding office in Canada is the Canadian Food Inspection Agency (CFIA) (https://www.inspection.gc.ca/), that country's federal department responsible for issuance of health certificates for animals traveling abroad. The Canadian Transportation Agency, or CTA (http://www.otc-cta.gc.ca/eng/service-animals), is another source of health certificate information for Canadians with service dogs who want to travel inside and outside the country. It also has a link to the Canadian Food Inspection Agency's animal health certificates.

An APHIS Form 7001 International Animal Health Certificate attesting to your dog's well-being and immunizations and signed by a licensed veterinarian, or the Canadian version of the document, is almost essential if you take your service dog out of the United States or Canada. Whenever the Form 7001 is mentioned in this book, the Canadian International Health Certificate for Dogs and Cats is its equivalent.

For travel from the United States through Canada, as well as bringing a proof of rabies immunization, it's a good idea to take along an APHIS Form 7001, though it is not strictly necessary.

Elsewhere it might be vital. For instance, if you suddenly suffer a health emergency aboard a cruise ship in the Caribbean, the captain might put you ashore at a country not scheduled on the itinerary in order for you to fly home for treatment. Having a Form 7001 for your dog might avoid trouble if you have no papers specific for that country.

For Mexico, you must carry a bilingual version of the Form 7001 signed by an APHIS-accredited vet and endorsed (as that country requires) by an APHIS Veterinary Medical Officer. The form must be filled in (no abbreviations; words spelled out entirely) either with a computer or typewriter—Mexico will not accept handwriting. The dog must be immunized not only against rabies but also against leptospirosis, distemper, and hepatitis.

Travelers coming from the United States to Mexico have a second option for dogs, a bilingual health certificate imprinted on an accredited vet's letterhead, with template language provided by Mexico. The certificate must also be typed without abbreviations. It does not need to be countersigned by an APHIS official.

You'll find detailed information about working with an APHIS accredited vet, these two forms, and other destination documentation in chapter 6, "That Annoying Paperwork."

## Service Dog Identification

If a professional organization trained your dog, it very likely will have given you a certificate attesting to the training as well as ID cards and a special vest identifying the dog's status. None of this is required by ADA rules in the United States, although it is in some Canadian provinces, but in case of difficulty and especially in foreign countries, the more official paperwork you have to establish your dog's bona fides, the better. Florida resident David Caras, whose black Labrador, Bobb, was trained by Southeastern Guide Dogs, agrees.

"Although papers, ID cards, and service dog vests are not legally required for a service dog, almost nobody knows this, and will probably refuse service or access unless you have at least the service dog vest," said Caras, who has made more than twenty flights with Bobb.

Some Americans with disabilities traveling in the United States with service dogs want the letter of the ADA followed and prefer not to carry certificates of any kind (except for rabies immunizations) or dress their animals in identifying vests. This is their right. For privacy's sake, some people do not want their disabilities advertised. Others would rather forestall any difficulty by using bright ID vests and certificates from their dogs' trainers.

Bobb, a Labrador trained by Southeastern Guide Dogs, has flown more than twenty times with his partner, David Caras, pictured here with David's niece, Natalie Chapman. (Photo by Barbara E. Chapman)

**Henry:** For travel in the United States and elsewhere, Trooper wears an official City of Evanston (Illinois) municipal tag on his collar identifying him as a service dog. His orange vest from Dogs for Better Lives also bears an official State of Michigan registered service animal patch, and I carry two ID cards. One is from Dogs for Better Lives certifying Trooper's training, and another identifies both of us as Michigan-registered. As is the Evanston tag, that state's plan is entirely voluntary, and the official patch has been useful in dealing with trouble not only in Michigan but also everywhere else in the United States.

Some service dog people, however, justly complain that business owners in Michigan may come to expect service dogs to wear that patch and may banish those who don't, even though the Americans with Disabilities Act says service dog teams cannot be asked for identification. I understand their point of view. Years ago I was happy that my disability was invisible. It helped protect me from strangers who would take advantage of weakness.

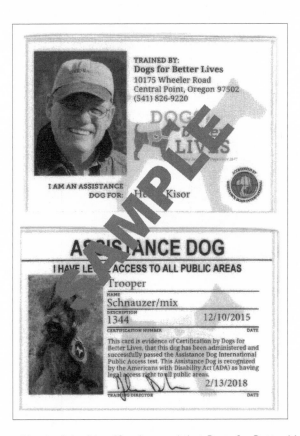

The front and back of the identification card that Dogs for Better Lives issues its clients. The certification may have legal weight in Oregon, but not in the rest of the United States. Nonetheless, though such identification is not required by the Americans with Disabilities Act, the card may persuade a reluctant manager of a public venue such as a restaurant that the dog and handler are a legitimate service animal team. (Dogs for Better Lives, formerly Dogs for the Deaf)

Today, however, I don't mind people being aware that I'm deaf. I'm a septuagenarian with a bad back and am sometimes wobbly on my pins, and a dog with a bright orange vest gives a warning heads-up not only to passersby on a crowded sidewalk but also to drivers in the street. So does the rollator—a four-wheeled walker with hand brakes—that I often use when walking more than a city block or so.

The voluntary State of Michigan service dog registration program with ID card and patch may help establish a genuine service animal's status in public venues, but it is controversial in the service dog industry. (State of Michigan)

Another good reason for care with identification is that it could come in handy for a service dog team traveling solo if the human partner should suffer an incapacitating accident or illness. First responders need to know what to do with the dog while its partner is taken to the hospital—and I've wondered about that, since Trooper and I often travel by ourselves.

Deborah Guy, a professional staff member in the School of Social Work at Marywood University in Scranton, Pennsylvania, knows of one incident in which an automobile accident victim and dog were airlifted to a hospital emergency department. The hospital social worker "was called in, checked for emergency contacts, and phoned them. The social worker stayed in the patient's room and took care of the dog until the patient went into surgery, then kept the dog with her until the emergency contact arrived. She even took the dog with her on her rounds in the dialysis unit."

Sometimes only a name and phone number is all that is needed for an emergency contact. But a wallet card or a typed memo specifying what to do with the dog—take it to a boarding vet, an animal shelter, or a friendly private home until the emergency contact arrives—might give a human partner further peace of mind. Such a document could be carried in a wallet or a purse, with a copy in the dog's vest pocket where first responders can easily see it.

Guy suggested that the information also be placed in the medical ID app on the handler's smartphone, so that it can be accessed without using a password. For example:

> Uses service dog. In the event of incapacitation please call wife Deborah at [phone number] and make arrangements for temporary boarding of the dog at a veterinarian or animal shelter until the emergency contact arrives or the medical situation is resolved.

Gilding the lily? Would the phone numbers on a dog's collar tags be enough? Maybe, but an excess of information never hurts.

# Your Dog's Best Behavior

It's a memorable day when your dog's trainers certify your team for public access and hand you the leash. But it's also the day when you become solely responsible (gulp!) for reinforcing your dog's obedience training. "It's a two-way street," said Suzy Wilburn. "You have to be a responsible handler if you want respect."

Internationally accepted guidelines specify that, in public, a well-behaved service dog:

- Does not pee or poop in inappropriate places.
- Does not beg for attention with the general public.
- Does not whine, growl, or bark unnecessarily.
- Does not show aggression to other dogs or people.
- Does not solicit or steal food from people.
- Does work calmly and quietly on leash.
- Does lie quietly beside the handler without blocking aisles or doorways.
- Does pee and poop on command. (Good luck with that.)

All are sensible rules, and your dog should, of course, respond appropriately to commands to stay out of trouble.

**Chris:** Service dog organizations are expert in selecting dogs with appropriate temperaments to serve people with specific disabilities. Guide dogs paired with blind or visually impaired partners typically are off duty when the harness comes off, while some dogs must be on the job twenty-four hours a day and are chosen for their high energy levels. Hearing dog Raylene, for example, once awakened me at 3 a.m. at the sound of a tornado a few miles from my house, and another time alerted me to a door knock in the middle of the night aboard a ship. But her high energy paired with a cheerful Labrador personality means she may be more interested in interacting with friendly people, when she has my permission, than a guide dog in harness would be.

● **Henry:** Trooper, a lively miniature schnauzer-poodle mix, does his hearing dog job almost perfectly. He boasts a 95 percent success rate at alerting me to the ring of my captioned telephone, jumping up on me wherever I may be in the condo and leading me to my office. He does the same for the doorbell, the blare of my smartphone alarm clock, the screech of the hallway fire alarm, the beep of my Instant Pot, even the call of my name from another room. His trainer also put him through his paces and observed our teamwork outside our home before declaring him fit for public access.

Phenomenal he may be, but he is first and foremost a *dog*. At lunchtime aboard ship during an early cruise together, we were making our way through the crowded buffet when, to allow a plate-laden fellow passenger to pass, I stepped aside and took my attention off Trooper for a quick moment. At that instant a waiter pushed a large multitiered cart full of desserts past us. The lowest shelf, laden with pies and tarts, was conveniently at Trooper's head height, and . . .

I was mortified. There were witnesses, both passengers and crew. But the captain never did summon us before the mast for a tongue-lashing.

Of course Trooper's food snatching violated a cardinal rule of service dog behavior, and he needed a round of firm retraining.       ●

No matter how highly trained they may be, dogs will sometimes be dogs, and their human partners should do their best to keep a weather eye out while traveling for situations that could lead to breaches in behavior.

The authors of this book, like most service dog partners, know that dogs are not robots controlled by buttons and switches. At times their partners live in fear that their animal, like a small child, will misbehave at absolutely the wrong time—and the dogs can pick up on that feeling of tension. Relax. If dogs blunder, that's the real world they live in. Simply recover and keep on keeping on—and keep working on the dog's training.

Service dogs are everywhere, even on motorcycles. This superbly trained boxer in Juneau, Alaska, would not budge from his perch on the bike while his partner, a combat veteran, sat within view at an outdoor coffee shop. When asked what the dog does for him, the vet said simply, "He takes care of me at night." (Photo by Henry Kisor)

## What to Expect in This Book

The following pages will help any service dog handler prepare for a trip in the United States or Canada, or elsewhere in North America. Chapter 2, "In the Air," treats airline travel. Chapter 3, "Riding the Rails," tells how to handle journeys on long-distance trains. Chapter 4, "On the Road," explores RV, automobile, and bus travel. Chapter 5, "Sailing the Seas," covers voyaging aboard cruise liners. Chapter 6, "That Annoying Paperwork," has been left for last for obvious reasons. Appendixes cover fine details.

# Summing Up

- Take trial runs to give your dog a little experience before an ambitious trip.
- Mind your dog's relief habits; keep to a schedule and train the dog to use a relief box.
- Prepare a "go bag" of food and meds suitable for the trip you're taking.
- Be wise about where you take your dog.
- Know the law and be ready to defend your presence.
- Call ahead to hotels, restaurants, airlines, and so forth, and let them know you are bringing a service dog.
- Carry a current rabies certificate and, if traveling outside the United States or Canada, at least an APHIS Form 7001 International Health Certificate or the Canadian International Health Certificate for Dogs and Cats.
- Carry ID cards, if your dog's training organization has issued them, and dress your dog in an identifying vest.
- Make sure your dog obeys all accepted service animal behavioral standards—and be ready to retrain him if he slips.

## Chapter 2

# In the Air

For some service animal teams, the hairiest part of flying is not in making reservations, going to the airport, finding a place to pee your animal, walking down the jetway, getting the animal placed at your feet, or settling into your seat to enjoy or endure the flight.

Sometimes the toughest row to hoe is getting yourself and your partner through the Transportation Security Agency (TSA) gauntlet—especially if you are older and have any metal in your body, such as knee replacements. Most people who trigger the metal detector will just get wanded, but if they also arrive with service dogs or miniature horses, they and their animals almost certainly will get the intimate full-monty pat-down, for that's the rule. Obtaining TSA PreCheck status (https://www.tsa.gov/precheck) helps a great deal. If you don't have PreCheck, it's not a bad idea to ask for a pat-down as soon as you arrive at the security gate with metal and dog. That's TSA's own rule anyway, though some agents may be unaware of it.

● **Henry:** The first time I flew with Trooper, I planned things poorly.

Our cruise ship had just tied up at the dock in Fort Lauderdale. It was 7 a.m., and my flight didn't leave until 2:45 p.m. Being the kind

Scout, a guide miniature horse, and his blind partner walk through Cincinnati/ Northern Kentucky Airport. Such horses often wear custom sneakers while traveling because steel horseshoes not only trigger security metal detectors but also damage wooden floors. (DanDee Shots/Wikimedia Commons)

of person who always has a nervous eye on the clock lest I miss my flight, I figured it was best to get to the airport early, hanging out in the first-class lounge until boarding time. Trooper could sleep, and I could get a little work done on the laptop.

We presented ourselves at the American Airlines ticket counter.

"Is *that* a service dog?" said the agent, skeptically eyeing the little terrier.

"He sure is," I responded. She shrugged and did not ask what service he performed for me. My breathy "deaf speech" was the tipoff.

"I see you're in first class," she said. "I'll give you a first row bulkhead seat. The plane is full, but there'll be plenty of space in front of your seat for the dog."

"Fine," I said. "Where's the first-class lounge, please?"

"We don't have one." My heart sank.

"Oh. Well, then, where's the dog relief area?" Trooper hadn't peed since using the relief box on the ship early that morning.

"Outside," she said, pointing through the entry doors to a grassy spot across the vehicle ramp.

"There isn't one after security?" I said.

"Nope," she said.

"So if I go into the airport now and come back out later to relieve him, I'll have to go through security again?"

"Yep," she said.

"Damn," I said to myself. But there was no choice. I'd just have to make the best of it.

It was still early and the crowds hadn't yet arrived. After a pee outside, Trooper and I presented ourselves at the TSA security gate. I put my carry-on on the moving belt, removing my shoes and belt as I was directed, but forgetting to take out my laptop. Then I stepped up to the agent at the metal detector.

As I always had, I pointed to my ear and said, "First, I'm deaf." Then, "Second, I have knee replacements."

"Step through with your dog," the agent said.

"*Beep-beep-beep!*" The steel in my knees and Trooper's collar tags triggered the alarm.

"Step over here," said the agent. "We'll have to give you a body search. Do you want privacy?"

"Naw," I said, having been through wandings and perfunctory patdowns many times, owing to the metal in my body. "Let's get it done."

There was a brief delay while the agent went to find the proper official to do the search.

"Is that your bag?" said another agent.

"Yes."

"You forgot this," she said sternly, holding up my laptop.

"I'm sorry," I said. "I was so concerned with the dog ..."

"Never mind. We'll let it through."

Pat-down Man arrived and led us to the mat with the foot marks.

"Stand here and raise your arms," he said. "Please keep control of your dog."

I stood with my arms straight out, holding Trooper with one hand on a leash so shortened that it nearly lifted him off the ground. The agent proceeded to pat and rub every square inch of my person, starting at my neck and slowly working his way down, lingering at the lumpier parts.

I could feel Trooper's unease through the taut leash as I held him at arm's length. He was still an inexperienced young dog. The lower the agent went, the more concerned Trooper became. My arm ached from holding back his scant but surprisingly powerful eighteen pounds.

"I'm sorry," I said. "He's never seen this before."

"It's OK," said the agent. "What's this in your back pocket?"

"My wallet," I said. I'd forgotten to put it into the bucket with my phone.

"Take it out and give it to me," he said.

I did and he opened it, looking for bad things. He handed it back. "Hold this in your other hand," he said.

Wallet in one hand and Trooper's leash in the other, I struggled sweatily to keep my arms up and out while the agent palpated every part of both knees, ending at the ankles, still keeping a wary eye on the nervous dog a few inches from his hands.

"Thank you," he finally said and stood up. I think we were both relieved.

Despite taking pains with my corpus, the officers did not touch Trooper at all. Maybe they figured the poop bags in the pockets of his vest couldn't be shaped into *plastique* and decided to wave him through. Only later did I discover this was a departure from TSA protocol. Dogs are supposed to be patted down.

I collected my things and, as Trooper sat calmly beside me, donned my shoes. I was conscious of all the agents watching us, some with smiles on their faces, some chuckling. The sight must have seemed funny to them. I doubt that they had seen it often.

For the next five hours we waited in various uncomfortable seats at several gates, moving only to stretch our legs.

Finally, ninety minutes before flight time, I took Trooper back to the security area.

"I have to take my dog out for a pee," I said. "I have to come back in this way, right?"

"Yes," said the TSA guy firmly. They don't let you catch a break.

Trooper and I went outside. There was a grassy and brushy area full of cigarette butts and other litter just to the left of the entry door, so Trooper and I didn't have to dodge traffic to get across to the official outdoor relief area.

On the way back we went through the whole thing again, from head to toe with another thorough rifling of my bag. (This time I remembered to remove the laptop.) Again Trooper quivered at the end of the leash. As before, the TSA agents fortunately were pleasant fellows with a sense of humor.

We flew home first class because it was our first flight together, and I wasn't sure how much room for Trooper coach class would offer. We had wanted to make this inaugural hop as easy and comfortable as possible.

He sat cradled in my lap during takeoff and landing, but slept all the way home on a little fleece mat atop the carpeted floor. Whew.

In retrospect, I should have checked the location of the relief areas before going out to the airport. I should have done the math—two hours at the airport before flight time, three and a half hours aloft and half an hour upon deplaning at O'Hare—or six hours in all, well within Trooper's bladder capacity, even with a delay of an hour or two. Then I could have peed Trooper outside at Fort Lauderdale before going through security—once. (There is now a post-security relief area inside Terminal 1.)

# Education Is Your Best Friend

Much of the foregoing misadventure could have been avoided by reading up on the TSA service animal rules. They're simple and clear:

- Inform the TSA officer that you are traveling with a service animal. You may provide the officer with the TSA notification card or medical documentation to describe your condition.
- You and your service dog/animal will be screened by a walk-through metal detector. You may walk through together or you may lead the animal through separately on a leash. You will undergo a pat-down if you are not screened by the walk-through metal detector.
- If the metal detector alarms, you and/or your service dog/animal will undergo additional screening, including a pat-down.
- If the service dog alarms, do not make contact with the dog (other than holding the leash) until the dog has been inspected by an officer. TSA will not separate you from your service animal. If you have concerns about your screening you can ask to speak with an officer.
- Service dog collars, harnesses, leashes, backpacks, vests and other items are subject to screening. Items that are necessary to maintain control of the service dog or indicate that the service dog is on duty do not require removal to be screened.
- If you need to relieve your service dog and must exit the security checkpoint, you and the service dog will need to go through the screening process again. You may request to move to the front of the line upon your return.
- Medication for service animals must go through X-ray or inspection screening. Separate medications and inform the TSA officer that you carry these items for your service dog.

A guide dog for the blind gets training experience going through security at an unnamed airport. Everyone seems to be enjoying the pat-down except possibly the dog, who may simply be going along with the process. (Photograph courtesy Transportation Security Administration)

Be aware that no TSA check is the same. Some agents are faster than others. Some skip a step or two. Some may want a companion to hold the dog's leash during a pat-down, but TSA's own rules forbid that.

● **Henry:** Once, during a madhouse holiday Friday morning at O'Hare, Trooper and I were sent to the TSA checkpoint for airline employees instead of the regular passenger security line. There a TSA agent insisted on separating me from Trooper while my steel knees were patted down, and afterward refused to let go of the leash until a supervisor arrived to examine the dog. It was a difficult moment for us both, but Trooper remained calm.

Later, when I informed the metal detector agent at the San Diego airport that I had steel in my body, he told Debby—who had already passed through without incident—to come back, then pick up and carry Trooper through the detector while my legs were wanded nearby. For some reason neither Trooper's collar tags nor steel splint in a hind leg triggered the machine, and the agents did not examine him.

Those incidents taught us never to expect TSA to follow its own rules.

Diane Munro experienced TSA inconsistency when flying with her hearing dog, Valley. "At Milwaukee, a TSA agent seemed unpleasant and determined to make things difficult," Munro said. "She demanded I take the vest, collar, and leash off my service dog and pass them through the X-ray belt. That meant I was forced to handle Valley hands-free. She and I had to walk through the metal detector separately. I prayed Valley would be 100 percent obedient despite the distraction around us, and listen to my commands until we could get to the other side and retrieve her collar and leash from the X-ray machine belt."

"Going through TSA security with a service dog by myself is added stress when I'm also dealing with personal carry-on items and laptops," said Munro. "Most agents are standoffish and don't seem to help in any way."

**Henry:** If a service dog partner has to be patted down, most dogs will go through the experience calmly, especially if they have been trained to do so. Some dogs may be edgy about new situations. One way to deal with that is to give the dog practice by having a friend use a smartphone or plastic coat hanger to simulate a wand as it is passed over your body. Another tip is for a friend to simulate full pat-downs so that the dog learns they are not a hostile invasion of your person. When a TSA agent pats down your dog, talk to the dog in a happy voice as you hold the leash, letting him know that everything's okay with what's going on. These strategies helped Trooper get used to people putting their hands on me, including several weeks of physical therapy during which he watched intently, then sleepily, as therapists manipulated my muscles and limbs.

If you have TSA PreCheck status, going through security will be quick and simple. Sometimes the airline will arrange for you to be given Pre-Check for that one flight.

"Certain passengers may receive expedited screening on occasion," TSA Media Relations told us. "However, if a traveler wishes to receive expedited screening on a consistent basis, they must enroll in one of the Trusted Traveler Programs" (https://ttp.cbp.dhs.gov).

The fee is $85, and the process requires an in-person interview and fingerprinting at an airport or TSA office. Be aware that at some facilities you may have to leave your dog outside during your interview because of the random presence of Customs and Border Protection bomb and drug-sniffing dogs. In that case, ask someone to come along with you to hold your dog in the waiting area.

If you pass muster, you will be free of having to fuss with your laptop, shoes, liquids, belts, and light jackets for five years. If you fly frequently, getting PreCheck status is a no-brainer. And if you often travel outside the United States, apply instead for Global Entry, which provides the PreCheck benefit plus expedited U.S. customs screening for international air travelers when entering the United States. Global Entry costs just $15 more, $100 for a five-year membership.

"We applied for Global Entry and have found that TSA PreCheck has been more than worth the cost," said Dianne Urhausen. "We were told by the TSA in Fort Lauderdale that we could not go to the front of the line if we took Henri outside to use the relief box. Being able to speed through security with PreCheck was a real time saver."

Canada's Trusted Travellers program is similar to TSA PreCheck and will speed service dog teams through security checkpoints across that country (https://www.catsa-acsta.gc.ca/en/trusted-travellers).

# Differences between
# the ACAA and the ADA

On a U.S. airplane you may notice the presence of a dog (perhaps well behaved, perhaps not) that doesn't seem to be a service animal at all. Rather, it's probably an emotional support animal. On U.S. airlines, both service dogs and emotional support animals are covered by the Air Carrier Access Act (ACAA), not the Americans with Disabilities Act (ADA). (This book does not discuss emotional support animals, only *service* animals.)

As of early 2019, the Air Carrier Access Act still lumped psychiatric service animals in with emotional support animals and allowed airlines to require documentation of a medical need for both. Late in 2018, the U.S. Department of Transportation had announced that it was reconsidering the rules of the ACAA, possibly making them conform more closely to those of the ADA, which recognizes psychiatric support animals (including those that deal with post-traumatic stress disorder) as trained service animals with public access rights. Such a change in the ACAA rules might mean, among other things, recognizing psychiatric service dogs as true service animals and forbidding breed discrimination such as the banning of pit bulls. At publication time of this book, the USDOT had not yet announced new rules.

The ACAA allows airlines to determine that a service or support dog is legitimate by means of written documentation or "credible verbal assurance." Having paperwork from your dog's trainer helps a great deal here.

In 2018, Delta and most other major airlines responded to increasing misbehavior by emotional support animals on board by requiring documentation to be submitted forty-eight hours in advance of a flight, a policy that at first included service dogs with the emotional support and psychiatric service animals. After protests from several organizations representing people with disabilities, Delta eliminated the forty-eight-hour requirement for service animals. The airline, as is customary in the industry, still requires service dog handlers to travel with a health certificate, immunization record, or other proof of vaccination current within one year of the travel date. Handlers are encouraged, but not required, to upload this proof to Delta's website before traveling.

## Other Dogs in the Airport

As if clearing security and weaving through throngs of people in a typical airport isn't stressful enough, you may encounter other service animals, emotional support animals, and plain old pet dogs as well as airport security dogs. Therapy animals roam departure areas, calming anxious passengers, in programs such as Pets Unstressing Passengers (PUP) at Los Angeles International Airport and the Wag Brigade at San Francisco International Airport.

Pets, however, are most likely to be cause for concern. "My dog has been attacked twice in an airport by pet dogs that have gotten loose from their owners," said Morgan W., who travels with Foley, a Goldador

Morgan W. travels often by air with his service dog, Foley, and recommends keeping an eye out for pet dogs running unleashed in the airport. (Photograph courtesy of Morgan W.)

(Golden Retriever/Labrador mix), a service dog trained by Southeastern Guide Dogs. "In the second attack, the dog didn't even have a leash or collar, so it was difficult to get the dog off my service dog. It was quite traumatic."

While airport rules usually require that pets be confined to a carrier or, at the very least, be kept on a leash, don't count on it.

## Planning Your Flight

It's always a good idea to notify the airline when you purchase your ticket that you are traveling with a service dog, an item that will be entered into your passenger name record. Some airlines offer this option online.

As the day of your flight begins, consider limiting your dog's water and food to help the dog extend its range before it has to visit the

Eric W. of Illinois and his dog, Nieko, waiting for a plane at a gate at O'Hare Airport in Chicago. (Photo by Sarah W.)

facilities. Sarah W. of Illinois did that with Nieko, her ten-year-old son Eric's assistance dog from Paws with a Cause in Wayland, Michigan. "Because we've had Nieko only a year, we've taken just one flight with him. He did beautifully. It was a short flight to Florida, and because I restricted his food and water prior to the flight, he did not need to use an airport pee facility."

Some professional service dog trainers withhold both food and water entirely on flight day. You may want to consult your dog's veterinarian or training team for a recommendation. If you haven't flown with the dog before, it's also a good idea to bring along some dry treats to help calm him during the flight.

Many service dog partners have developed a reliable air travel routine for long flights. "When flying, I always feed Dapper on his regular morning schedule," said Mary Seamon, a Californian whose Labrador service

Eric W. of Illinois uses his dog, Nieko, as a footwarmer while in flight. (Photograph by Sarah W.)

Dapper, a seasoned traveler, is ready to go to work whenever his partner, Mary Seamon, schedules another coast-to-coast flight. (Photo courtesy of Mary Seamon)

dog was trained by Palmetto Animal Assisted Life Services (PAALS) in Columbia, South Carolina. "If I'm flying earlier in the morning, I feed him on his regular schedule but give him half a meal. On a late morning flight, I would give Dapper a whole ration. I then feed him his regular afternoon meal when we arrive."

Your dog must lie in the floor space in front of your seat. This can be a problem on small commuter-style airliners with two-and-one or two-and-two coach seating, especially if your dog is a big one. Some airlines will make a first row bulkhead seat available for a service dog team at no extra charge, although some travelers prefer to avoid bulkhead seats and are able to squeeze themselves and their dogs into a tiny space. Sometimes extra coach seat room is available. Ask for it when you make your booking, and the extra inch or two you might get for a modest upcharge could make a big difference in your comfort. In any case, ask for a window seat.

"We tend to fly Southwest, and they are awesome," said Melanie, who has made forty-five flights since 2012 with Paddington. "Because of his size we always get the bulkhead row, and on one flight they blocked out the middle seat for our row, even though the plane was full. If I am not traveling with my husband, which happens often as Paddington and I go to conventions and universities to participate in research, no one has ever asked to be in a different row or away from us. As we have waited to board, people have said they hoped they would be next to us. They also say things like 'He is so calm!' I respond, 'That is part of his job.'"

● **Henry:** On longer (three- or four-hour) domestic flights, I will often try to book first class or premium economy class, even though Trooper is a small dog. First class is expensive, but to us the extra space is well worth the premium. We'll opt for seats in the first row behind the bulkhead where there's plenty of room for Trooper to lie on the floor between my wife, Debby, and me. I'm an arthritic septuagenarian, and trying to fit both my creaky legs and a terrier into a tiny coach space can be awkward and painful.

If my flight is a long one, such as New York to Seattle—six hours in the air, plus an hour or more on the ground for the dog's relief—I may break the trip into two flights. I will try to schedule the connecting stop at an airport with a service dog relief area *inside* the security-sanitized part of the terminal. If I have to leave the secured area to go outside to relieve the dog, I'll add another hour (or two, depending on how crowded the airport is) to the layover to get back through TSA.

I also always inform the airline upon booking a flight that I will have a service dog. Even though the dog flies free, I'll ask for a seat with more leg room than the cheapest ones, even if I have to pay extra. If the agent can give it to us, we'll get it. And sometimes the airline refunds the difference in fares between the lowest-priced seats and the slightly more expensive comfortable ones. Sometimes, when we called ahead, the airline also nominated us for TSA Pre-Check status, and the security theater was far less onerous. ●

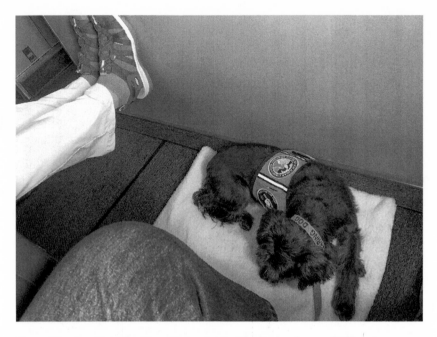

Henry Kisor's schnoodle, Trooper, snoozes with plenty of room in first class during a flight from New Orleans to Chicago. (Photograph by Henry Kisor)

Service dog partners with flying experience advise that airlines sometimes permit you to check a suitcase containing your animal's food and other needs at no charge, even when passengers' bags are subject to a fee.

Special assistance at the airport can be a lifesaver, especially if you are traveling alone or using a walker, cane, or wheelchair while juggling a dog's leash. Preboarding the plane is a helpful courtesy frequently offered to service dog teams that allows you time to arrange your gear and settle your dog and yourself ahead of the crowd.

Mary Seamon said that for the most part, she has had "wonderful experiences" flying with Dapper. "There have been a few problems with wheelchair pushers (mostly at Dallas–Fort Worth) who were afraid of him," she said. "In fact, one pusher kept swerving the wheelchair toward Dapper. When I told the pusher to stop, he left. Another passenger offered assistance. Another time, the pusher insisted that we would have to go through a revolving door into the baggage area. Again, I had to insist that it would be potentially dangerous for Dapper. We took the long way around."

● **Henry:** Special assistance upon arrival at your destination can indeed be interesting. Years ago, I was on a plane to Kansas City for a convention of hard of hearing people when I spotted a middle-aged woman with a service dog a couple of rows behind me. The woman was going to the convention, too, and the dog was fast asleep at her feet.

When the plane landed and I emerged from the jetway, a wheelchair and attendant were waiting at the gate. That made me chuckle. Even today, airlines often offer wheelchairs upon arrival to deaf and hard of hearing passengers, much to their amazement. Hope the chair isn't for that woman, I thought.

A few minutes later she, the wheelchair, and its attendant rolled by. She was on her feet and the dog in the chair. She'd given it a little too much veterinary sedative to relax it for the flight. It was out cold.

That evening, however, the pup was bright-eyed and bushy-tailed, and everyone who had arrived on that flight was happily dining out on the story.

Speaking of wheelchairs, I recently flew from Chicago to Montreal. My wife, Debby, had booked my ticket over the phone with Air Canada, asking for a window bulkhead seat in coach to make room for Trooper. When I showed up at the ticket counter to pick up my boarding pass, there was no TSA PreCheck symbol on it. The counter agent said that an O'Hare special services attendant would take me through the TSA Special Services line for the regular inspection, then to the gate . . . in a wheelchair.

"I'm deaf," I said, astonished. "I don't need a wheelchair."

"That's the rule," she said.

Was I going to make a fuss and miss my flight? No. So I climbed into a wheelchair, Trooper in my lap, and was wheeled to the security area past long lines of impatient travelers. I felt embarrassed and humiliated and had to endure the usual full-body pat-down as well.

Afterward I emailed TSA's media relations people and was subsequently told: "I can tell you that this is not a TSA rule. This sounds like an airline policy. I find too often that frontline airline workers blame TSA for company-imposed policies (carry-on bag size restriction is another example). TSA will gladly screen a passenger with a service animal whether they're in a wheelchair or standing."

Shortly later, Debby and I both applied for TSA's Global Entry status.

But if you *do* need wheelchair assistance, make arrangements with your airline in advance for an airport attendant to assist you from plane to plane or to the baggage claim area. When service is good, tips aren't required, but they are appreciated—and help attendants remember the special needs of people with service dogs.

If you encounter unforeseen difficulties with bookings and service at the airport and are unsure what to do, you could ask the airline to contact a Complaint Resolution Official. CROs are responsible for resolving disability-related issues that have escalated beyond an initial interaction with airline personnel. Each air carrier is required to have one or more designated CROs on site or available by phone. ●

## Dog Relief Spots

"We know every doggie relief area in most airports," said Melanie, a frequent flyer with Paddington. "It is nice that they are finally getting relief areas *inside* security."

Since August 2016, the Department of Transportation has required all airports in the United States handling more than ten thousand passenger boardings a year and receiving federal financial assistance to provide animal relief areas for each terminal within the sanitized security area. While most big-city airports have complied, some are dragging their feet, and so it's a good idea to check them out while planning your flights. The website https://www.petfriendlytravel.com/airports

lists those with areas both within and outside of security. So does the handy Where to Go app for iPhones and Android devices.

Other airports still keep their animal facilities *outside* security, usually in grassy areas near parking garages. It's always advisable to go online and search for airport maps to pinpoint the locations of relief areas instead of arriving at the airport and relying on agents and officials who may not (and probably won't) have a clue where they are. But don't be surprised if the maps are not accurate and a long trek is involved to reach the closest relief location.

"A couple of years ago, while on a flight to Washington, D.C., we had a stopover in Salt Lake City," said Flo Kiewel. "I had researched the airport before leaving home, and the airport maps indicated there was a service dog relief station outside of each airline's arm of the airport. When I got there, I was unable to locate a single dog relief station."

Airport service animal relief areas inside security areas now provide a more convenient option than leaving the terminal in search of grass. (Photo by Robert Goodier)

"On the return trip I asked an airport employee for directions to the dog relief station, and they led me all the way across the entire airport on foot, as there are no shuttle buses. AJ angled toward every single potted plant along the way and sniffed around the bottom of the pot suggestively. I kept him going forward until we finally got outside, but at that point he didn't wait to arrive at their three-foot-by-six-foot designated area. The airport employee glared at me. I just shrugged and said, 'Too bad, he got as far as he could.' I don't know why they changed to one single station at one end of the airport, but they were very unsympathetic about the inconvenience."

If your dog has never used an airport relief box—usually a four-foot-by-four-foot enclosure filled with artificial turf, sometimes with a faux fireplug and self-cleaning plumbing—it's not a bad idea to train the pooch well ahead of time with a similar box in your back yard. If there are no distractions, they usually catch on quickly, and the familiar scents of a well-used airport box may encourage them. Not, however, if the airport uses bleach, ammonia, or other harsh and often toxic chemicals to clean the boxes. The odor will warn you away.

"Henri has no issue with using indoor pet relief areas," said Dianne Urhausen. "She used the indoor area at Seattle-Tacoma and it was so much more convenient than taking her outside and then back through security."

Sometimes a dog will turn up its nose at the fake grass in post-security airport relief areas. This is more likely to happen if you relieved the dog outside just a hour or two before. If you know your animal's schedule, try to follow it. A dog that *has* to go *will* go.

## In the Air

If your dog has never flown before, it may be nervous, especially on takeoff when the engines suddenly spool up and fill the cabin with thunder, and when the flight is turbulent. To prevent this, you might ask your vet for a mild sedative of the kind often given to sensitive dogs on the Fourth of July. (Many trainers, however, are adamant against drugging dogs for travel. It's up to you.) Usually a dog will decide during its first flight that airplanes are all right and just lie down and go to sleep.

Urhausen gets double duty from a car harness she bought for road trips with Henri. "I carry the harness onto the airplane with me when we fly, along with a strap and carabiner clip, in case there is turbulence on the flight," she said. "So far in five plane trips I have not needed to use it."

During longer flights, some service dog handlers ask the attendants for ice chips to give the dog piece by piece. This will slake the dog's thirst and add to its comfort without filling its bladder.

Because airline lavatories are tiny, there won't be room for the dog if you have to go. If a familiar companion's not present to hold your dog's leash while you visit the facilities, watch your own liquid intake.

Mary Seamon, who often travels solo with her mobility service dog, suggests planning carefully about using the human restroom. "Flight attendants may be too busy to watch your dog," she said. "Establishing a friendly relationship with a seatmate may be your salvation."

● **Henry:** I always pick up Trooper and cradle him in my lap during take-offs and landings. He sleeps happily on the floor through mild turbulence. I suspect that he thinks he's riding in a car over rough roads.

Airlines will always try to give you a window seat, but sometimes that doesn't happen. In that case, make sure no part of your dog juts out into the aisle. Passengers rushing to the washroom and flight attendants shoving drinks carts never seem to spot what's in front of them.　　　　　　　　　　　　　　　　　　　　　　　　　　　●

● **Chris:** Raylene curls into a ball at my feet against the window wall as soon as I unroll her travel mat and place it on the cabin floor. The mat helps keep the big Lab clean and provides some comfort when the floor becomes icy cold. She seems to fall asleep immediately and only occasionally stands up to stretch and rearrange herself.

Once on board, I offer ice chips if my dog seems restless. She views them as treats, and they help keep her hydrated in dry aircraft air without creating the need to pee too soon. I bring training treats in my carry-on bag to offer only sparingly and praise her when she settles back down after a stretch. ●

Najawarie took her *Altdeutscher Schäferhund,* Moon Moon, from Paris to Montreal aboard the Canadian budget airline Air Transat.

"Neither of those airports have indoor service dog bathrooms. Montreal has one right outside the terminal, but you have to go through customs before reaching it. The flight was seven and a half hours long, but from where I was staying near Paris to my destination near Montreal the trip took about twelve hours.

"I was nervous about Moon Moon having to hold his bladder that long, so took a 'belly band' just in case and didn't feed him for twelve hours before the flight, giving him just enough water to keep him hydrated.

Chris Goodier books coach bulkhead seats for extra floor space where a large service dog like Raylene can curl up at her handler's feet. (Photo by Robert Goodier)

"But he did great and never asked to go. I had to motivate him to pee when we went outside the airport at Montreal. He mainly wanted to sleep."

Najawarie said she reserved her flight several months ahead and made arrangements for her dog with Air Transat via email. "They were very understanding and kind. They asked some basic questions, such as if Moon Moon was able not to pee or poo during the flight, whether he had already taken a flight, and whether he had experience or training that would assure the trip would go well. They also asked for a letter from my doctor specifying that I need a service dog. Air Transat also said to check in at least an hour before the flight, have Moon Moon wear a service dog vest, and keep him on leash at all times."

Upon approving the dog, the airline offered a seat with extra foot space and even reserved a space for Moon Moon. "When the day of the flight came," Najawarie said, "the airline personnel spotted me quickly

Najawarie, a young woman from Quebec, with her psychiatric service dog, Moon Moon, who was trained in France and flew with his partner from Paris to Montreal, a seven-and-a-half-hour flight. (Photo by J. Christophe/Photographie)

in the queue and gave me check-in priority, and even offered to take my cabin luggage for free to the airplane so I would have less to carry with me."

At the security check, "they understood it was stressful for me and the first time Moon Moon had been through it. They took all the time I needed and never rushed me."

The flight, she said, went smoothly. "The flight was full. The only free seat was the one they held out for my service dog. The attendants offered water to Moon Moon several times and spoke to me often to make sure I was feeling well."

At Montreal she had a similar reception. "From the beginning to the end of that trip, everyone was so kind and helpful that they went way beyond my expectations. Canada is really welcoming to people with service dogs."

## Individual Domestic Airlines

Most every U.S. major airline's requirements for service dogs are similar to each other, but some are more generous than others in allocating space. Provided the flight isn't full or oversold, you might be lucky enough to be put next to an empty seat so that your dog has room to sprawl a little in the knee space. Don't expect it, though. Here, for illustration, is **American Airlines'** service dog policy. Its specifics are common to most other mainline carriers:

> Service animals, including emotional support animals, are welcome at no charge if they meet the requirements. They must fit on your lap, at your feet, or under the seat, and cannot block the aisle. For security reasons, you won't be able to sit in an exit row when traveling with your service or emotional support animal. If your animal doesn't fit within the allowed space, you may need to rebook on a flight with more open seats, buy a ticket for the animal, or transport the animal as a checked pet. Animals must be trained to behave properly in public and they won't be permitted in the cabin if they display any form of disruptive behavior that can't be successfully controlled, including growling, biting, and jumping on or lunging at people.

Dogs that meet the Air Carrier Access Act definition of service animals are exempt from the following requirement: "To travel with an emotional support and psychiatric service animal in the cabin, you must contact the Special Assistance Desk with all required documentation at least 48 hours before your flight. Document validation will include American Airlines contacting your mental health professional." This documentation requirement has become almost uniform at all U.S. carriers.

"For ACAA-defined service animals, either an identification card or credible verbal assurance is acceptable at check-in." (It should be pointed out that people with invisible disabilities, such as diabetes or seizures, who use service dogs are challenged frequently by most airlines.)

American invites service dog handlers to contact its special assistance team by phone (800-433-7300 or 800-543-1586 TDD) or online (https://www.aa.com/i18n/travel-info/special-assistance/service-animals.jsp). The company's website provides more details on destinations with restrictions such as Hawaii, London, Edinburgh, all other cities in the United Kingdom, Japan, and New Zealand.

**United Air Lines'** policy is nearly identical. Trained service animals "are animals that receive specific training to perform life functions for individuals with disabilities." These animals must sit in the floor space below your seat, must not extend into the aisle, and must behave properly in public. United allows service dogs in training in the cabin if accompanied by their trainers and if they are older than four months of age. The airline does not recognize as service animals pets that have been trained as therapy animals. United also reminds travelers that "there are restrictions regarding the entry of service animals into Hawaii. Customers planning to travel to Hawaii should contact the Hawaii Animal Quarantine Branch manager directly for quarantine requirements. The twenty-four-hour phone number is 1-808-837-8092. You may also view animal quarantine information at the Hawaii Department of Agriculture (https://www.hdoa.hawaii.gov) website."

Why is Hawaii so tough on incoming animals? It has an extensive stray dog problem and takes pride in being a rabies-free state, so it quarantines all incoming pets for up to 120 days. Service dogs are exempt from quarantine but must jump through complex hoops to get onto the islands. For full details, see chapter 6, "That Annoying Paperwork."

**Delta Air Lines'** policy bans "pit bull type dogs" as service or support animals as well as animals under four months of age because of rabies vaccination requirements. The airline also encourages, but does not require, passengers to send in advance notice of a flight with a service dog as well as fill out a Trained Service Animal form. It does require a rabies certificate, as all airlines do.

**Southwest Airlines'** policy is similar to that of American, United, and Delta. In addition, customers "traveling with trained assistance and emotional support animals on an international itinerary are solely responsible for researching and complying with applicable laws, requirements, and/or procedures of each country on the customer's itinerary with respect to the acceptance of the animal."

## OTHER DOMESTIC AIRLINES

**Alaska Airlines** allows service dogs, including trained psychiatric service animals, cats, and miniature horses, and service animals in training if accompanied by their trainers. "Advise the customer service agent upon arrival at the airport that you are traveling with a service animal to ensure we have your animal accounted for on board the aircraft. Documentation is not required when traveling with a trained service animal. However, our employees are trained to ask certain questions to determine the classification applicable to your animal."

**Allegiant Airlines** "requests" that passengers traveling with a "fully trained service animal" have a veterinarian complete a "trained service animal form" that certifies the animal "is fully trained to mitigate a physical disability by performing a specific task" as well as evidence of rabies immunization and that the animal has not "bitten or injured/ attacked a person or another animal." Pit bulls or "pit bull-type breeds" are not allowed.

**Frontier Airlines'** rules are basically similar to those of the other carriers, except that it "will accept fully trained psychiatric service animals as trained service animals." The airline adds, "We reserve the right to refuse to accommodate an animal in the cabin if requested documentation is not available or if the animal is considered aggressive or disruptive."

**JetBlue** welcomes service animals but won't allow service animals in training, nor will it permit as service or emotional/psychiatric support animals "hedgehogs, ferrets, insects, rodents, snakes, spiders, sugar gliders, reptiles, non-household birds (farm poultry, waterfowl, game bird & birds of prey), animals improperly cleaned and/or with a foul odor, animals with tusks."

**Spirit Airlines** accepts service animals and says "you will be asked at the airport to verify the service the animal provides." Those using psychiatric service dogs must submit three forms at least forty-eight hours before a flight: a mental health professional form, a veterinary health form, and a passenger acknowledgment form."

**Sun Country Airlines** says service animals are welcome and "must remain seated on the floor at the passenger's feet and cannot obstruct an aisle or other area used for emergency evacuation." It adds, "when traveling outside the U.S. and its Territories, please ensure documentation of the animal's health (e.g. vaccinations, health certification, etc.) is up-to-date and readily available for customs agents to avoid delays or the possibility of the animal being quarantined."

## NON-U.S.-BASED AIRLINES

Most non-U.S. airlines that fly to destinations in North America and the Caribbean follow much the same onboard rules that domestic carriers do, and transport service dogs for free, but for flights to destinations outside the United States, they require official (not fake) documentation for the dog. Here are a few:

**Air Canada**'s service dog policy for flights between Canada and the United States says the airline "is subject to the U.S. Department of Transportation's rule on 'Non-Discrimination on the Basis of Disability.'" It adds that if the passenger has "purchased a ticket with an Air

Canada operated flight through a US-based airline," the ticket will "then bear the code of the US airline, e.g. United Airlines' UA 7811."

For all other flights, including those from Canada to other countries in the Northern Hemisphere, the rules are as follows:

Certified, professionally trained service animals which are assisting customers with disabilities are carried, free of charge, in the passenger cabin at the customer's feet. The animal must be harnessed and certified as having been trained to assist a person with a disability by a professional service animal institution (as a requirement under the Canadian Air Transportation Regulations).

If you plan on travelling with a service animal, we require that you:

Inform Air Canada Reservations at least 48 hours prior to departure. However, we will make every effort to accommodate requests made within that time frame.

Be at the airport for check-in at least one extra hour ahead of the recommended check-in time.

For exceptions on travel to international destinations, please consult specific government regulations of any countries you are travelling to. [These can be extraordinarily complex. Do your homework well ahead of time—six months doesn't hurt.]

Air Canada Signature Service (formerly International Business Class): Visually impaired customers may be seated in International Business Class and may travel with a service animal such as a seeing-eye dog, provided the animal travels under the Suite's footstool and/or seat at all times.

Those traveling with psychiatric service animals must advise Air Canada Reservations 48 hours in advance and provide supporting documentation in the form of an original letter on the letterhead of a licensed mental health professional whose care the traveler is currently under.

● **Henry:** When I booked that aforementioned Chicago–Halifax trip with a two-hour layover at Montreal, the Air Canada agent said that if I checked my bag through, I'd have to get it at the Montreal baggage carousel and take it through Immigration and Customs, then recheck it to Halifax, finally reentering through security. An hour (if the plane was on time) didn't give much time for getting the bag, transiting Immigration, then going outside, peeing Trooper, and returning through security, so I carried the bag aboard.

Also, Air Canada wanted an extra US$25 for each of the bulkhead seats but said if I called Air Canada Medical and satisfied them that I was deaf, they'd refund the money. I did and they did. My trip wasn't as eventful as Najawarie's on Air Transat, but it was satisfactory all the same.

**Air France**'s rules are basically the same as Air Canada's, except for "On flights longer than eight hours, we may ask you to demonstrate that you are prepared to handle your dog's hygienic needs (primarily the natural need to relieve itself)." Presumably this is done with absorbent belly bands or "pee pads" in the lavatories.

**British Airways** uses the term "assistance dog" and defines it as "one that has been trained to assist a person with a disability or medical condition and has been determined as being able to travel safely in the aircraft cabin." The dog must have "documentary evidence confirming that it has been trained," must wear "an identifying jacket/harness," and must "remain under your control at all times." British Airways also recommends a safety harness, a fleece bed, and absorbent pads to be placed under the fleece.

**Lufthansa:** The German airline requires "a training certificate for your dog from a recognised training institute" but does not specify how the institute is recognized. The dog "must be trained to be obedient to your commands and must behave appropriately in a public space. . . . If your dog does not behave in an appropriate manner, Lufthansa may transfer the dog to the cargo hold at an additional cost or refuse to transport the animal." Also, the airline recommends securing the dog with a harness rather than a collar, and "out of consideration for the other passengers, we request that you bring a muzzle with you for your dog."

Many other airlines, some of them very small, fly to the Caribbean and Central America and have similar rules for service dogs. Before booking, go on their websites and check out the details of their policies. Always inform them at least forty-eight hours before flight time that you are bringing a service dog.

## FINALLY: CHECK FOR CURRENT INFORMATION

Always check out the countries' national websites before flying from the United States or Canada to other countries including those in the Caribbean or Central America. Other sources of information are the USDA APHIS and Canadian CFIA and CTA websites.

All these countries require considerable documentation of one sort or another, and some require import permits for visiting service dogs, even those that are visiting the country for just a few hours. Be aware that immunization rules can vary from island to island and country to country.

As was pointed out in chapter 1, "The Basics," an APHIS Form 7001 (or the Canadian equivalent) is a must almost everywhere, and some countries require that U.S. and Canadian forms be countersigned by *government* officials (at APHIS regional veterinary services endorsement offices), not just an accredited vet. Some countries also want their own health forms filled out.

Getting certificates and permits to bring your animal into a foreign country can take months as well as treks to your nearest APHIS office. Don't leave the paperwork until the last minute.

See appendix 4 for details about the animal import requirements of various countries in North America. These requirements are constantly changing; *don't rely on this book for the freshest information*. Rather, contact the countries' consulates or websites for that.

---

## Summing Up

- Before going through airport security with your dog, familiarize yourself with TSA service animal rules.

- If you have metal in your body, give your dog a few "dry runs" with the help of a friend willing to simulate a TSA pat-down.
- For a smoother trip through security, enroll in TSA PreCheck or Global Entry.
- Consider limiting your dog's food and water before a flight.
- Ask the airline for a bulkhead seat, if you wish, or a coach seat with extra room.
- Arrange for special assistance in advance and at the check-in counter if you have a mobility disability.
- Locate airport animal relief facilities online, both outside and inside the security-sanitized zone.
- Go online to check the service animal policy of the airline you are flying.
- When flying outside the United States or Canada, investigate animal import rules and documentation for your destination.

## Chapter 3

# Riding the Rails

It's just after 2 p.m. in Chicago. You and your service dog have just boarded Amtrak's *California Zephyr* for a two-day, two-night trip to San Francisco Bay. You're a bit worried. Where's the pup going to go when he's got to go? And if the dog is fussy about going, are you in danger of getting left behind at a station way out in the middle of nowhere? What about the dining car? Will you have to leave the dog alone at your seat or in your compartment?

The conductor appears in the door to your bedroom. "Tickets, please, and how can we help you with the dog?" she says.

"Where can I take him out for his business?" you ask. "Will there be time?"

"Don't worry," says the conductor. "Amtrak welcomes service animals, and we'll be sure to give you enough time. The best times to relieve your dog are service stops, crew change stops, and fresh air stops, which we'll announce on the intercom, or your attendant will tell you. Your car attendant will watch out for you and make sure you and your buddy are back aboard before the train leaves."

Trooper on a planter along the river outside Chicago Union Station, the only natural facility there. Even Amtrak's police dogs use the planters for relief. (Photograph by Henry Kisor)

"Whew," you say.

"By the way, the first fresh air stop is Galesburg at 4:38 p.m.," the conductor says. "That's a checked baggage stop, so we'll be there for about five minutes. There'll be a nice strip of grass just a few steps away from your car."

You feel better, especially when the sleeping car attendant comes in and shows you on his timetable other likely stops for your pooch. There is, you learn, plenty of opportunity for short walks.

Not long afterward, a dining-car attendant comes in to take dinner reservations. You've heard that Amtrak dining cars employ community seating, placing at each table four people who may be strangers to each other.

"Will there be room under the table for my dog?" you say. You worry that four pairs of human legs in a close confine will be too much for him to handle.

"We'll give you two reservations," the attendant says. "One for you, one for the dog. There'll be plenty of room on the floor for him."

Again you sigh with relief.

"Of course, if you wish, you can dine in your room—or at your seat if you're in coach," he says. "Your attendant will bring your meals. It's all up to you."

Things are going to go well, you say to yourself. And so they do.

## What It's Like to Ride the Train

Traveling by Amtrak or VIA Rail with a service animal around the continental United States and Canada can be both relaxing and convenient. Dog and partner get to see the country up close. The scenery on the western routes in particular is majestic.

You can ride from city center to city center without expensive taxi trips to and from airports way out of town. There are no stern security agents at big-city stations to rifle through your bags and pat you down while you try to control a dog on leash. Once in a long while a passenger and their luggage might be taken aside in a big-city station for a random check, but that happens infrequently.

If you ask Amtrak or VIA for special help, you will almost certainly get it. In large staffed stations, for instance, you can tell an agent that you have a service dog for a disability, and that agent will gladly escort you and your chum to the train. (Increasingly, though, smaller Amtrak stations are becoming unstaffed, and you may be on your own.)

At big-city U.S. terminals, an Amtrak police officer teamed with a dog sometimes will watch as passengers file down the platform to their train, but that's as much for sniffing out drugs as it is for safety from terrorists. All the same, if you spot such a team, keep yourself between your dog and the Amtrak dog. Well trained as they may be, police dogs are still dogs. They can suddenly lunge when they see others of their kind, nearly pulling over their handlers.

**Henry:** Whenever I spot an Amtrak dog team, I'll pick up Trooper and carry him past the potential danger. He's not afraid of big dogs, by the way, and he won't turn down a chance for a friendly playtime with any fellow pooch he might encounter.

Trooper's first train ride—on a suburban Chicago commuter train—frightened him. He quivered in my lap as the horn blew and the train pulled away, but after a few miles he calmed down. Since then he's eager to go and even leaps into the vestibule when we arrive at train-side.

Sometimes other passengers take a dim view of dogs in their presence, service or not, just as they do in airport waiting areas. At Union Station in Portland, Oregon, Flo Kiewel and her cocker spaniel, AJ, were "getting some stares from the old ladies because there's (sniff) a *dog* in the first class lounge."

AJ, who tends to take notice of other dogs, "is always jumping up when he sees someone pulling their luggage along behind them, thinking that's maybe a dog," Flo said. "So a train pulls in and people begin getting off and heading for the station. AJ is putting his paws up in my lap and looking out the window to check out everybody's luggage.

"The old lady across from us says with surprise, 'Oh, he really does know when a train is here and tells you!'

"I made the mistake of explaining his interest in the luggage, and she went back to being mildly disgusted with his presence. I just smiled."

## Trains and Planes Are Not the Same

Be aware that the policies of Amtrak and the airlines in the United States are not identical, for they follow different federal laws. Airlines (which follow the Air Carrier Access Act) allow emotional support animals to ride on the floor next to their owners, but Amtrak (under the Americans with Disabilities Act) does not, although genuine service dogs have the run of the train except, of course, the dining car kitchen. (Amtrak does permit *pets* under twenty pounds, including emotional support dogs, but they must be confined to carriers and can ride only up to seven hours.)

As time goes on and more and more people with service dogs travel aboard Amtrak, the onboard and station crews are becoming accustomed to their presence. Many crew members, however, have had unpleasant experiences with fraudulent "service dogs" and may be skeptical at first. But once persuaded that your companion is a bona fide service animal, the dog lovers among them will bend over backward to make your trip a pleasant one. Of course, there will be indifferent attendants and conductors who will go by the book but no further.

On VIA Rail, incidents with fraudulent service dogs are all but unheard of, according to a VIA official, primarily because the Canadian railroad has been diligent about asking for documentation. (More about that later in this chapter.)

## Advance Planning

Taking a service dog on the train in either the United States or Canada has become remarkably easy, whether you go by inexpensive coach or in a costlier but comfortable sleeper room. Advance planning, however, is a must, as it is in any form of travel.

First, how long is your dog able to go before needing to be relieved? Trooper has a capacity of about eleven hours before accidents are likely to happen, but for his comfort we try not to go past eight hours. Five or six hours between relief stops is about right. A dog that's full enough will happily go—and quickly instead of sniffing around aimlessly and frustrating impatient conductors.

Mature service dogs, especially those that have traveled widely, will be happy to use just about any hard surface to pee or poop on. Younger and inexperienced animals may prefer grass, bushes, trees, or other natural targets.

A broad courtyard at Raton, New Mexico, was a welcome grassy oasis for Trooper and Henry Kisor on the *Southwest Chief*'s long trek through the arid desert Southwest. (Photograph by Deborah Abbott)

**Henry:** When he was a rookie, Trooper, a California dog by way of rural Oregon, absolutely had to have a natural bathroom, but since then he has become more accustomed to man-made "plumbing" such as light posts, stone walls, and telephone poles. He still prefers a nice bush or clump of grass, but sometimes he has no choice.

Don't worry about being left behind at a station stop. Just make sure your car attendant knows you are getting off with your dog, and *stay close to the train within view of the attendant and conductors.* They will make sure the train doesn't leave without you. Amtrak and VIA regulations both say the needs of service dogs *must* be accommodated, even at quick station stops. The train *has* to wait for you.

Don't abuse the privilege, however. The crew will like it best if you consult with them at the beginning of a journey about the most appropriate stations to relieve your dog. Crew change and engine service

During an Amtrak *Empire Builder* stop, Trooper makes use of the artificial grass and faux fireplug on the platform at the St. Paul (Minnesota) Union Depot, the only such railroad relief facility for service dogs in the United States. (Photograph by Henry Kisor)

stops, seven to twenty minutes long, are ideal. Baggage handling stops are shorter at five minutes or so, but usually provide sufficient time.

Whenever you go outside the train at a baggage stop, keep an eye out for the baggage cart up near the front (sometimes rear) of the train. When the cart pulls away from the baggage car and heads for the station, it's time to get back aboard.

At the beginning of every trip, when your attendant introduces himself or herself and the conductor stops by to check your ticket, it's not a bad idea to explain the needs and limitations of your disability, especially if they're not visible. Sure, in the United States the ADA guidelines do not allow inquiries into your medical history, but in the real world that can be a problem if you're not open about it.

● **Henry:** Here's an example of the need to be upfront. Sometimes, if the conductors are trying to make up for lost time, they might announce that at the next stop only one car will be open for board-ing and deboarding, so things can be kept moving swiftly.

This means that you might have to carry or lead your dog through five or six cars to the appointed one. If you are young and fit, go along with the scheme.

When it happened to Trooper and me, it was a near disaster. As a septuagenarian I deal with arthritis, a bad back, and a very poor sense of balance. On the *Capitol Limited* from Chicago to Washington one day, the conductors announced fifteen minutes before arrival in Cumberland, Maryland, ordinarily a leisurely crew change stop, that only one door in one coach would be open there—and it was five cars away from ours—instead of stopping the train twice at the short plat-form, once for the sleepers and once for the coaches. Getting Trooper from car to car through a rocking and jolting train and through the gauntlet of sprawling legs in the coach and lounge car aisles (and the dining car, too) was a sweaty, heart-pounding exercise for me. Not good at all.

Had my attendant opened our sleeper car door at the other end of the train, Trooper and I would have been back aboard even before the conductors had started boarding passengers.

Since then, upon boarding I always explain to my attendant my physical limitations and how difficult it is to get Trooper through the train at single-car stops. The attendants pass on the information to the conductors. ●

## Feeding and Watering Your Dog

So far as service dog supplies are concerned, neither Amtrak nor VIA provides animal food. You'll need to pack sufficient provender for your dog, plus a couple of days' extra in case of extreme delay. Though they don't happen often, freight train derailments and weather extremes can put your train many hours—even an entire day—behind schedule. It's a good idea to pack at least two extra days' worth of kibble. Bottles of water are free in the sleepers and can be purchased in café cars, or you can use the train's potable water spigots. As well as collapsible plastic food and water dishes, some service dog handlers bring along small fleece blankets, folding them several times for their dogs to sleep on.

And, of course, poop bags—lots of them.

## Selecting Your Accommodations

Amtrak passengers with disabilities enjoy a 10 percent discount on rail fares, and so do their companions. Passengers with disabilities traveling on Amtrak *Downeaster* trains from Boston to Portland, Maine, are eligible for a 50 percent discount. Children aged two to twelve travel for 50 percent off, and if they have disabilities, get another 10 percent off the discounted child's fare. Service dogs travel free. Sleeper charges are upgrades from the coach rail fare, and the price of a room is the same regardless of how many passengers are in it.

You must provide written documentation of your disability at the ticket counter and when boarding the train. Acceptable documents include a transit system disability card, a membership card from a disability organization, a letter from a physician, a Medicare card if you are under sixty-five, a U.S. Department of Veterans Affairs "Service Connected" ID card, or a disability parking placard issued by a state department of motor vehicles.

A coach seat is the cheapest way to ride either Amtrak or VIA. If you are taking a day coach trip that is seven hours or fewer in length, you needn't worry about relief stops, but if there's much of a delay, you might want to talk to the conductor about taking your dog off the train for relief even at a quick station stop where checked baggage is not handled. Little suitcase symbols on the downloadable timetables indicate where baggage is handled.

Amtrak no longer prints paper timetables to put in stations and on trains, so you must download them from Amtrak.com.

In coach, there's always plenty of carpeted leg room on the floor in front of your seat for a dog. Dogs are not permitted on the seats. It's best to ask the attendant for a seat next to the window so the dog doesn't accidentally sprawl into the aisle and get stepped on.

Your dog's temperament can be as important as your budget in choosing accommodations. Coaches are constantly busy and sometimes noisy, even on long-distance overnight trains, with people coming and going at all hours. Phlegmatic breeds such as Labs are more likely to handle any hubbub with aplomb, excitable terriers perhaps less so.

**Henry:** Trooper and I don't often travel in coach, primarily because we usually take long-distance overnight trains and prefer sleepers for those. Many coach passengers are unaware of service dog etiquette, especially small children. Some will try to pet or talk to Trooper without asking me and may even ignore my request that they keep their distance. As a cute and fuzzy small terrier, he simply is irresistible to the public. For such a dog, conditions are often better in the less crowded and quieter sleepers and business-class cars.

On many long-distance double-decker Amtrak Superliner trains, some coaches offer lower-level seating areas for senior citizens and passengers with mobility disabilities. Close by these quiet areas are large bathrooms accessible by those with mobility disabilities. They have plenty of room for both you and your dog as well as a wheelchair.

The view outside from below is less impressive, but booking a lower-level seat on a Superliner means you don't have to take your dog down the stairs from the upper level to the lower, then up again after a relief stop. An attendant will bring your meals if you'd rather not deal with the stairs and the sometimes perilous trek through several cars to the dining car.

Walking between bucketing and rocking Amtrak train cars can be dangerous for dogs and anyone else with bare feet. The moving steel footplates between the cars can slice like scimitars. If your dog is small, carry it from car to car. If your dog is big, best to wait if you can until the train is stopped at a station.

If you are planning a long-distance, perhaps overnight, train trip, the first thing to do is to decide what kind of seat you want for yourself and your dog. The pricing begins with coach seats, followed in ascending order by business class on some trains, sleeper roomettes, accessible sleeper rooms, family rooms, and full bedrooms.

● **Henry:** In both double-decker Superliner and single-level Viewliner sleeping cars, Trooper, my wife, Debby, and I have found that the best accommodations for us are the full bedrooms. They have two bunks, a shower, and a toilet. The upper berth is standard bunk width, but the bottom has a three-quarter-full-size bed large enough for both members of a service dog team. These full bedrooms are sticker-shock expensive, but Debby and I usually amass enough points on our Bank of America Amtrak credit card to pay for most of them. ●

Many dog handlers choose the less expensive roomettes. If two adults are traveling with a dog, the quarters are very tight when the rooms are made up for the night, but you can share the lower bunk with your dog—if it is small, twenty pounds or less. Bring a small blanket for the dog to sleep on, or ask the attendant for a folded sheet. Yes, Amtrak officially says no dogs on the beds, but crew members who live in the real world understand that sometimes that rule has to be bent.

The Superliner roomettes do not have bathroom facilities. If your dog isn't content to be left alone in the room for a few minutes (this is where a human companion comes in handy), you must take your dog to a bathroom in the corridor with you. Frankly, there's no room in most of the Superliner bathrooms for both of you, unless your dog is small, about fifteen or so pounds.

● **Henry:** Trooper and I have managed to squeeze into a Superliner bathroom several times, but only just. Simply turning around in the

Henry Kisor and Trooper in their preferred Amtrak accommodation, a full bedroom. Trooper sleeps on a fleece baby blanket spread on the seat. (Photograph by Deborah Abbott)

tiny bathroom with the presence of a fuzzy companion is nearly impossible. Sometimes I have to open the door, then back in and pull Trooper in with me, a maneuver that always raises curious eyebrows on passersby.

Viewliner roomettes, found on single-level trains east of Chicago, have toilets en suite, so booking such a room if you're a solo traveler with a service dog is not a bad idea at all. That is, if your dog is small enough to share a bed with. Two passengers and a dog can make do if they are all small, skinny, and like each other very much.

Slightly more costly than a roomette is the accessible bedroom (often still called by older crew members Room H, for "Handicap," the old designation). Each Superliner or Viewliner sleeping car has such a bedroom for passengers with mobility disabilities. Those are the roomiest accommodations and have their own bathroom facilities, but are sold first to passengers "with a disability who travel with a wheeled mobility device." There's room (and a bunk) for a human companion as well as space for a wheelchair and a service dog on the floor.

Amtrak says passengers booking accessible bedrooms must provide "written documentation of your disability at the ticket counter and when boarding the train. Acceptable documentation includes:

- Transit system ID card for persons with a disability
- Membership card from a disability organization
- Letter from a physician
- Medicare card, if under 65
- Veteran's Administration ID with 'Service Connected'
- Disabled/Accessible parking placard issued by a state Department of Motor Vehicle (photocopy is acceptable)"

If an accessible room is not sold by two weeks before departure, it will be released to the general public. You have to call Amtrak to book that room; it can't be done online.

● **Henry:** On one occasion I could get only a Superliner roomette for Debby, Trooper, and myself, but the day before departure I checked once more—and the accessible bedroom was available. We called Amtrak and scored that room for a modest upgrade charge.    ●

Family bedrooms (for two adults and two children, no shower or toilet) are also available on the Superliner trains, but they can cost almost as much as full bedrooms, especially in high-demand summer months, and they're only on the lower level. However, even with all the beds made up for the night and occupied, there's room on the floor for your dog. Some service dog teams have found that riding on the lower level makes getting off at relief stops a bit easier, because they don't have to negotiate the narrow stairway up to the car-length corridor.

All Amtrak sleeping car accommodations, by the way, include all meals on the train. This helps justify the often high cost of the rooms.

Whatever accommodations you select, **it's smart to call Amtrak (1-800-USA-RAIL) ahead of time with your reservation number, if you have one, and date of travel as well as the train number, and let them know you're bringing a service dog.**

Don't be surprised if the agent sounds skeptical and asks what the dog does for you. Sometimes inexperienced telephone agents will ask what the dog does for you *on the train*, which is irrelevant. Sometimes a clueless agent will tell you it must be in a crate. In these cases, the agent is just mistaking traveling *pet* requirements for service dog accommodations. If you have trouble, ask for a supervisor.

Once persuaded, the agent will place a note about the service dog on the train's passenger manifest, and if all goes well, the crew will be anticipating your dog's needs. If you've taken the trouble to ask that the manifest include your dog, the crew will be more likely to accept the pooch as a genuine service animal. Fakers rarely take the trouble to call ahead, instead bluffing their way aboard trains.

If a coach attendant has read the manifest and knows you're coming, you'll often be placed at a bulkhead seat with extra room on the floor—sometimes the seats reserved for wheelchair passengers. Same with business class on short-haul trains.

## What to Do En Route

On boarding your train, tell your coach or sleeper attendant that you must get off at certain stops to relieve your dog, and ask that the conductors be informed. Sometimes attendants haven't had time to study the manifest, especially if they are late substitutes from the "extra board" rather than regular crew.

If your dog is quick to go and doesn't care whether he goes on concrete, grass, or dirt, you're in luck—the checked baggage stops will be

Henry Kisor and Trooper take a breather during their exercise hike up and down the long platform at Albuquerque, New Mexico, where Amtrak's *Southwest Chief* stops for an hour to refuel. (Photograph by Deborah Abbott)

fine. Some heavily patronized baggage stops are long enough for the conductors to announce that smokers can get off for a few puffs. The official Amtrak term for these events is "fresh air stops," but the crews still call them "smoke stops." The longest stops of all are those for train servicing and crew changes—twenty minutes to a full hour, sometimes more if the train is on time.

But if your dog is slow to go and does best on grass, brush, or trees, you'll need to plan more carefully. Veteran attendants and conductors often will know good grassy places, but some won't have a clue. It's often helpful to consult Google Earth on a computer or smartphone before taking a train trip. You just enter "Amtrak" and the name of the town and state, and a map showing the location of the station will appear. If you zoom in on the station, there'll be a detailed close-up view showing any greenery around.

If you're traveling on VIA Rail in Canada, however, be aware that the Google Earth resolution is often crude for small towns in the middle of nowhere. Greenery will be hard to see in those images.

Of course, during the winter months in the northern and western areas of the United States as well as most of Canada, snow will cover everything. Provided your dog knows what snow is all about, that shouldn't be a problem in most places.

If a train is running very late, the conductors will try to keep every stop as short as possible. Some scheduled five-minute stops, for example, will take less than thirty seconds if nobody's getting on or off and there's no checked baggage. The train may not stop at all if a station is a "flag stop," and no one is scheduled to board or detrain. Sometimes, however, the train may actually be running ahead of time because of slop built into the schedule—but it will not leave an individual station before the scheduled departure time if it allows passengers to board and not just detrain. You can sometimes get lucky and have a few extra minutes on the ground.

● **Henry:** Aboard long-distance trains, you can take your dog to the dining car if the dog is comfortable under the table. In the beginning Trooper wasn't, and I couldn't keep an eye on him because the edge of the table blocked the view underneath. We took meals in our bedroom instead; the sleeper attendants are all too happy to bring them for tips, and we tip well—$10 per night, plus $5 for each meal.

With time Trooper learned to lie quietly under the table on a little eighteen-inch-by-twenty-four-inch roll-up fleece mat that softens the hard floor. He soon learned that when the mat is unrolled, he is expected to lie down on it—and stay. We also learned that if the dining car lead attendant forgot to offer a reserved space for Trooper, asking for it usually worked.

In the summers, when Amtrak long-distance trains are often sold out, it's often better to take your meals in your room rather than take your dog to the dining car and either stuff the pooch under the table with four pairs of legs or let it occupy a seat space that the staff would rather use for a human passenger. At less busy times, the lead attendant will be happy to reserve two spaces at a table, one for you and one for your dog. (Sometimes Debby and I go to the dining car in shifts while the other stays in the room with Trooper.)          ●

Do take your dog to the lounge cars, especially those on the double-deck Superliner trains on western routes and some eastern runs. Many of the bench seats face outward with lots of room out of the way for a dog. Fellow passengers will be friendly and will want to talk about your dog. Be ready, however, to warn overeager dog lovers about approaching a working dog without your permission. Most will understand.

If your dog has a tendency to be an opportunist, you'll have to keep a weather eye out for tidbits on the floors of the dining and lounge cars and try to kick them aside before your dog pounces. Americans are messy travelers.

Once in a long while you may encounter a fellow passenger who declares an allergy to dogs, setting up a potential conflict of competing rights. Amtrak puts the needs of passengers with disabilities first—it says more allergens are brought aboard trains on people's clothes rather than on the animals—but in such cases it's just good manners to volunteer, if you can and doing so is not physically difficult, to take your dog to another car. Leave the decision, however, to the attendants and conductors.

## For Passengers with Visual Disabilities

Riders who are blind and travel with companions can rely on them to help get around the train as well as find good spots to relieve service animals at station stops. Those who travel alone can be confident that onboard Amtrak personnel will step in with plenty of assistance.

Attendants, for instance, will help you get from your room or seat to the dining or lounge car. At station stops they will offer to stand on the side of you opposite to your guide animal and offer their elbows for guidance to a relief area. If they don't, just ask. Give them time, however, to get other passengers and luggage off in front of you.

It's worth mentioning that Amtrak crews particularly like guide dogs, for they know these highly specialized dogs are the calmest and most highly trained of service animals.

## For Wheelchair Users

The platforms at almost all Amtrak stations, even unstaffed ones, are equipped with small brown metal sheds inside which lie mechanical wheelchair lifts. Each lift can accommodate a chair, a rider, and a dog. Once the passenger rolls into the lift, a gate is closed and a station agent or car attendant cranks a handle to raise or lower the lift to coach or sleeper door height.

Amtrak personnel say the lifts are easy to operate, but because they're so infrequently used, there's often a moment of learning while the crew members refamiliarize themselves.

Incidentally, the lifts are present at every Amtrak station on the western routes but are usually not needed (so far) because the double-decker Superliners on those routes employ built-in ramps on the cars that have wheelchair access. Superliner doors open close to the platforms.

If you are a wheelchair user as well as a service dog handler, always call Amtrak before departure to make sure either your train is equipped with a ramp or your final station has a lift that is in service.

## For Miniature Horse Partners

Amtrak will carry service miniature horses, but it is *absolutely essential* to call ahead to arrange accommodations. If a service horse team is traveling in a sleeper, it can be accommodated *only* in an accessible bedroom. The other rooms are just too small, and negotiating a Superliner's narrow stairway upstairs is very difficult for a miniature horse.

In a double-deck Superliner coach, the team will be accommodated in a coach with lower-level seating. On a single-level eastern train, a wheelchair lift is usually necessary to get horse and partner up into the train. Remember, not all stations may have working lifts. Best to ask when booking your ticket on the phone.

# Railroads in Alaska

Amtrak does not operate in Alaska, but that state is one of the United States, so the Americans with Disabilities Act applies there. Service animals are welcome aboard Alaska Railroad passenger trains, including the famous Denali Star between Anchorage and Denali National Park, and aboard the White Pass & Yukon narrow-gauge tourist train that wends between Skagway and Whitehorse in the Yukon.

# Railroads in Canada

**VIA Rail Canada:** Like Amtrak, the Canadian national passenger railroad welcomes service dogs, but with a few differences.

The biggest is that, unlike Amtrak, VIA Rail not only requires proof of rabies immunization but also may ask for documentation that your dog is a bona fide service animal trained by a government-approved facility. In some cases it may even ask for a note from a doctor attesting that you must travel with a service dog.

As with Amtrak, lower-level customer service agents who handle bookings from passengers with disabilities may not be fully informed about service dog policies, may confuse them with pet policies, or may be overeager at asking for documentation. If this happens, ask for a supervisor.

If you are flying into Canada to take a train, be assured that customs and immigration at Canadian airports will accept a service dog provided its handler is with it, has a current rabies vaccination certificate, and carries documentation proving the dog was trained by an approved organization.

● **Henry:** As mentioned in chapter 1, "The Basics," when Trooper and I travel by train in Canada, we carry ID cards from Trooper's training outfit, Dogs for Better Lives, and the voluntary State of Michigan service dog registry program—as well as his immunization record and an APHIS Form 7001 international health certificate signed by

Trooper's veterinarian. That last is not strictly necessary, but, again, an excess of paperwork never hurts.

As on Amtrak, service dogs always travel free. VIA also will give the dog its own seat space (and ticket) without charge in coach or business class on short-haul trains (which Amtrak doesn't), and even offers a discount on a bedroom for two aboard some overnight trains so that you and your dog have plenty of room to move around at night.

So far as rail fare is concerned, VIA does not offer a 10 percent discount for persons with disabilities and their human companions, as Amtrak does.

But VIA will allow a service dog team to pay roomette fare for a bedroom for two (saving up to CAN$1,000), provided the tickets are booked by telephone—and you can prove to the railroad's satisfaction that you are a legitimate service dog team with the required documentation.

**You must call 1-888-842-7245 to book your tickets. If you are deaf or hard of hearing, the TTY number is 1-800-268-9503.**

If you have a disability that does not allow you to travel without a human companion, VIA will allow your two-legged helper to travel for free, even in a sleeper room, as well as your service dog. This could save you as much as CAN$2,800 on a Toronto-to-Vancouver trip.

Of course the railroad wants documentary assurance that you *need* a companion. There are two forms of proof:

1. Your doctor could fill out an official "Confidential Medical Certificate for Passengers Requiring a Support Person." It's good for a year.
2. If you're a Canadian citizen and carry a membership card in one of several VIA-recognized disability organizations, that may be all you need to take along a support person for free.

For details, including a copy of the medical certificate, see https://www.viarail.ca/en/travel-info/special-needs/accessibility. For other details, check the "Traveling with a guide dog" link.

Like Amtrak, VIA asks that passengers with disabilities book their tickets by phone (as above) rather than online, so that a note can be put into the train's manifest for attendants to best serve their needs, and this is especially important if you're taking an overnight train. If you're riding a short-haul train on the spur of the moment, however, you can just show up at a station before the train arrives, and VIA will happily deal with you and your service dog. (But carry that paperwork with you!)

You should also be advised that, in international fashion, VIA uses twenty-four-hour time, not the twelve-hour clock of the United States, and that its week begins on Monday, not Sunday. For example, Train No. 1, the *Canadian*, leaves Toronto during the off season on Days 3 and 6

Trooper and Henry in the bustling Montreal Union Station during a transcontinental adventure on VIA Rail from Halifax, Nova Scotia, to Vancouver, British Columbia. (Photograph by Johannes Urbanski on Henry's iPhone)

of the week—that's Wednesday and Saturday, not Tuesday and Friday, as it would be below the border. That's important to know when you're reading the VIA schedules and planning a trip.

To confuse matters further, most of the rest of Canada follows U.S. practice and starts its week on Sunday.

At any time, Canada's most famous train is the celebrated *Canadian*, the four-night journey from Toronto through the Ontario forests, the Great Plains, and the Canadian Rockies to Vancouver on the Pacific Ocean. Riding this train is like stepping back in time to the days when your grandparents rode in luxury coast to coast across the nation. That train's cars, both coach and sleeper, consist mostly of single-level stainless steel streamlined cars from the 1950s that have been through several rebuildings over the decades.

For a passenger with a service dog, the classic one-person sleeper roomette is fine during the day, but at night the bed covers the toilet. If you're of an age that needs to arise at least once a night, raising the bed is clumsy and noisy and forces you to put the dog out into the aisle while you do the job. This is a good reason why VIA will allow a passenger with a service dog to book a bedroom for two for the price of a roomette for one. For service dog handlers who also use wheelchairs, VIA provides in each of the famed boat-tailed Park observation cars from the 1950s a roomy and luxurious wheelchair-accessible bedroom for two, and the price for passenger and qualified human companion is no more than that for two old-fashioned open berths covered with curtains, still a feature in the sixty-five-year-old *Canadian* sleeper cars. The dome of this car is the place to be during a ride through spectacular scenery. On the other hand, a passenger who uses a wheelchair may need help getting from the bedroom through the very narrow corridor a step up to the lounge in the rear, and trying to navigate the stairs from lounge to dome may be unwise. So is trying to negotiate the narrow vestibules between cars.

Still, meals from the superb dining car will be brought to your room—and to your seat if you're in coach. In the *Canadian* coaches, there are wheelchair tie-down spots next to accessible toilets, and VIA will provide lightweight wheelchairs narrow enough to negotiate the aisles to those spots. See appendix 1 for more details about the *Canadian*.

The modern Renaissance cars on the Montreal-Halifax *Ocean* run were born as *Nightstar* cars for overnights on the English Channel Tunnel runs, but when that scheme fell through, VIA Rail bought them for a song. They are considerably smaller and sleeker than the 1950s equipment.

There are no Renaissance roomettes, so everyone pays the same rate for a double bedroom on the *Ocean*. At least one wheelchair-accessible bedroom with bath is available on every *Ocean*, as is a coach with a wheelchair tie-down and accessible bathroom among the two-plus-one seating (one row of seats along one side, two rows along the other).

Some Renaissance coaches can be found on the Quebec-Montreal-Toronto day runs, but most of those regional trains use Canadian-built lightweight aluminum "LRC" coaches. These latter coaches have roomy wheelchair spaces with tie-downs next to accessible bathrooms.

Jean and Tom M., the Ontarians who travel with Jean's service dog, Cha-Cha, suggest choosing business-class cars rather than the less expensive coaches on the "corridor" between Quebec City, Quebec, and Windsor, Ontario.

"Experience has taught us that children almost always travel in coach, whereas they almost never ride in business class," Tom says. "Children have a hard time being cooped up on the train for extended periods. And so it is only natural that they seek out Cha-Cha to play. But she is either working or resting while on the train and cannot engage with the children without compromising herself.

"And on the rare occasion that there has been a child in business class, they have been the child of a diplomat or someone of similar station in life—as opposed to the free-range children back in coach."

● **Henry:** Trooper and I recently booked a VIA business-class ride on the corridor from Montreal to Toronto and loved it, especially the roomy, leather-covered seats and excellent at-seat food and bar service. There was, however, a minor problem.

For some reason VIA had booked us into the wheelchair space, a low table facing two side-by-side seats with Trooper next to the window. That would have been fine, but in a last-minute scheduling change Trooper and I lost those seats to a little girl in a wheelchair and her parents and were put into two facing seats in a single row on the opposite side of the aisle. Little girls in wheelchairs take precedence over everything else, and I had no complaint about being moved—but Trooper was now on the aisle where people could see, touch, and speak to him.

A number of times I had to say "Working service dog! Please don't interact with him!" Most passersby took that in stride, but one elderly woman insisted that she had the right to speak to him. That woke Trooper suddenly from his sleep, making us both uncomfortable.

The VIA crew took Trooper's side and asked the woman not to harass him again. Still, I wished we could have found a window seat for him in a double row. The car, however, was full. We had to make do.  ●

VIA Rail insists on issuing tickets and boarding passes to service dogs, although they ride free. (VIA Rail)

Vince F., a Washington State resident who travels with Otto, a graduate of Dogs for Better Lives, had a less bumpy experience. When his wife, Sally, told VIA that they were bringing a service dog on the train from Quebec City to Montreal after a St. Lawrence River cruise, the Canadian railroad said it would upgrade them at no charge from two seats together to four, two rows of two seats facing across a low table—and gave Otto his own seat space and ticket.

That facing-seat arrangement is common on many VIA trains. For service dog handlers, there are two other major physical differences between Amtrak and VIA Rail cars.

First, while the slashing footplates in Amtrak vestibules are dangerous, those on VIA trains are much less so. Even when a Canadian train is bucketing along at 140 kmh (87 mph), the tight passageways between cars are safe for a service dog to traverse on foot if supervised. Just be careful that a small dog doesn't get a claw caught in the quarter-inch gap between buffers.

Second, while Amtrak dining cars feature rigid banquette seating, VIA diners have either movable chairs or seats that fold up and back. You can spot your dog at your side within full view instead of under the table in a dark jungle of human legs.

**Rocky Mountaineer:** This private Canadian Rockies luxury train network between Seattle, Vancouver, Lake Louise, Banff, and Jasper does accept service dogs according to British Columbia and Alberta law, but a representative pointed out that the trains do not stop between these major stations, and the journeys range from eight to twelve hours long. That is a long time for a dog to go without relief—if there are no delays.

As with the rest of Canadian transportation, documentary proof that the dog has been specially trained is required.

## Rails in Mexico

**Copper Canyon Railroad:** "Sadly, the train company (Ferrocaril Chihuahua al Pacifico) and some of our hotels do not allow service dogs at all," said a representative of one of several tourist companies that offer rides on this famous train between Chihuahua and Los Mochis.

The only other operating passenger railroad in Mexico is the **Tequila Express**, a luxury tourist train running on weekends from Guadalajara, Jalisco, to a tequila distillery in Amaltitan. To our inquiry, a representative responded, "Up to now the train to Tequila does not have special service for people with disabilities that we know of. Please contact them directly for more information: +52 (374) 74207 00 Ext. 6767."

One commuter rail system is the **Suburban Railway of the Valley of Mexico Metropolitan Area**, and under construction is a commuter line from Mexico City to Toluca. There are also four light rail or rapid transit systems in Mexico City, Guadalajara, and Monterrey.

## Individual Trains

Appendix 1 contains station-by-station schedules and descriptions for several of the most popular American and Canadian passenger trains. These will help you locate the best stops to relieve your service dog. Knowing where they are often will give you confidence that you and your dog will be able to negotiate a train trip without difficulty.

## Summing Up

- When planning a train ride, consider your dog's relief needs.
- Pack sufficient food and treats for your dog.
- Let the conductors and attendants know *your* needs as well as your dog's.
- Always make sure the conductors and your car attendant know when and where you get off the train to relieve your dog, and always stay within their sight.
- You have three choices of accommodations: inexpensive and roomy coach seats, quieter business class on some trains, or more costly roomettes or full bedrooms on overnight trains.

- You can take your dog to the dining car, but you may prefer to remain at your coach seat or in your sleeper room, where attendants will bring your meals. (Be sure to tip.)
- Be careful when moving between cars, especially on Amtrak, where the sharp footplates are dangerous.
- It is a good idea to call ahead with Amtrak so that crews are ready for you. In Canada, providing documentation is essential for VIA Rail rides.

## Chapter 4

# On the Road

The open road may be calling you for a weekend getaway, camping trip, resort vacation, or distant family wedding. Or perhaps you may be traveling on business. Whatever your trip's purpose, driving in the United States can be liberating for service dog partners—you can skip the hassles of expensive paperwork, artificial dog relief stations, airport security, sardine seating, and checked luggage fees. You and your dog can enjoy privacy and freedom, often at a lower cost than you'll pay for air tickets.

"I've traveled by taxi, Uber, plane, and car," said Morgan W, who travels with his service dog, Foley. "By car is by far the easiest, as I can control everything from where he sits to when we stop."

Although fuel costs are higher north of the border, it's equally easy to head for Canada. Bring along a copy of your dog's rabies certificate—it's always a good idea, regardless of your destination.

If you don't have a car or recreational vehicle, you can rent one or hit the road by bus "and leave the driving to us," as the Greyhound Lines' commercials promised back in the 1950s.

And with twenty-first century technology, you can reach in your pocket and summon a shorter ride using your smart phone.

# Using a Taxi or Ride-Sharing Service

For a short hop, you may want to get around by taxi or by Uber, Lyft, and other ride-sharing companies. However, there have been well-publicized incidents in which drivers refused to transport passengers with service dogs, and lawsuits ensued.

Melanie said she has traveled easily with Paddington in taxis and hotel vans, trains, planes, and even a riverboat in Tennessee, but "at the airport in Los Angeles, a taxi driver refused to take us on. An airport employee was herding the taxis for riders, and she waved him on. I think he had to go to the back of the line again."

Ride-sharing car drivers can be equally difficult. Suzy Wilburn reported that a graduate of Southeastern Guide Dogs was bypassed twice in a row while standing with his guide dog at an appointed spot awaiting pickup.

**Henry:** Trooper and I have found Uber and Lyft cars particularly useful, although there have been plenty of news stories about their drivers refusing to take service dogs—and it has happened to us. Sometimes rideshare drivers who stop and pick us up appear a little dismayed about Trooper, but when I explain he either sits on my lap or lies on the floor, they're fine with it. They usually know the law about service dogs. But not all do, or they pay no attention to it.

Once, in Washington, D.C., an Uber driver spotted Trooper as he slowed to pick us up, then sped up and hightailed it away without stopping. He may have had a religious belief that dogs are unclean, or perhaps he was allergic or otherwise had had a bad experience with a dog in his car, but whatever the reason, his refusal to pick us up violated both federal law and Uber policy.

Another Uber was close by and picked us up in less than five minutes.

But I was irked. This sort of thing should not happen. What if a service dog and its handler called for a ride in the middle of the night in unfamiliar and possibly dangerous territory and were refused?

Letting the incident go without complaint could mean some other person with a disability might be imperiled.

So I went online and filed a complaint on the Uber customer help page. (The page actually has a box to check for "service dog issues," since there have been so many of them.)

After a brief exchange of emails in which I described the incident in detail and, instead of threatening a lawsuit, just asked that the driver be re-educated, Uber responded: "At the conclusion of our investigation, the partner you reported has been provided with additional information regarding legal obligations and their Uber account has been reactivated. They have confirmed that they understand their legal obligations. Should we receive a second report of this nature, their account may be subject to permanent deactivation."

That was good enough for me. When possible, persuasion is always better than litigation. That saves time and effort. (Some people think I'm naive, but going to court requires time, trouble, and treasure.)

In Toronto a few months later, however, three consecutive Uber drivers passed by in ten minutes without stopping before a fourth picked me up. If I had been a Canadian, I'd have filed a stiff complaint with the proper Ontario authorities, but as a visiting American didn't want to get embroiled in an international incident. So I went through the same online exchange with Uber customer help. The following week Uber Canada sent out a broadcast message to all its drivers reminding them of its new and stiffer service dog policy. Coincidence? Maybe not.

Canadian human rights laws allow taxi and rideshare drivers with either religious scruples or physical difficulties to refuse to carry a service dog team—but, according to Uber's new rules, drivers must stop on the spot and arrange another ride for the partners.

Other service dog handlers may have different problems. Yes, Trooper, being a small terrier, sits on my lap rather than the seat, often mollifying potentially hostile drivers—but what about seventy-pound Labs?

● **Chris:** When I've used Uber with my Lab, Raylene, I have directed her toward the back seat floor, but sometimes there has not been enough room there for a large dog. At times, she has had to jump in on the back seat itself as she would in our car, and has ended up half sprawled on my lap. I brushed stray black hairs off the leather seats and tipped well. The drivers did not seem to care. My guess is that they see a lot worse from kids and drunks, to name just two problem categories. ●

● **Henry:** I asked Uber about big dogs, and the company said its policy is to suggest to drivers that they carry blankets or towels to put on the back seat for service dogs, but that's at their discretion. (Uber views its drivers not as employees but as independent contractors, so it allows them certain leeway in its policies.) ●

## Going by Bus

Bus operators offer budget-friendly scheduled service between cities, escorted motor coach tours, and, of course, transit services. Even though you'll sacrifice some space and freedom compared to traveling in your personal vehicle, you'll never have to deal with directions, parking, repairs, and refueling. Catch up on your reading, look at the passing scenery, and you might discover that bus travel suits your style perfectly.

There should be no difficulty with acceptance of a service dog on a municipal transit bus. In some localities the dogs must sit or lie on the floor, and that can be a problem if the bus is crowded. In Windsor, Ontario, a woman with a twenty-pound service bichon frise put the dog on the seat next to her because, she said, he was so small and was jostled around when the bus was moving. The driver and his supervisor demurred, saying "the consensus across the transit industry was that a dog on a seat on his own doesn't have the ability to hold on to a grab bar if the bus takes a tight turn." The obvious solution in such cases is to hold a small dog on one's lap and cradle a large one between one's knees.

Before boarding shuttles, vans, or buses, service dog partners can speak with the driver to request seating that will best accommodate the dog. (Photo by Robert Goodier)

Elsewhere the rules may be different. Pets can ride free on the King County metro buses in the Seattle area but must pay a fare if they can't sit on their owners' laps. Service dogs ride for free and normally either stay on the floor without blocking the aisle or sit on their handlers' laps—but if an unoccupied seat is available, they can sit on it.

As for long-distance bus travel, it isn't what it used to be in both the United States and Canada. The days when every small town in the middle of nowhere had a bus stop are long over. Today most bus travel runs on U.S. interstate highways from city to city and on major Canadian roads as well.

There are distinct advantages to bus travel. It is inexpensive compared to air and rail travel. Most modern intercity buses are clean and relatively comfortable, with roomy seats, a bathroom aboard, tray tables, and even Wi-Fi.

Increasingly, buses and trains share the same terminals in cities big and small, making the transfer from one mode of travel to the other easier. Layovers between buses can be lengthy, sometimes requiring overnights.

There are, of course, drawbacks. Seats aren't as comfortable as those on trains, and there's no space to get up and move around. That can be hard on a dog as well as a human. Some runs attract rough characters who may make more genteel riders uncomfortable. For a few service dog handlers, there is no other choice. For others, buses can be a happy adventure.

All interstate bus lines say they accommodate service dogs, but some seem to accommodate them better than others.

Certain bus lines (Trailways, Jefferson Lines, Peter Pan among them) sternly say no dogs are to be on the seats and that they must lie within the customer's space—that means on the floor in front of your seat and not in the aisle. Some will allow them to ride on the customer's lap. (Good luck if you've got a Lab.) Other bus companies don't mention it at all.

Though service dogs are carried free on all bus lines, it's often a good idea to buy two seats so that your dog has plenty of room on the floor at the next seat—or *on* the seat, if the driver is willing to look the other way. (Don't count on this. You can't predict what the driver will do.)

The bus lines all say your dog must be under control on a leash. Some carefully define what a service dog is and does, perhaps as much for the edification of riders without disabilities who might object to a dog's presence as for a warning to anyone who might want to bring aboard a pet. Greyhound, for instance. says:

> Service animal means any guide dog, signal dog, seizure response dog, psychiatric service dog, sensory signal dog or other animal individually trained to assist, work or perform specific tasks for an individual with a disability.
>
> The service provided by a service animal, includes, but is not limited to, guiding individuals with impaired vision, alerting individuals with

impaired hearing to intruders or sounds, standing guard over the individual during a seizure, detecting the onset of a psychiatric episode, providing minimal protection or rescue work, pulling a wheelchair, fetching dropped items or disrupting repetitive movements that are common to individuals who are autistic.

Greyhound has an email address for questions or complaints about disability access (ADAsupport@greyhound.com). So do most of the other bus lines.

- **Henry:** As with the airlines and Amtrak, sometimes low-level customer service representatives won't have any idea how to handle queries from a service dog handler. For a trip from Chicago to St. Paul, Minnesota, I asked Megabus's online customer service not once or twice but three times for the itinerary of intermediate stops and if I'd be able to take Trooper off the bus at one of them for a pee. Each time I received a different response.

  One rep said, "Unfortunately, we do not have such itinary [sic]. We're sorry but we do not have authorization to let anyone off at locations other than our designated bus stops which are for drop-offs and pickups only."

  The second said, "Drivers are permitted to make stops when the bus ride is 8 hours or more. If the route you're traveling is less than that, the driver is not allowed to stop."

  The third said, "Just ask the driver to stop when the dog must go out."

  I asked for a supervisor, who responded:

  "I do apologize for the incorrect information being sent prior. Breaks are usually on trips five hours or more but the location and when is to the discretion of the driver. On your trip you are able to ask your driver if they would be able to make a rest stop soon."

  "Able to ask"? With some asperity, I emailed the company's ADA compliance department, asking where the intermediate stops were.

  Milwaukee and Madison, she said. Or elsewhere on the route if needed, for I would be a passenger with special needs, and all

I would have to do is ask the driver. And sorry, she added, for the confusion.

When I made that trip, the Milwaukee stop wasn't so convenient, because there's no grass in the intermodal station area—just concrete and gravel. Madison was fine, because the stop is in the middle of downtown with grass and brush close by. I was astonished, however, that the ADA person did not tell me (nor did the Megabus website say) that the bus stopped at a service plaza with a fast-food restaurant off an interstate highway just outside Mauston, two-thirds of the way to St. Paul. There was lots and lots of lawn at that twenty-five-minute stop.

As for the ride itself, buses are buses and their quarters are cramped, but it was OK. The bathroom aboard the bus did have plenty of room for both Trooper and me. He slept atop a baby blanket on the seat next to me. He had his own adult ticket so he could have his own space on the floor if need be. The driver didn't care.

The only real negative I carried away from the trip is the Megabus "terminal" in Chicago, a lonely curbside stop at Polk and Clinton in the middle of a mostly industrial area. There are no benches and no shelters. Trooper and I would have hated to wait for that St. Paul bus in driving rain or snow on a cold day. ●

Trooper at the Megabus "terminal"— actually a street corner in an isolated industrial neighborhood— in Chicago. (Photograph by Henry Kisor)

Gayle Crabtree, a Tennessean and a Megabus rider who regularly travels with her spouse and service dog, Tomlin, offers this advice:

1. Buy your service dog a ticket. Megabus is a discount bus carrier so the cost for three round-trip tickets from Knoxville to D.C. came to less than $110. At these prices, there isn't any reason to skimp by not buying a ticket. Both of you deserve to be comfortable.

2. Cover the Megabus seat. Someone will sit in the seat after you leave who may not appreciate dog fur. Take a minute to cover the Megabus seat well with a sheet or towel. It only takes a minute to get it done. My service dog sat in the aisle while I got this done, and the driver even helped.

3. Bring a water bowl, treats, and toys. Always, always, always do this. I figure that he may not eat or drink, but offering it means that we're doing our job.

For a short while Trooper took an interest in the proceedings aboard a Megabus from Chicago to St. Paul, but after a while he curled up on a blanket and let the miles pass by while he slept. (Selfie by Henry Kisor)

4. Tip the driver (or at least say a meaningful thank-you). The goodwill helps pave the way for the next person who brings a service dog on Megabus.

As for Greyhound, its ADA compliance department had this to say:

Our drivers will make announcements and provide information regarding upcoming rest stops, rest breaks, departures, arrivals and transfers—at which time you are more than welcome to allow your service animal to eliminate.

The first row of the bus is reserved for the elderly, customers with disabilities and unaccompanied children. While some disabilities and needs may be obvious, others are not and may be served by several different representatives of Greyhound along the way. *It is essential that you ask for assistance at each location where you may need help, in-*

Gayle Crabtree's service dog, Tomlin, is a veteran rider of intercity buses. (Photo by Gayle Crabtree)

*cluding with each driver if you should have different drivers for multiple legs of your trip.* (Greyhound's italics)

So there it is. It's all up to you . . . and the driver.

## Travel by Car

Car rental companies in the United States must follow ADA guidelines, and some rent to people traveling with pet dogs. For a service dog handler, companies should waive "no pet" policies and pet deposits. However, they have the right to charge the renter for damage a service dog might cause.

If you own a car, your dog is already accustomed to hopping in and enjoying the change in scenery. It's a good idea to restrain the animal in one way or another to keep him from becoming an unguided missile in a crash and suffering grievous injuries. Some people use crates strapped to a back seat or in a cargo area of a sport utility vehicle. Some prefer padded "playpens," while others use harnesses threaded through shoulder belts.

"I use the Sleepypod Clickit Utility dog harness for Henri when we are taking long trips in the car," said Dianne Urhausen, who also takes it along on airplane flights. "I don't use it for short trips around town because it is a bit of a hassle getting her buckled in to the seat belt. I chose the Sleepypod because it was recommended by *Consumer Reports* and the Center for Pet Safety. Henri is not crazy about it because it does keep her from moving around in the back seat as much as she would like, but she tolerates it."

● **Henry:** At the suggestion of one of Trooper's trainers, we purchased a $35 "hammock" that straps over our minivan's front and back seat headrests and provides a soft U-shaped area that protects him from pitching to the floor in sudden stops. We leave that arrangement in the van even in city driving. On long auto trips we also place large pillows against both rear doors to provide padding against T-bone collisions. ●

● **Chris:** What should you pack on road trips? Along with the travel packing suggestions outlined in chapter 1, "The Basics," I bring one of Raylene's full-size beds from home, multiple plastic waste bag rolls, bowls for food and water, fast-drying towels, her grooming kit, documentation, training treats, and toys. I carry bottled water in case the local supply is questionable and a larger supply of her dog food than I expect to need. And I always bring along my dog's first aid kit. (More detailed information follows in this chapter.) ●

On a long trip, you might experience frequent variations in temperature, humidity, and elevation. Time zone changes will alter the dog's eating, sleeping, and waking routines. But if you remember to pace yourself, you and the dog both will have time to adapt and get the most out of your destinations. Remember the rule of threes: drive only three hundred to four hundred maximum miles per day, stretch your legs (and the dog's) at least every three hours, and pull into a hotel or motel by three in the afternoon.

Some days, of course, you won't drive at all; you're already there. Try to spend at least three to five days at high-demand locations like the Grand Canyon or Yellowstone National Park and, as early as possible, reserve a hotel inside or very close to the park. It saves time and energy to be in the center of the action and use free shuttle services that are often provided. A similar approach is effective for visiting urban areas like Washington, D.C., New Orleans, Los Angeles, and New York City that attract hordes of tourists.

A good strategy is to cover a lot of ground starting first thing in the morning, enjoy a leisurely lunch, and relax in the afternoon. Lining up with dozens of tourists in the midday heat and leading a tired, panting service dog onto a packed shuttle bus is no fun. You can always head back out later after the day-trip crowds have subsided.

Another strategy is to avoid heat and crowds by vacationing in the off-season, possibly in the spring or fall. However, some national parks like Glacier, Crater Lake, and Mount Rainier have only brief summer seasons. Everglades National Park is best visited in the winter, Yosemite

Service animals like hearing dog Raylene are permitted in all buildings at Colonial Williamsburg. (Photo by Robert Goodier)

is jam-packed in May, and many of Yellowstone's facilities, including campgrounds, close by mid-September. Spring is prime time in Washington, D.C., and it is likely to be mobbed. So research your destination before booking anything.

## Tours and Attractions on the Road

Whether you use a car, RV, or bus for your road trip transportation, you'll probably want to explore area attractions. With a little online research, you may learn about facilities well designed for people with disabilities, information that will help you and your travel companion have a smooth visit.

"Disney, for instance, is very good about service dogs," said Dianne Urhausen. "Something I never noticed until I took Henri to Disneyland is that there are designated relief areas in the grassy areas in the park. Look for a dog symbol, and there will be a gate to let you in behind the fence."

At Disneyland your dog can stay at your side during most, if not all, of your visit. "Service dogs can go on some of the rides with you," Urhausen said. "We took Henri with us on Small World, the Jungle Cruise, the Mark Twain Riverboat, the raft to Tom Sawyer Island, the Disneyland Railroad, and the Monorail."

Assistance dog Henri accompanied Dianne Urhausen on many Disneyland rides such as Small World, the Jungle Cruise, and the Mark Twain Riverboat. (Photo by Dianne Urhausen)

While having fun in such a park, remember to keep an eye on your dog's scavenging just as you do back home. "I never noticed how much popcorn there is on the ground," Urhausen said, even though Disneyland employees are constantly sweeping up.

When planning your itinerary, remember that physical constraints mean some places are hard to visit with a service dog, such as Antelope Canyon, a photogenic attraction near Page, Arizona. "Lower Antelope has too many stairs (read ladders) too steep for a dog to use, and they are steep enough that you couldn't carry a dog," said Vince F., Otto's partner.

Mesa Verde National Park welcomes service dogs on public trails and facilities, but many of the cliff dwellings also have ladders, as well as narrow paths and steep drop-offs. "Balcony House, Cliff Palace, and Long House cliff dwellings have ladders, ranging in length from 6 to 30 feet, which may prove difficult and unsafe for a dog," advises the National Park Service website.

● **Chris:** It's usually important to notify tour operators when space will be needed for a service dog. I'm encouraged by reservation systems that now proactively ask if you are traveling with one. Xanterra Parks and Resorts' reservation service, for example, offers a service dog booking option when visitors confirm Glacier National Park's famous Red Bus Tours. Since the historic "Red Jammers" were built in the 1930s when people were smaller, space is at a premium. A big dog can take up as much room as a child, so it makes sense for the tour operator to know one is accompanying a passenger. Ideally the driver-guides usually will receive this information in advance, although our driver cast a doubtful eye at placid Raylene and asked, "Does the dog like children?"

The Yosemite Area Regional Transit System (YARTS) also incorporates the option to enter your requirement as a service dog partner into its online reservation system for scheduled bus rides into the Yosemite Valley.

Some hotels and RV parks provide complimentary (or inexpensive) van or bus shuttle services to airports, cruise ship piers, or tourist locations. Reservations are usually required. On a recent trip to New Orleans, we stayed a few nights and booked a time slot for the shuttle into the city, advising the office that I would be accompanied by my dog. The following morning, the driver pulled up, saw the dog, and pleasantly advised that she "probably will be no problem," but he would need to first ask all the other passengers if they had any objections to her presence.

As a service dog partner, you already know you'll encounter uninformed, inexperienced, or seasonal employees during your travels.

"Be prepared to react calmly to vendors of different cultures who are new to the United States, because they might not be completely clear on ADA laws and rights," said David Caras, human partner of the black Lab Bobb. "Be ready to encounter resistance from teenage employees

At New York's Niagara Falls State Park, service dogs are welcome wherever patrons are permitted to go. Raylene was offered a child-size raincoat for a ride on the *Maid of the Mist*. (Photo by Robert Goodier)

who might not know the ADA. All they understand is that they are told by their manager not to let dogs into the store, restaurant, etc. Ask for the manager."

Sometimes well-meaning employees aren't sure how to accommodate a service dog appropriately unless you explain your needs right away in a straightforward way. (For example, "That front seat will be ideal since it offers room for the dog at my feet.")

● **Chris:** Happily, you'll meet people who go out of their way to be sure that you and your dog can fully participate in a tour, like the gracious young woman who offered child-size plastic rainwear to keep Raylene dry as we cruised around Niagara Falls aboard the *Maid of the Mist.*　●

## Camping

Touring national parks, seeing jaw-dropping natural wonders, and immersing yourself in attractions you've only read about are all pleasurable elements of the classic American camping trip. Sharing long hikes, exploring deserted beaches, and sitting around campfires are all fun for the dog, too. But hauling a trailer over the mountains, maneuvering a motor home around tight corners, and driving through unfamiliar megacities all call for more time, planning, and concentration than usual.

You won't need suitcases to travel in a trailer or motor home. Instead, you'll create a microcosm of your home by loading clothes, linens, kitchen gear, food, medications, toiletries, tools, books, charging cords, cameras, travel confirmations, paper goods, and your dog's daily needs into cupboards and compartments. With plenty of space for extra stuff, it's easy to bring the frivolous and forget the important, so a packing checklist is important.

Life on the road is easier if daily supplies are easy to reach. For example, a kitchen drawer or shelf near the sink can be equipped as the dog's feeding depot with a plastic bin for food (refilled weekly from a big bag),

For long road trips, the familiar scents of a dog's bed and toys can make an RV feel like a second home. (Photo by Christine Goodier)

a plastic measuring cup, spoon, and containers of whatever supplements or medications you give your dog daily.

- **Chris:** After more than twenty-five thousand highway miles with Raylene, I've learned that dogs and RV trips are a great match. A cupboard above the front door of our RV holds Raylene's first aid kit, grooming supplies, a towel for rainy days, a spare leash, and a few toys. Just inside the door are three handy hooks to hold gear needed for our constant exits and entrances: her harness, leash, and working vest.

  My dog, like most, loves exposure to new sights, sounds, and sniffs, yet I think she takes comfort in the familiarity of our RV, her second home. As her partner, my job includes finding safe places to stay and fun things to do during our trips.

Most people have mastered online booking for hotels, and finding an overnight spot for RV or tent camping is just as easy. With a cell phone or tablet, it's easy to use an app such as AllStays Camp and RV that pinpoints your location, provides interactive maps of the region, and includes links to websites, reservations systems, and traveler reviews for all nearby campgrounds.

(Since large RVs are notorious gas-guzzlers, another handy crowd-sourced app is Gas Buddy, which identifies nearby gas stations and displays recent fuel prices, with the cheapest at the top of the list.)

You can choose a basic RV park, splurge on a pricey resort, or save money at a modest campground on public lands. National, state, provincial, county, and even city parks have some of the most beautiful campgrounds in North America and the best hiking for exercising your service dog. Lesser-known locations managed by the U.S. Army Corps of Engineers, Bureau of Land Management, and National Forest Service contain campground gems, too, often in remote, sprawling, scenic settings.

Should you reserve or just wing it? Spontaneous people enjoy setting off with no plan except to go where the road leads, while others savor research and reservations. Either approach can be fun. There are more than thirty thousand campgrounds in the United States and Canada, and hundreds of thousands of campsites, so reservations aren't always necessary. But because of a strong economy, increasing popularity of RVs, and the sheer numbers of retiring baby boomers, book ahead for your "can't miss" destinations.

If you are a die-hard, spontaneous road-tripper, it's good to know that managers of truck stops, Walmarts, and Cracker Barrel restaurants may let you spend the night in an RV free at the edge of their parking lots, depending on local regulations. You might not sleep as well there, but your dog probably will be perfectly happy.

Wherever you stop for the night, your service dog will usually have canine company. It's rare to find a campground or RV park in the United States or Canada that discourages dogs, although many impose restrictions on the breed, size (by weight), and number of pets per unit and may occasionally charge a small fee. Some have designated relief areas with free waste bags or even provide fenced dog parks, and almost all campgrounds have plenty of outdoor space for long walks.

Campgrounds typically inquire about pets when taking reservations and provide rules on their websites, reinforced by handouts when you check in. Here's an example from a state park:

- Pets must be confined, leashed or under the physical control of the owner at all times. Leashes may not exceed six feet.
- Pets are not allowed in restrooms or park facilities including swimming areas, playgrounds, and beaches.
- Pets cannot be left unattended for more than 30 minutes. Pets cannot be tied to trees, bushes, tables, or facilities even when the owner is present.
- Pets must be well behaved at all times and must be confined in the camper's unit during quiet hours (11 p.m.–7 a.m.).
- Pet owners are required to pick up after their pets and properly dispose of pet droppings in trash containers. "Mutt Mitts" are provided at each restroom facility.
- Any pet that is noisy, dangerous, intimidating, or destructive will not be allowed to remain in the park.

Your working dog is not a pet, of course, and you should not need to pay a pet fee at any campground. Let the staff know you are traveling with a service animal when you reserve and check in. You have the right to be accompanied by your service dog in locations such as visitor centers that may be off-limits for pets. For the most part, though, you should observe the same commonsense rules that pet owners must follow.

Don't forget to keep a sign in a front window of the RV that reads "Service Dog Inside" so that rescue workers or firefighters will be alerted to your dog's presence in an emergency.

## Keeping Your Dog Healthy

Would you know your dog's microchip number if you were separated far from home? Could you give an unfamiliar vet the dog's medical history during an emergency? If you were incapacitated, could your travel companion answer questions about your dog?

As we outlined in chapter 1, "The Basics," you have nothing to lose by traveling with copies of all your dog's official records. This includes the latest rabies certificate, spay certificate, microchip registration form, updated list of inoculations, and copies of ID cards from the animal's training program and from the International Association of Assistance Dog Partners if you are a member.

Create a one-page summary to staple on top and list all relevant information about your dog—your name and contact information, your APHIS-accredited vet's name, address, phone number, the dog's date of birth, breed, color, and so on. Add the dates and descriptions of your dog's most recent treatments for parasites (external: flea and tick topical application and internal: heartworm preventive chews) by both brand name and scientific name.

A first aid kit for the dog is essential, and it's a good place to keep your dog's packages of flea and tick treatments as well as heartworm medication, too. Rather than assume you can give your dog over-the-counter products made for humans, ask the vet to recommend a saline eye wash, antiseptic for wounds, antibiotic ointment, insect bite cream, motion-sickness medication, and antihistamine for allergic reactions. If your vet recommends unflavored pumpkin puree for minor digestive upsets, pack a can (and can opener) or, better yet, a supply of single-serving "Patch Up" brand foil pouches.

Bring a rectal thermometer (one designed for human use is fine) and Vaseline to lubricate it, tweezers to remove splinters or ticks, a styptic pencil, and alcohol prep pads. For collecting pee and poop samples, carry a sterile specimen cup and fecal sample container. Since someday you might need to wrap a wound until you can get to an emergency vet, carry a supply of nonstick gauze pads, a roll of hurt-free tape to attach them, and rolled gauze or self-adhering elastic wrap or "vet tape." (In a pinch, use a clean towel and a roll of duct tape.)

If you schedule a veterinary wellness checkup before a long road trip, you can discuss both the dog's current health and your upcoming itinerary. Review food, supplements, flea and tick treatment, and heartworm prevention medications to be sure they are still appropriate for your dog's age and physical condition.

Ask about destination-specific recommendations. For example, if you are headed to a hot, humid climate, your vet might suggest that the dog be vaccinated for leptospirosis, a bacterial infection that can be picked up from contaminated soil or water in lakes and even dog parks. Ear infections are also common in tropical locales, and the vet can suggest a cleaning product and regimen. Bring the vet a list of any concerns you have, such as bee stings or snakebites.

Keeping to your routine of regular walks will help keep the dog from gaining weight, which can be a health problem for many breeds such as Labradors. It can be a challenge to arrange a good workout, but sometimes you can find safe fields or beaches deserted at dawn. Scan the scene for hazards, unclick the leash, and toss a ball. A few good runs and some happy zoomies will burn off excess energy.

## Road Trip Hazards for Dogs

● **Chris:** One scorching Arizona morning, I stepped out of our twenty-five-foot motor home into the arid glare of an interstate highway rest stop, looking for the usual designated pet area. After a fruitless search for grass, I led Raylene to a tidy, cactus-free pebble field by the sidewalk. During her lengthy sniffing session, I passed the time gazing at the distant mountains and, just as Raylene squatted, squinted toward a sign: "Poisonous snakes and insects inhabit the area." We escaped unbitten, but that sign was a reminder that our surroundings were changing daily, and so were potential hazards. The dog was depending on me for her safety, and I needed to stay alert.

Another time, we sat by our campfire in Quebec's Forillon National Park and watched a porcupine lumber beneath our RV, continue past our chairs, and climb a tree at the edge of our campsite. Raylene wagged her tail, fascinated, as I gripped her leash. Later I learned

Stay vigilant when you take your service dog on a road trip into unfamiliar surroundings. (Photo by Christine Goodier)

that porcupine quills can be quite painful to remove and create nasty infections for another animal after a tussle.

No matter how well trained they are, service dogs can sometimes unwittingly invite an attack by approaching, barking at, or otherwise threatening an unfamiliar animal. Prevention, of course, is better than a cure when it comes to all injuries, including snake bites. Ask for local knowledge about where and when snakes have been spotted in the area. On a hike in snake country, stick to the trail or path. Keep the dog away from piles of brush, firewood, or rocks that might conceal snakes looking for rodents.

Along with random reptiles and mammals that seek only to go about their business undisturbed, we may encounter angry birds, spiders, fire ants, and more when we're out and about. If your dog's habit is to sniff, nose to the ground, for fascinating scents and snacks on recreational occasions, keep an eye out for edibles like nuts and berries, too.

● **Chris:** Labradors, like many dogs, think of life as a buffet. We were awakened one morning in Florida by the sound of Raylene throwing up a dozen orange queen palm seeds, each about an inch in diameter. She had scavenged them from beneath a tree in a fenced location while my attention was elsewhere. I was relieved when my vet assured me that they were not toxic, but she warned me that other palm tree seeds can be. ●

While many of us subconsciously expect the magnificent national parks of America and Canada to be as highly managed as Disneyland, they are filled with potentially harmful natural elements. Often danger is compounded by visitors' poor choices, and unfortunately dogs sometimes become victims. At the Grand Canyon, one tourist tossed a ball over the edge, activating his pet dog to jump after it into the abyss. People embark every summer on lengthy hikes down into the heat of the canyon packing very little water, sometimes with fatal results while being accompanied by their trusting dogs.

In 1981, after a California man parked his truck at Yellowstone National Park, his unleashed dog jumped into a boiling thermal pool, followed by the distraught Californian who was attempting to save it. Before he (and the dog) died, the man was heard to say, "That was a stupid thing I did."

Yes.

National Park Service rangers have to cope with the aftermath of such preventable tragedies. They are also understandably protective of their wildlife, knowing that when there's an overlap with domestic creatures, diseases can be introduced or exchanged. Individual park superintendents set policies for their locations when it comes to dogs in general, including service dogs. In larger parks especially, you'll find the specifics on the official website.

Yellowstone, for example, advises that "service animals are allowed in all facilities and on all trails unless an area has been closed by the

Henry Kisor and Trooper enjoying a hike in the Painted Desert of the Petrified Forest National Park in Arizona. Hiker and dog need to be leashed together and to leave no sign of their passing. (Photograph by Deborah Abbott)

superintendent to protect park resources." A permit is not required when taking your dog along to visit frontcountry attractions and thermal areas with boardwalks where pet dogs are barred, but if you plan to enter the backcountry, you will need to apply for a free permit.

The website warns: "Please be aware that having a service animal in the backcountry may put you at increased risk for confrontations with wolves, bears, and other wildlife. There are recorded instances of domestic dogs killed by coyotes within Yellowstone and numerous instances of dogs killed by wolves and bears outside of Yellowstone. Wolves are very territorial and may perceive domestic dogs as competitors and act aggressively toward them putting you and your animal in danger. If you must take a service animal with you in the backcountry, keep it on a tight leash at all times and sleep with it in your tent at night. In addition, thermal features pose a special risk to all animals. Boiling water in pools and thermal channels can cause severe or fatal burns if your animal decides to take a drink or go for a swim. Your safety and the safety of your animal are not guaranteed."

Another National Park Service concern is proper dog poop handling. "Service animal fecal matter must be picked up and disposed of properly. Fecal matter should be disposed of in a trash receptacle, toilet, pit toilet, or if none of those are accessible (such as in the backcountry) it should be buried in a cat hole dug a minimum of 6 inches deep and a 200 feet from water sources, campsites or trails."

Frontcountry or back, be vigilant, keep your dog close on a leash, and be sensitive to policies that will protect you and your dog. Along with the aforementioned coyotes, wolves, and bears, you could run into elk, bison, mountain goats, and foxes in some locations.

● **Chris:** At Rocky Mountain National Park's Moraine Park Campground, I led Raylene out of the RV at 5:30 a.m., and we both noticed food trash strewn across the road from our campsite. An hour later, a newly retired couple emerged from their tent and told their story of an overnight visitation. A black bear had opened the door of their Toyota 4Runner as they slept, removed a big plastic food storage box, and helped himself to popcorn, candy, and beef jerky, leaving behind only two bear-size paw prints next to the car door handle and one untouched bear-shaped honey container. The woman got up in the night to walk to the bathroom and discovered the door of the vehicle open and a coyote snacking on the leftovers.

I'm glad my dog and I did not have any unexpected encounters with the bear or coyote across the road. This episode was an example of why park rangers are so specific on how to keep a clean camp. Food boxes should go inside a hard-sided RV, in a vehicle trunk, or *under cover* inside a car if there is no trunk. Rocky Mountain National Park rangers place numerous "Bear Boxes" around campgrounds for shared food storage. Our tent-camping neighbors failed to heed the instructions posted everywhere.

As rangers say, "A fed bear is a dead bear," because wild animals return for more easy pickings, sometimes attack panicky tourists, and often end up relocated or euthanized. Dog food will attract bears, too, and should be stored just as carefully as people food. Bring food and water bowls inside at night or—better yet—feed your dog indoors. ●

# Meeting Other Dogs

● **Chris:** With Raylene at my side, I approached the Lewis and Clark Interpretive Center on the banks of the Missouri River in Great Falls, Montana. After a steamy summer morning on the road, I looked forward to touring the air-conditioned center's exhibits about the historic Corps of Discovery. We walked to the ticket window, Raylene sat, and an enormous, barking, black beast bounded toward us, thwarted in the nick of time by a volunteer who grabbed his collar.

Buddy, a Newfoundland dog, was apparently on-site to represent Meriwether Lewis's companion animal, Seaman, and easily outweighed Raylene by a hundred pounds. He parked his considerable

Other dogs can present an obstacle, even friendly ones like this Newfoundland dog at the Lewis and Clark Interpretive Center in Great Falls, Montana. (Photo by Robert Goodier)

bulk to block our entrance, rewarded by coos and chuckles all around from the volunteer staff, and stared hungrily at Raylene until someone finally dragged him off to the center of the lobby. I decided we would skip a closer encounter with the Seaman reenactor, and we headed for the exhibits.

Service dog handlers know that many dogs are probably friendly and just want to exchange sniffs. It's your call whether to permit a meeting, just as it's your decision whether to allow anyone to pet your partner. You never have to apologize or worry about hurt feelings if you'd rather not allow either encounter, whether your dog is on duty or not.

A bigger hazard is that unfriendly dogs with bad intentions can appear out of nowhere, especially since many people consider leashes optional. Amy Bosworth, a Texan, had firsthand experience with this problem.

"Holiday and I mostly traveled by car and never really had any major issues with lodging," said Bosworth. "Our one upset was her getting attacked by another 'service dog' checking into a hotel. Poor Holiday was trained to be passive, and a larger dog approached her aggressively as I was checking in. The manager later told me the dog was a seizure alert dog-in-training that had wandered away from his handler. Most encounters we had in public were just neutral. The best compliment we could get was 'I didn't even see a dog down there.'"

Bosworth's first dog, Holiday, a border collie, and her current partner, Marvel, a pointer, both came from Service Dogs Inc., a nonprofit organization in Dripping Springs, Texas, that trains dogs from animal shelters for people living with hearing loss or mobility challenges.

The best you can do is keep a wary eye out and avoid dicey situations. If you see dogs roaming freely while you are on a tour, visiting an attraction, or staying in a hotel or campground, immediately notify the manager or park ranger's staff. When other visitors ignore leash rules, they often will be directed to leave with no refund.

Many RV parks, such as those flying the KOA banner, provide fenced dog parks for leash-free exercise and socialization. Rest stops on interstate highways often have open, grassy areas or even fenced pens for dog walks. To avoid confrontations, wait until other dogs leave or, better yet, find another place where you can take a long walk and exercise your partner on the leash. Since some pet owners do not pick up after their dogs, even when free bags and trash cans are staring them in the face, that pleasant-looking fenced park could be a petri dish for all sorts of pathogens.

Should you carry pepper spray? It is highly restricted in Canada, and although it is legal (with some restrictions) in all fifty of the United States, many localities have strict regulations pertaining to possession and use of this product.

## Summing Up

- If you don't have access to a car, use a taxicab or a ride-sharing service such as Uber for short trips, or book a bus for longer journeys with your dog.
- Protect your dog while traveling in your car with a harness or other restraint system.
- Pace yourself on long road trips for your dog's well-being and your own enjoyment.
- Notify tour operators in advance that extra space will be needed in vehicles for your service dog.
- Travel with your dog's complete medical records and carry a first aid kit for emergencies.
- Be vigilant in unfamiliar locations for potential hazards to your dog's health, including other dogs with bad intentions.

Chapter 5

# Sailing the Seas

● **Chris:** Never has hearing dog Raylene performed her job better than one evening at the start of a cruise when my husband arose at two in the morning, groped along the unfamiliar wall for the bathroom door, and, disoriented, stepped out into the corridor. The heavy door closed and locked behind him, and his repeated pounding and knocking to get my attention was futile since I could not hear it. Raylene, however, woke up, pounced with her paws on my side of the bed, and kept it up until I stirred and realized someone was missing. She received a yummy treat from me that night, and a lot of praise and petting from Bob, who was spared a trip to the front desk in his underwear. ●

## Before You Make a Deposit

Can you take your service dog on a cruise? Usually, but not always, so find out before paying a deposit. Most ships that carry passengers in U.S. waters are registered in countries such as the Bahamas, Panama, and the Netherlands, and relatively few fly the American flag. In 2005,

Dianne Urhausen and her assistance dog, Henri, relax together on a cruise through the Panama Canal. (Photo by Peter Urhausen)

the United States Supreme Court decided that most (but not all) provisions of Title III of the Americans with Disabilities Act apply to foreign cruise ships in American waters, and this was reinforced by a settlement the U.S. Department of Justice reached with Carnival Corporation in 2015. By law, you can bring your service animal (as defined by the ADA) with you on sailings that embark and disembark from U.S. waters or those of its territories.

But note the phrase "in American waters." The ADA does not apply to lines operating cruises that do not embark or disembark at any U.S. port. This means if you are considering flying to a faraway ship (cruising in Europe, Asia, etc.), you should verify that your service dog will be welcomed on board. Ask for written confirmation before making a deposit even if it is a familiar cruise line that you have sailed before in American waters.

If you are Canadian, be aware that as of early 2019 there are no national or provincial laws that *specifically* give Canadian service dog partners the right to take their animals aboard foreign-registered cruise ships, although the Canadian Human Rights Act might be invoked in such cases. Still, some large cruise lines that do business in U.S. and Canadian waters do allow Canadian service dogs aboard as a courtesy, because Canadians make up a large segment of their clientele. Always check with the line before booking.

Take time to also research the specific ship you are considering, too, since some physical features may simplify getting around with your service dog, and not all ships are created equal. Ask your travel agent questions or contact the cruise line's accessibility staff.

"I have found that the age of a cruise ship makes a great deal of difference to a wheelchair user," said Dianne Urhausen. "The newer ships have automatic doors to all outside decks, to the public restrooms, and to the cabin and a threshold ramp out to the balcony."

"On the older ships I have sailed, the only automatic doors were on the pool deck," Urhausen said. "This makes it difficult to access outside decks with your dog and is especially problematic if the relief box is located on an outside deck. It really takes two people to assist you out to the deck, one to hold the door and one to push you over the threshold (the thresholds on older ships are higher and create a barrier to get outside unless you have an electric wheelchair or someone to push you)."

It's also a good idea to investigate your itinerary before making your deposit to find out if your dog will be allowed to accompany you when you go ashore. If it is, familiarize yourself with paperwork local authorities might require, and gauge how much lead time you'll need to obtain it. (Take a moment to read chapter 6, "That Annoying Paperwork," for more details.)

It is entirely your responsibility, with the help of a qualified veterinarian, to be sure your dog meets port requirements for any itinerary. The travel agency and cruise line do not handle such documentation for you and usually will not be knowledgeable about what you'll need anyway.

Dianne Urhausen prepared her assistance dog, Henri, to be a good traveler with several short practice trips before embarking on a long cruise. (Photo by Dianne Urhausen)

Finally, if you use a wheelchair, electric scooter, walker, rollator, or cane while also managing a service dog, you may want to choose an itinerary that mostly visits ports where the ship can dock at a pier. In some parts of the world, the crew must ferry passengers into the island or town on small tender boats that may be difficult to board if you have limited mobility.

## The Cruise Line's Paperwork

When you make a deposit, ask your travel agent (or the telephone representative if you are booking directly with the line) to enter a notation in your record that you are traveling with a service dog. At the same time, note your preferences for a dining time and table size. Many cruise lines offer an option to request a fixed time (either an early seating around 6 p.m. or a second seating about two hours later) and fixed table location in the main dining room, yours for the duration of the cruise. Or you can choose an "open seating" arrangement whereby you reserve night by night or simply check in at the manager's desk when you feel like eating.

Table size options vary by ship, but the number of seats usually ranges from two to eight. Solo travelers are typically assigned to a large table with a mix of passengers. If you are traveling with friends or family members, have your booking numbers linked with the appropriate table size request. (More about dining considerations later in this chapter.)

The next step is to write down your booking number and contact the line's department for "special access" or "special needs" right away. This is a task you should handle yourself, not delegate to a travel agent.

Most lines have a special needs form, sometimes found online, to fill out and send back to them. (If they do not provide a form, send a letter without delay with your name, booking number, sailing date, and requirements.) This form or letter gives you an opportunity to state your disability-related needs and also your expectations regarding the dog's relief box and your dining room arrangements. You should receive an emailed acknowledgment that the form has been received.

Upon receiving word that you are traveling with a service dog, many lines will send you an additional policy form for you to read, sign, and either send back or bring to the pier. The cruise line may ask you to provide more information, such as the type of tasks the dog performs and its name, breed, size, and age. These forms clarify the company's expectations—for example, that you understand the requirements of each port of call, will bring your own food for your dog, and will keep the dog out of the pools and hot tubs. Appendix 3 goes into detail about the policies of each cruise line that uses American waters.

After making your final payment, usually two or three months before departure, you'll complete an online check-in and receive a boarding pass and ticket contract for each of the human travelers in your party. These documents are typically sent in electronic form for you to print out and bring to the ship, although, like the airlines, some cruise lines such as Celebrity now have smart phone apps for check-in and offer the option of presenting the bar code on your phone to be read as you enter the terminal. You'll be given a link to order or print luggage tags. Attach these to bags that you will check with dock workers after arriving at the pier, and use extras for your hand luggage in case it goes astray.

We recommend that you call and/or email the line's special needs department about a month before departure to reconfirm that they are aware you are bringing a service dog and have notified the ship.

## Packing Your Dog's Supplies

The cruise line is not responsible for providing your dog's food or medications. Bring it all yourself, although for a long cruise you might be able to make specific arrangements at least sixty days in advance, at your expense, with some companies. (Holland America Line is one example.) Depending on the size of the dog and the length of the voyage, some cruisers bring a separate suitcase (and sometimes a steamer trunk) for the dog's supplies. Bring dishes for food and water, a first aid kit, a few toys, treats, and a blanket or mat with the familiar scent of home.

There are no veterinary services on board ship, and you may have difficulty finding a vet in a foreign port of call, so be sure to bring along your dog's first aid kit and consult with your vet if you have any concerns.

It's also a good idea to pack a life jacket carefully fitted to the dog. Cruise lines often provide life jackets for them, but the fit is hit or miss.

## Embarkation Day

Consider traveling a day or two early and booking a "fly and cruise" package at a hotel with transportation included to the pier, especially during the winter when storms can shut down airports. Many cruise lines offer pre- and post-cruise packages that can help smooth the way on embarkation day.

Pay particular attention to specified boarding and sailing times on your documents. We suggest arriving at the pier as early as possible rather than stressing yourself and your dog by running late. When you approach the cruise terminal, your luggage will be collected at the sidewalk, and you will go into the building through airport-like security procedures. Upon seeing your dog, staff members may direct you to a special needs line for security and check-in. An elevator is usually available if you prefer not to take your dog on escalators.

Before boarding the ship, you will be expected to present your dog's paperwork (see below) at either the security gate or the check-in counter, so hand-carry all documents, including your own boarding pass and passport. Keep cash, prescription drugs, and other hard-to-replace items in your hand luggage, too. Checked bags will be delivered to your room a few hours later.

Human passengers receive plastic room keycards at check-in. Dogs, alas, do not. Crew members will scan your card each time you board or depart the ship and whenever you make onboard purchases.

● **Chris:** I look for a patch of grass just before entering the terminal so that Raylene has a last chance to relieve herself. Boarding can be delayed for hours by random events (like a bomb threat that shut down the Port of Miami before one of our cruises and a medical emergency that halted baggage loading in San Diego before another). To be sure the dog's needs can be met while we languish in a packed waiting lounge, I stock my tote bag with extra meal baggies and bowls for her food and water. At some ports, a full water bottle may not make it through security, but there are bathroom faucets and sometimes vending machines inside. ●

● **Henry:** The day after boarding ship, when the initial flurry of passengers at the guest relations counter has died down, it's not a bad idea to introduce yourself to the port paper (or documentation) officer and the guest relations director (called hotel director or manager at some cruise lines). They could become your best friends on the high seas.

The port paper officer can give you a heads-up about the ports of call where officials are likely to want to examine your dog, and whether fees to do so will be requested. The guest relations director, who often will take you to meet the port officials in a ship's lounge, is the person to see if the relief box materials are unsatisfactory or if any particular needs crop up during the voyage. ●

# Your Dog's Paperwork

As outlined in more detail in chapter 6, "That Annoying Paperwork," you will need to bring your dog's most recent rabies vaccination certificate and a Form 7001 International Health Certificate issued by a veterinarian, along with any country-specific forms (also available from the vet) relating to your itinerary. We recommend working well in advance of your departure with an APHIS-accredited veterinarian who is likely to be most familiar with the local regulations and required documents for bringing animals into international ports.

Before your sailing date, the accredited vet must inspect your dog and sign the forms; if you are traveling to certain countries, a regional APHIS office must endorse, countersign, and stamp them. Remember, you will be "importing" your dog into those countries even if you step ashore for only a few hours. As explained in chapter 1, "The Basics," samples of the forms are available on the APHIS website, https://www.aphis .usda.gov/aphis/pet-travel.

Make at least two copies of your dog's original documents. Keep one copy in your packed luggage as a backup and use the other copy for check-in at the pier on embarkation day. Retain your originals in your hand baggage and later in your stateroom. After the ship's administrative staff has copies in hand of your dog's paperwork, they'll carry the ball and incorporate it into detailed documentation required for each port of call before local officials will "clear" the ship and allow passengers ashore. Sometimes your original documents may be temporarily requested by the ship's staff for local officials to view.

● **Chris:** Occasionally you may be required to bring the dog to a lounge and appear in person. Some local officials give the dog just a brief glance, but others may choose to perform a pat-down or more thorough examination. On a recent cruise that stopped in Cozumel, Mexico, a federal officer from OISA (the Animal and Plant Health Inspection Office) looked closely at Raylene's ears, skin, and paws and provided me with a copy of the ship's inspection certificate to take ashore as proof that the dog had passed review. I was thankful that Raylene, like most service dogs, was trained from puppyhood to stand or sit quietly while being touched by veterinarians and other strangers.

**Henry:** You never know what's going to happen. The night before our cruise ship called at Puerto Quetzal, Guatemala, we received a message from the ship's port paper officer that the Guatemalans had asked for Trooper to be present for inspection even though we had no health documentation for that country for him and planned to stay on the ship instead of going ashore. That made me a little nervous. Should we have obtained a Form 7001 for Trooper specifically for that country? What would happen?

A pleasant surprise, that's what. Two amiable officials from the Guatemalan Ministry of Agriculture sat down with us, cooed at Trooper, warmly ruffled his ears, remarked approvingly about his calm demeanor, and examined all the documentation we had brought for other countries. Satisfied that he had had all his required immunizations, the officials invited us to bring him ashore and issued us a permit to do so. And so we did.

**Chris:** When ashore, you also might be challenged by a representative of a local port authority, as we once were after a long ride by tender boat from the anchored ship into a dock at Honduras. I had failed to bring copies of the paperwork with me, cannot hear, and do not speak much Spanish, so lip-reading was futile. Fortunately my husband came ashore right behind me, caught the gist of the request, and explained that all the papers were back on the ship. After a brief standoff, the port guard gave up and allowed us to proceed. So take a copy of your dog's papers with you when you leave the ship.

Some countries such as the Bahamas may impose a legitimate import fee for pets (usually waived for service dogs), but your research, or a conversation on board with the ship's staff, should reveal that fact in advance. Upon arrival in other countries, more than one dog handler has been asked on the spot to pay an unanticipated fee to go ashore. How should you handle this situation, if it ever happens? That's up to you. I probably would calmly explain that I was not advised of such a fee by the embassy and did not come to the cruise ship prepared to pay it. As others have reported, chances are the official will persist a little, eventually give up, and finally wave you away. Ask the advice of your port paper officer.

**Henry:** When Debby and I tendered ashore with Trooper at Cabo San Lucas, Mexico, a customs agent stopped us at the pier and said, "Papers for the dog, please." Having been forewarned by Chris's experience, I fished them out of a shirt pocket.

"Is that Trooper?" called another agent from a nearby desk.

"Yes," Debby said, astonished.

"Let him in," the second agent said. "He's OK."

Later we speculated that the port authorities had studied the documents—which carried not only Trooper's breed mix but also his name—that had been faxed to them from the ship's port paper officer the day before, and had decided that Trooper was good to go.

It's also possible that the Mexican authorities at Puerto Chiapas two sea days to the south, who had examined Trooper aboard ship and checked his papers before allowing us ashore, had called ahead to Cabo and given their colleagues a heads-up.

Whatever the truth, we were gratified. Mexico may have no official policy about service dogs, but in some places they just seem welcome.

## Can't the Dog Just Stay on Board?

It's understandable that many people give up after learning about some ports' requirements and decide to keep the dog on board. In recent years, however, Bahamas officials have informed cruise passengers traveling with service dogs that an import permit is required whether or not the dog will go ashore. Laws pertaining to animal export change constantly, and other countries might decide to follow suit.

Try very hard to comply with the animal import requirements of the countries you will visit for another good reason. If you or your traveling companion have a medical crisis during the cruise or an accident ashore, it might be necessary for you to leave the ship and either check into a local hospital or be evacuated for medical treatment. Having thorough paperwork for your service dog partner could simplify an already difficult situation.

If you don't get the country-specific documentation for that destination, you may get a call from the ship's office reminding you that your dog cannot go ashore there. The staff will alter your onboard record in the computer system to reflect this fact.

When they scan your ship card at the gangway, security will get a pop-up message on their screens that you are traveling with a service dog and that you don't have permission to take the dog ashore in that particular port of call.

But if you have travel companions to help you while ashore, depending on the nature of your disability, you might be comfortable leaving the dog on board with a friend or family member for a few hours. Don't be surprised if the cheerful "ding-dong" of the key reader turns into a disapproving "thunk-thonk" when the crew scans your key card at the gangway. A ship's officer will be summoned, and you can explain that your canine travel companion is staying on board.

Important: Cruise lines generally do not permit service dogs to be left unattended in the stateroom, even tied up or in a crate. So you *must* arrange for someone else to stay with your dog. The cruise line will not provide this service, but some people report having made informal dog-sitting arrangements with a staff member on board.

## "Where Does Your Dog Go to the Bathroom?"

"If I had a dollar for every time I'm asked that question, it would certainly pay for a dinner in a fine specialty restaurant on board!" said

Rosalyn "Roz" Silberschein, a Southern Californian who made fifteen cruises with her first service dog, Brenda, and now is accompanied by a successor service dog, Horton. Both of her dogs were trained by Canine Companions for Independence.

It's the number one (and number two) question other passengers ask service dog handlers aboard ship, and the answer is: at a relief station provided by the cruise line at a location it determines. A typical station should consist of a wooden box (approximately four feet by four feet), a filler such as grass sod or garden mulch, and a trash can for disposal of solid waste bags. Bring your own bags.

It can also be the number one source of anxiety when you plan your first vacation with a service dog. Will your dog have an appropriate place on board for relief? Even though some service dogs will make do with any old surface on command, you can't help worrying about whether your dog will accept a strange box out in the middle of the ocean. To calm your nerves, address the issue before you sail.

When you notify the cruise line that you are bringing a dog, ask their accessibility department by phone or email where the box will be located on that particular ship. The location varies from line to line and from ship to ship. If you want a cabin conveniently close to the relief box, it's not a bad idea to ask where it is on the particular ship you are booking. Advise the accessibility department of your dog's weight and breed, and discuss the box size and filler the ship will provide. Some companies offer grass sod on request from U.S. departure ports. As mentioned earlier in this chapter, it's important to confirm your preferences by letter or email, receive a written acknowledgment that you'll be traveling with a service dog, and reconfirm a month before you sail.

Upon boarding the ship, go directly to the guest relations desk (also known as guest services, front office, purser's desk, and so on) to confirm the box location. You may get a blank look or be told to return later, but persist in obtaining this information so you can investigate and introduce the dog to this new reality. Embarkation day is busy, but some cruise lines will summon a staff member to escort you and your dog to the box.

Often, if more than one service dog is aboard, the ship will provide separate boxes in either the same deck location or close to the handlers' staterooms. Sometimes the dog's name and/or stateroom number will be displayed prominently on a printed sign above the box.

● **Henry:** One November I took Trooper on a Caribbean cruise aboard Holland America's *Nieuw Amsterdam.* The relief box aboard that ship was located far forward on the promenade deck under the bow overhang, protected from the elements. Before that voyage was over I decided to book an Alaska cruise the following June on the older ship *Amsterdam* and, with the agreement of the onboard bookers, chose a stateroom across from the forwardmost elevator so that Trooper and I wouldn't have a long walk to the relief box. The inexperienced bookers didn't think to call to ask where it was on the *Amsterdam,* nor did I.

Lo and behold, when we boarded the *Amsterdam* for Alaska, we learned that the box was located far away at the very stern of the ship on the lowest passenger deck, open to the air but protected by an overhang. That made for quite a trek each time Trooper needed to go. It didn't really matter, for we both needed the exercise.

Nonetheless, before the end of that cruise, when I booked a Panama Canal cruise on the same line's *Westerdam,* I chose a cabin squarely amidships so that it didn't matter which end of the ship the relief box was on. Just before sailing, however, we were offered a bargain upgrade to a better cabin with a balcony . . . at the stern. We couldn't resist.

As it turned out, the relief box on this voyage was way up at the bow. Naturally, Trooper and I got lots of exercise. But now, on booking, I always ask where the box is. ●

● **Chris:** You never really know where you'll find the relief station and what it will contain until you get there. On one cruise, I requested sod in advance, but the box was filled with a hamster-cage mixture of fine sawdust and shavings. The lightweight stuff flew about like a dust storm in the crew-only corridor, settling on the dog's fur, my hair, and the passageway floor. My room steward arranged to have mulch brought on board at our first port of call.

Another time, I walked my seventy-pound Lab to the designated location and couldn't help laughing at the size of the box, tailor-made for a Chihuahua. The crew quickly replaced the box with a larger one before we sailed.

On yet another cruise, the station featured flat slabs of cardboard, centered by small squares of grass sod, neatly lined up for the three service dogs on board. Dog urine, however, instantly drained in rivulets onto the surrounding deck through which dogs and their handlers walked. After I brought the problem to the hotel manager's attention, the crew built watertight wood boxes and purchased mulch ashore on Kodiak Island in Alaska.

After a small square of sod on flat cardboard proved unsatisfactory, a ship's crew quickly constructed a more functional four-foot-by-four-foot plywood box station for the three service dogs on board. (Photo by Robert Goodier)

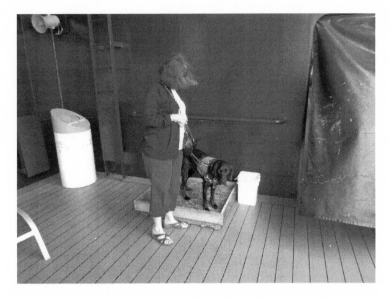

On some ships, service dog teams will find the relief box located on an outdoor deck exposed to wind and rain. (Photo by Robert Goodier)

Other service dog partners report that they, too, have encountered a variety of makeshift, unsatisfactory filler material ranging from sand and shredded newspapers to hard paper pellets that wedge themselves uncomfortably in the dog's paws. Some handlers even resort to packing a roll of artificial grass to cover such problem materials, while others get assistance on board.

"We have had bark chips and mulch as the fillers for the relief box," said Dianne Urhausen. "We have requested sod but have never had it in the box. The mulch that was used on our Alaska cruise was very fine and tended to blow around in the wind and made a mess. Henri didn't like it (although she did use the box) because it was too soft, and she would sink down into it. Our cabin steward wetted the mulch down and that made a firmer surface and solved all of the problems."

What to do about an unsatisfactory relief box? Speak up and give the ship's staff a chance to fix any problems. As noted above, you can try addressing the issue with your cabin steward, since on some cruise lines the housekeeping department is in charge of the relief box.

Some stateroom balconies have sufficient space for a service dog's relief box, a location that can be a lifesaver for passengers with mobility challenges. (Photo by Dianne Urhausen)

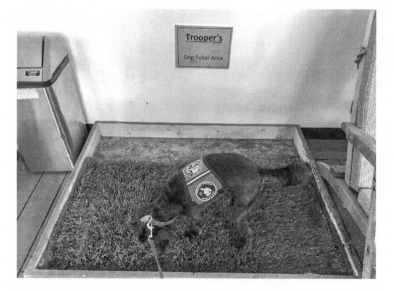

When more than one service dog is aboard ship, some cruise lines offer separate relief boxes and identify them with prominent signs. (Photo by Henry Kisor)

If a change is not made, return to the guest relations desk and state your needs, both verbally and in writing. Be specific: "On deck five aft, please replace the flat cardboard with a four-foot-by-four-foot wooden box filled with grass sod for my service dog as soon as possible," for example. If an improvement is not forthcoming after the first day, ask to speak to the ship's guest relations manager.

● **Chris:** On our first cruise together, Raylene awakened me as our ship rolled through stormy seas, and we lurched through deserted corridors to her relief station location, outside toward the bow of the ship, two levels below our stateroom. Approaching a set of doors, the dog increased her pace until suddenly we were stopped in our tracks by red warning signs taped across all the exits: "Heavy Weather—Deck Closed." Luckily a friendly crew member happened by at that moment and helped me maneuver under the tape, shove open the heavy glass door against the wind, and step out onto the dark, rain-swept deck with Raylene so she could relieve herself at the box. The ship's staff refused to change the location. (The solution from an officer was, "Oh, it's OK, you can just duck beneath the tape.")

On other sailings, the crew placed the box in a small space at the end of a long, windy corridor blocked by a "crew only" barrier I had to climb over. To reach it required a walk through high winds on a wet, slippery exterior deck. Aside from the detrimental effects on hairdos and evening clothes, these were not safe locations for me or for my dog. ●

It's worth studying the deck plan and asking when you book if the ship has a protected area for the relief station that can be reached by doors leading from the inside passenger corridors, such as some of the Holland America Line vessels have.

As Dianne Urhausen pointed out, many lines' newer ships may feature automatic sliding glass doors to exterior decks and public restrooms, a welcome modification for users of wheelchairs, walkers, or canes. However, older vessels still employ mostly wooden or glass doors

Speak up if you encounter unexpected problems, such as a closed-off deck where the ship's staff has placed your dog's relief box. (Photo by Robert Goodier)

that are heavy to pull and hold onto against the wind, especially for someone juggling a dog's leash, lest the door slam shut on both of you.

"On our Panama Canal cruise," Urhausen said, "we were on an older ship, and it was impossible for me to access the box by myself in the location where it was originally placed since it was on an outside deck without automatic doors and I was unable to even get over the threshold without assistance."

If these potential issues concern you, one possibility is to request that your dog's box be placed in a crew closet or stairwell close to your stateroom. An even better solution, if you book a room with a large enough balcony, is to specify that the dog's box (and a trash can) be placed on it. Some lines are reluctant to consider this option, but many service dog partners with mobility disabilities have been able to make such arrangements after boarding following a bit of discussion.

"Having the relief box on our balcony makes a huge difference in my enjoyment of our cruises," said Urhausen, who tried communicating with the shore-side access department before the cruise and was not successful in getting them to agree in advance that the relief box would be on her balcony.

"Once we are on the ship, we immediately go to guest services and ask to speak with the hotel director. So far, we have been able to get the box moved from an outside deck to our balcony," she said. "Not having to get dressed first thing in the morning to take Henri to use the box and not having to trek to another deck on the opposite end of the ship at night makes a world of difference."

Finally, if you have a small- or medium-sized service dog who buys into the concept, you may already have used pee pads or an artificial turf and tray system (all sold in pet stores or online) from time to time. Some dog partners successfully create their very own relief station on the balcony and bring along garbage bags for cleanup. If you drive to your departure port, you could check this gear with the rest of your luggage the ship will deliver to your stateroom. If you are flying, box it up and hire a porter.

## Dining on Cruise Ships

While cruising for the first time with her young service dog, Brenda, Roz Silberschein and her husband, Morey, were seated in an elegant ship's dining room, perusing the long menu. A waiter tapped her on the shoulder.

"Your dog is in the middle of the restaurant!" he said.

She immediately peered under the table, but Brenda was gone. The sociable black Lab had sneaked away and sniffed a path around the room, snarfing tidbits from the floor and visiting other diners. Now she was standing in the middle of the dining room, surrounded by passengers, her leash grasped by the maître d'.

"I wanted to die," said Silberschein, who quickly retrieved Brenda and tethered her to her chair, a practice she highly recommends. Of course, Brenda had violated the ironclad service dog behavior rules, but she soon redeemed herself, performing daily tasks for Roz during an eight-year career before retiring at age ten. Together, they took fourteen more cruises and traveled to Mexico, Brazil, Spain, Hawaii, France, Switzerland, Germany, Italy, and Alaska.

As noted in chapter 1, "The Basics," dogs will be dogs. As handlers, we can find ways to help them succeed in minefield environments like ships where tempting food is present around every corner.

● **Chris:** When I fill out the cruise line's "special needs" form, I request a dinner table alongside a wall or partition, ideally in a corner near the entrance, so I can place Raylene on the floor beneath the table by my side against the wall. I avoid curved banquettes; they look nice, but it's difficult to settle a large dog's body around a metal table base. She ends up too close to where servers come and go, and it takes vigilance to keep alerting them that the dog is at their feet.

Your table request usually makes it from the shore-side office to the ship's dining room manager, but not always. Soon after boarding and sorting out the relief box, I head for the dining room to look for our assigned table's location. If it won't work, I explain that a table out in the center of the room is bad news for a big dog with a long tail. Dining room managers are experienced problem solvers and have always found more suitable tables for us.

Since a service dog entered my life, the fixed early evening seating seems to work best for us at a table for two (or a larger one when friends or family cruise with us). After Raylene has been fed and walked, she is likely to settle under the table and snooze for a couple of hours while we enjoy a leisurely, multicourse dinner. ●

● **Henry:** At breakfast the buffet restaurant floors almost always are crumb-strewn from late-night dining, and we have to search out tidy spots. In the dining room I once had a hard time finding a regular

table out of foot traffic for Trooper until we explained our predica-
ment to a savvy maître d', who put us next to a waiter station with a
large overhang under which Trooper could shelter out of the mad-
ding crowd. At a specialty frequent-cruisers luncheon in the dining
room, we stood helplessly amid the swirling mob until an equally
adept headwaiter spotted us and found us a table next to a tall col-
umn that kept Trooper out of harm's way.                              ●

In a ship's buffet restaurant, Trooper 'down-stays' on a fleece mat out of the way
under a table while his partner goes for breakfast. (Photograph by Henry Kisor)

Roz Silberschein emphasizes that the right location can be crucial when she dines with Horton. "Be very careful where you place your dog, because a host of waiters will be coming and going all around you, and you don't want them to step on him. If you hate where the table is, ask to speak with the maître d'. If there's a seat against a wall or railing, that would be good. Always remind the staff that there is a dog on the floor."

She stresses the importance of not feeding the dog in the restaurant area—and never feeding him "people food" on board a ship.

"I sometimes carry a piece of kibble or two and give him one after leaving the restaurant, praising him for being such a good dog," she says.

For breakfast and lunch, your table will not be reserved. Sometimes, usually on sea days rather than port days, the ship's main dining room will be open, and you can remind the manager when you arrive that you'll need a table against a wall. More often, however, cruise lines serve breakfast and lunch (and a casual dinner option) in a cafeteria-style buffet restaurant on an upper deck near the pool with some outdoor seating. You'll probably find it easier to leave your dog beneath your table rather than try to take him with you while you visit the buffet lines and stations, juggling a plate or tray.

"In the buffet or outside eating areas, you can place your dog in a 'down-stay,' hooking the leash around the leg of the chair or table, away from any public walkway," Silberschein says. "Against a wall, window, or railing would be best. Start to walk away, then turn around, and as a reminder hold up your hand with the 'stay' command. Go get your food, and when you come back to the table where your dog has not moved from where you placed him, watch the faces of the folks nearby—they're amazed and know if that were their pet back home, he'd be all over the place or whining or barking. Never stay away too long, and don't forget to praise him on what a great job he did."

But be sure you have confidence in your dog's ability to hold that 'down-stay' command, Silberschein warns. "When Horton was attached to a chair in a restaurant on his very first cruise, it was a *Marley and Me* moment after I walked away. I turned to check on him, and he was looking for me, towing the chair behind him. I was so embarrassed, to say the least. It was my mistake to expect too much from a novice two-year-old. Horton is a much more secure service dog now. He will keep watching for me but will not move."

● **Chris:** If you decide to book specialty restaurants, which usually involve a surcharge and provide an extra-upscale experience, be sure to talk with each restaurant's manager about your table requirements.

On our first cruise with Raylene, my husband stopped in after boarding and informed a man at the podium in the ship's French restaurant that our family had reservations later in the week and that we were traveling with a service dog.

"A dog?" was the incredulous response. As Bob began to explain, the man rushed off in search of a manager.

"A dog?" the maître d' repeated, gazing at my husband for a long moment with raised eyebrows. Similar responses ensued at another specialty restaurant and from other crew we met. The ship's personnel just did not seem familiar with the idea of service dogs on board.

Still, the maître d' of the elegant venue rose to the occasion. With a flourish he seated our party of four in a private wine room at a round table designed for ten. We feasted on lobster flamed in cognac at our table with great flair and topped off the gala evening with a bottle of champagne. Raylene slept through her third birthday party under the enormous table, and no one stepped on her tail.

## Shipboard Life

● **Chris:** After you unpack, arrange a comfortable bed for your dog, either next to you on the floor or in a spot where the dog can always see you. Some cruise ship staterooms have a small sofa that you can cover completely with tucked-in beach towels (ask your room steward for a supply and explain their purpose) to thoroughly protect it from dog hair. I bring a little blanket topper and a few toys from home, and Raylene settles in comfortably. I fill her water bowl from

On embarkation day for a cruise, ask your room steward to provide a beach towel or two you can use to completely cover the sofa. (Photo by Robert Goodier)

Aboard ship Trooper sleeps atop a pillow wrapped in a fleece baby blanket and placed on the sofa. (Photograph by Henry Kisor)

the tap (she has never experienced digestive problems drinking the ship's water) and place it in the bathroom, on the balcony, or on top of a plastic mat in a place where the room steward and I will not trip over it. ●

● **Henry:** When we travel on cruise ships or stay in hotels, we fold a fleece baby blanket around a pillow and place that on the sofa (or sometimes the floor) for Trooper's bed. (One of the advantages of a small service dog is that the accoutrements we have to carry for him are also small.) ●

The next order of business on embarkation day (after finding the relief box, confirming your seating in the dining room, and preparing for the dog's stateroom needs) is to attend a mandatory safety drill. Cruise ships sometimes provide life jackets for dogs, but they often come in only two or three sizes and are ill-fitting. It's not a bad idea to bring your own, carefully matched to your dog before sailing. The chances that the dog will ever have to use one are almost infinitesimally small, but you—and the cruise line—will feel better. It's usually not necessary for passengers (or dogs) to wear life jackets to the safety drill, but the cruise line will advise their required procedure. Just stow the dog's jacket in the stateroom closet atop those intended for humans.

You'll also want to find an outdoor deck area suitable for exercising your dog on sea days. Some ships still have wide, full promenades that allow you to walk a complete circuit around the vessel. Many newer ships have more limited exterior decks that require reentering the ship to cross to the other side. Jogging tracks on upper decks tend to be narrow and, well, filled with joggers.

If you have any energy left after all the first day's formalities are done, stroll through the ship and glance inside lounges and theaters to identify likely places to sit. Cruise ships almost always have seating areas or rows designated for passengers with disabilities, but latecomers and cocktail servers may not notice a dark-colored dog in a dark room on a dark carpet once the show is underway. As you become more familiar with the ship, you might discover ideal places such as a row of several

Henry Kisor and Trooper on one of their many daily exercise treks around a cruise ship's promenade deck. (Photograph by Deborah Abbott)

seats abutting a wall or partition. Try to arrive early so you can snare a spot like that out of the traffic flow where you can settle your partner on the floor against the wall.

When you bring the dog into public areas, obviously you must observe all of the line's policies you have read and signed. Here's one example from Celebrity Cruises: "Your service animal is welcome to accompany you in all public areas, including dining venues. However, they may not sit on furniture or eat from dining room tables. Due to health regulations, they are not permitted in pools, whirlpools or spas."

Another from Holland America Line reads, "I understand that it is my responsibility to ensure that my service animal is on a leash or harness when in public areas of the ship, refrains from sitting on any surface other than the floor, stays out of the saunas, hot tubs, pools or the 'beach' area surrounding the pool, and does not eat in the public areas of the ship."

# Interacting with Crew and Other Passengers

● **Chris:** Raylene and I were on our first cruise together when our partly filled elevator stopped at a floor to admit more people. My large black dog stood quietly by my side on the dark carpet, apparently unnoticed by the other passengers. "Back up," I commanded her in what I thought was a low, yet masterful, voice. She did—along with the rest of the wide-eyed passengers who glanced at me and dutifully shuffled back toward the rear of the car.

Usually, though, you and your partner are highly visible to others, and you will have to deal with the reactions of passengers and crew to the dog's presence. Many of them will beam in delight, but some will grimace in disapproval. My husband overheard one woman say, after a long delay in boarding due to a bomb scare, "Oh, great, a dog. This is the cruise from hell!" There's nothing you can do about those who just don't like dogs, and you'll have to develop a firm but friendly way to deter those who want to rush up and smother them in cuddles and kisses. ●

● **Henry:** I just hold up a hand, smile, and say, "He's a working dog and needs to be let alone to do his job." That usually solves the problem. Frequently I'll take him "off duty" in a passenger lounge and let folks sit down and pet him. While he basks in their attention, I'll do a little promotion for service animals in general and Trooper's training organization—Dogs for Better Lives—in particular.

"How much does it cost to bring the dog aboard ship?" asked one passenger. Judging from her accent, I would say she was from somewhere in Eastern Europe and had never heard of service dogs. She seemed astonished that they were not only allowed but also carried free. More often, an expression of sudden understanding wreathes the faces of curious passengers when they realize what that box of sod on the deck is for.

I've found that Filipino and Indonesian service crews are much the same as Americans and Canadians in their views of dogs aboard. Some are indifferent, a few are disapproving, and one or two are absolutely terrified of dogs. Others miss their own dogs at home and want a fur fix in the worst way.

One of those was a cabin steward, a young woman from a small village near Jakarta. Every morning she would collapse to her knees upon entering my stateroom and gather Trooper into her arms, gushing and cooing. He would squirm in delight. Sometimes the scene got a little sticky, and her fellow cabin steward had to remind her that *they* had a job to do. ●

"The crew have not seen their pets for many, many months, and some even shed a tear when they see my dog," Roz Silberschein said. "I totally understand. Then there are the crew who are absolutely terrified of my dog. Horton weighs ninety pounds, has a huge head, is pure black, and if you don't know what he's trained to do, he can look frightening."

Other service dog partners have dealt with the problem of overly friendly passengers by asking the ship's cruise director to insert a short item into the announcement sheet placed by the door to every stateroom each morning. The item could say something like: "A service dog for a person with disabilities is aboard ship. Please avoid distracting him from his job by attempting to pet him or even speaking to him when he is in public areas. The dog's partner will let you know when it's OK to come over and say hello."

A cruise director once did that for Silberschein. "The 'blurb' was perfect," she said. "We even scheduled a 'Meet and Pet' in one of the lounges for folks who wanted to know more about service dogs as well as throw a ball and play with Brenda."

● **Chris:** A lot of passengers stop me to ask questions, tell stories, or show me pictures of their pets back home (frequently Labs like Raylene), and they get a little misty talking about the ones who have "crossed the Rainbow Bridge." Many will nicely ask if petting is ever permitted. I have Raylene sit first, then give her the command, "Say hello." She loves it since she knows a treat may be coming from me and because she enjoys the attention. She also knows that jumping on strangers is verboten.

● **Henry:** As a young dog, Trooper sometimes greeted friendly people by eagerly putting his front paws up on them. As an inexperienced service dog handler, I first explained that because he's a small hearing dog, he was trained to jump up on me (big dogs nudge their partners), but after a visit and a refresher lesson from his Dogs for Better Lives trainer, we cured that behavior. ●

● **Chris:** On one cruise, a toddler became quite enamored of my big dog and rushed toward her every time she spotted us coming. Raylene, who rarely encounters children, happily tolerated fingers in her mouth and tugs on her ears, with doggie grins and tail wags. When the father scooped the child up to depart one afternoon, the anguished wails and screams could be heard the length of the deck. I'm convinced a rumor spread throughout the ship that Raylene had nipped off one of those wee fingers. ●

## Tipping

If you have cruised before, you will be aware of the line's gratuity policies. Often, a set amount per person will be charged to your shipboard account each day, to be paid by credit card at the trip's conclusion. If you booked during a special promotional period, these standard gratuities may have been included in the price you paid. Ask your travel agent before you sail if you are at all uncertain about what your fare covers.

When you travel with a service animal, the staff and crew often will make extra efforts to be sure your needs are met. It's appropriate to say thank you, both verbally and by offering *extra* cash tips. If you want to include notes of appreciation, too, ask the guest services desk for paper and envelopes. It's nice to extend your extra tips as you go along or you can wait until the last night of the cruise.

● **Chris:** The dining room manager who took care of our request for a better table location, the room steward who vacuumed up my dog's hair from the carpet, or the waiter who anticipated my needs by pulling extra chairs out of the way each time I arrived and departed with the dog, all were people who smoothed the way and made our cruises extra enjoyable. They earned the extra gratuities we provided. I've learned that onboard employees really appreciate it when I also write a brief note mentioning them by name to give to the hotel manager. ●

● **Henry:** We do the same. My wife, Debby, is in charge of writing the bread-and-butter notes to the hotel manager, and I make sure to give a green handshake to each crew member who has helped us.

## Excursions Ashore

Upon arrival in port, after local authorities have cleared the ship, announcements will be made when you can go ashore. Be sure to bring a bottle of water and a collapsible bowl for your dog. You'll also need to bring along your room key card for the crew to scan as you exit, and a copy of your dog's documents. Then you'll simply proceed with your dog down a gangway ramp to the pier. You'll do the same procedure in reverse when you return to the ship, with the addition of a security check.

Sometimes, however, the ship cannot dock and instead must anchor offshore and use tenders—small boats of varying sizes—to ferry passengers into port. Crew members will assist as each person steps off a platform and onto the tender.

● **Chris:** At times, the ocean swell may raise and lower the water level between the boarding platform and the tender. I wear sturdy, flat shoes and a cross-body bag so I have both hands free, and I keep Raylene close on leash while we wait our turn to board the tender. I ask a travel companion (or a crew member) to get into the tender first, face me, and be ready to receive my dog. I start walking and urge her to quickly step or jump forward into the tender door (with a command like "Up" or "Let's go!") and toss or hand the leash to my companion. Then I can safely board myself with the assistance of the crew. We try to find seats against a bulkhead in the front or back of the tender so I can prevent Raylene's tail and long legs from being stepped upon. ●

145

Most cruise lines offer a variety of shore adventures that range from an hour or two of bus sightseeing to day-long helicopter flights. The lines typically contract with independent local tour companies to arrange visits to venues as well as provide transportation and refreshment.

There are two downsides to these excursions. First, they are quite expensive compared to booking an independent but equivalent tour on your own. Second, many of these contract venues are artificially created just for cruise ship passengers. Think of a fake Wild West town with bad guys on horseback shooting blanks, and you'll get the idea.

There is an upside to contracted tours, and it is an important one: if your bus breaks down or otherwise is greatly delayed, the ship will wait for you—or if that's not an option because of tides, the danger of departing through a narrow channel after dark, or fines for tarrying too long at a dock, the cruise line will get the tour group to the next port and cover lodging and food on its dime.

Many veteran cruisers who know what they're doing will book with less expensive independent tours. Usually the tour operators are savvy about sailing deadlines, know the port officials, and have backup resources. Most often, people who miss the ship do so because of rental car trouble, getting lost in town, or losing track of time while swimming or shopping.

If you're new to cruising, being able to rely on the cruise line to take care of you aboard and off the ship is definitely more relaxing. After booking your cruise, research the tour offerings to find out if some are likely to deliver enjoyable experiences for you and your dog. Talk to the ship's shore excursion staff, ask questions, and be ready, as always, to roll with the punches during the tour.

● **Henry:** Once, at a raptor rehabilitation center in Sitka, Alaska, I was sitting in the front row for a keeper's show-and-tell with a juvenile bald eagle, with my wife, Debby, holding Trooper's leash beside me so that I could photograph the proceedings. When the keeper brought in the bird, Trooper immediately wanted to roughhouse, and the eagle wanted to rip him to shreds. Before matters got out of hand, Debby towed Trooper to safety in an anteroom.

My thoughtless mistake was not anticipating a possible problem. Although the rest of the center was hospitable to service dogs, I never should have taken Trooper into that room. At the best of times, canines and eagles are never chums, for they are both predators. ●

Now the big question: Will the contracted tour operator in a foreign country accept your service dog? It will in the United States and Canada, that's for sure, but what about Central American and Caribbean ports?

● **Henry:** I asked Holland America Line's accessibility people whether HAL-affiliated foreign shore tours would accept a service dog, and they suggested I go ahead and book the tours and then let them know which ones. I did, and they spoke to the tour operators, asking if a service dog would be a problem. None objected, and some even said dogs were welcome and they'd give us seats at the front of the buses. ●

Some service dog partners have reported rejection from tour bus drivers in some ports. When this happens, it's best to shrug and go along with the rejection. The ADA does not apply in foreign countries, many of which have no disability rights laws.

## Other Dogs

You may encounter other service dog teams on board the ship, but usually these dogs, like yours, will be quiet and trained to ignore other animals. Going ashore may present a different scenario, depending on your itinerary. We suggest that you ask the staff at the shore excursions desk about the potential presence of other dogs during tours you plan to take.

● **Henry:** Recently I spent four hours on a tour bus with Trooper in rural Mexico without getting off because scores of unleashed dogs frequented the sites the bus visited, including a town square. Most of those dogs, of course, just lay lethargically in the shade out of the hot sun, but several got up and approached us. Obviously, you don't want to run the risk that your very expensively trained service dog will be either attacked or greeted by another that might be full of parasites, as one Mexican tour guide warned us.

Police dogs may be present when you disembark, too. For example, at Cabo San Lucas, Mexico, federal police K-9s are used as drug sniffers at the port's tender dock. (When their handlers spotted Trooper, they considerately pulled their dogs out of the way in order to avoid a confrontation.) It's also not uncommon to see a police dog in the customs area at major U.S. ports such as Miami or San Diego. Keep an eye out to avoid any unexpected encounters.  ●

## Reentry into the United States

When you disembark in the United States (or fly home from a foreign port of disembarkation), remember that you will be "importing" your dog into the United States. You will pass through passport control staffed by U.S. Customs and Border Protection agents. In theory, the Centers for Disease Control and Prevention (CDC) (https://www.cdc.gov/importation/traveling-with-pets.html) and other government agencies require that pet dogs and cats brought into this country be examined at the first port of entry for evidence of diseases that can be transmitted to humans or might be a threat to American livestock.

Your service animal may or may not be examined as you disembark, collect your luggage, and go through passport control. Your ship's officials presumably already have provided the dog's documentation to U.S. officials as part of their clearance procedures, and passport control agents in our experience do not request it. However, keep your set of the dog's original papers in your hand luggage.

● **Chris:** After disembarking from a cruise at the Port of Miami, I was escorted with my dog to a separate room to meet with a uniformed official who examined her coat, eyes, ears, teeth, and paws. He asked a few questions about our itinerary and wanted to see her papers, which I was able to produce. The process delayed us about forty-five minutes, but luckily we did not have a tight connection to a flight to worry about.  ●

## Less Complicated Cruising

If your life is hectic enough already, consider an itinerary that visits only ports in the United States and Canada, such as a cruise along the Pacific Coast, an Alaska cruise out of Seattle, or a New England and Canada cruise from the Eastern Seaboard. Canada is a service-dog-friendly country, and tour operators in U.S. ports follow guidelines set by the ADA.

U.S. ports of call, other than those in Hawaii, require very little paperwork from a service dog team. You will need a rabies certificate and a Form 7001 issued by your vet because airline and cruise line personnel typically expect you to present it when you check in. Same with Canadian ports.

Appendix 3 reviews the published service dog policies of most of the cruise lines that sail in U.S. waters and call at U.S. ports. Appendix 4 has detailed information on Animal Import Regulations for many ports of call, including those in Hawaii.

Henry Kisor and Trooper aboard a harbor ferry in Halifax, Nova Scotia. Canada does not require heavy-duty documentation for service dogs from the United States. (Photo with Henry's iPhone by an unknown fellow tourist)

# Summing Up

- Always check with a cruise line (or have your travel agent do so) about the line's service dog policy before booking a cruise.
- Fill out the cruise line's special needs forms and advise them of your expectations, especially what you want for the dog's relief box.
- Pack enough food and meds for the entire cruise plus a few days' extra.
- Pay particular attention to required documentation for foreign ports, including proof of rabies vaccination, international health certificates, and dog import permits.
- When arriving at the cruise terminal, have copies of all your dog's documentation ready to give the ship's personnel.
- Upon boarding ship, make sure the relief box's location and filling meets your dog's needs.
- Next, consult the dining room maître d' to reconfirm your request for a suitable table for the duration of the voyage.
- Survey the ship for protected places to sit, such as in the theater, where your dog won't be stepped on.
- Be ready to fend off friendly fellow passengers who want to interact with your dog.
- Never leave your dog unattended aboard ship, even in your stateroom.
- Tip well for exceptional personal service.
- When booking foreign shore day trips, ask the cruise line's excursions department to obtain advance permissions to bring your dog with you.
- For reentry into the United States or Canada, keep your dog's original documents in your hand luggage in case officials request it.

Chapter 6

# That Annoying Paperwork

**Chris:** The final morning of a two-week Hawaii cruise, my husband, Bob, and I sat next to a woman at breakfast who had booked her trip, looked forward to it for months, and boarded the ship without investigating whether any special documentation might be required for the small seizure alert dog that was sitting on her lap.

"Hawaii is supposedly part of the United States, and they wouldn't even let me take my dog off the ship!" she complained. Another assistance dog on board the ship trotted ashore next to his partner's wheelchair without a problem.

I felt sorry for the woman and learned a lesson that has proven to be invaluable ever since a hearing dog came into my life: never assume your service animal can travel without the right paperwork.

## Why Is It So Complicated?

The good news: many countries (including foreign cruise ship ports of call) allow a service dog or a pet dog to enter as long as the animal meets the government's health requirements and has official documentation to prove it. However, your service dog can't always accompany you on your foreign travels. As of this writing, many countries, such as Bermuda, restrict importation of certain breeds. Others, such as Jamaica, refuse entry for any dogs unless they meet narrowly defined criteria. Still others may require a lengthy quarantine.

Virtually every country, including the United States, requires that the dog have a current rabies certificate. Some countries may require additional inoculations, verification that the dog has been spayed or neutered, a microchip number, and proof that the animal has been treated for internal and external parasites. Rabies-free regions typically require titer tests—advance blood work that measures the response of the dog's immune system to the rabies vaccine.

Why so difficult? Think of it this way: even though you may be vacationing for a week, traveling on business for a few days, or just stepping ashore in a cruise port for a few hours, you actually are temporarily "exporting" your dog and "importing" it into a foreign country that has a vital interest in protecting its own animals and citizens from diseases.

## Where Can I Find the Requirements for My Destinations?

When you're reviewing your bucket list, you can often get a fairly accurate read on what will be involved in a few minutes at no cost. If you are in the United States, just log onto https://www.aphis.usda.gov, the U.S. Department of Agriculture Animal and Plant Health Inspection Service (APHIS) Veterinary Services website, for a wealth of international animal export information. Yes, it is true that your service animal is not a pet. But the same foreign governmental requirements usually apply to both, so click "Pet Travel" at the top of the home page. Under the banner, "Take your pet *from* the United States to a foreign county (Export)" you'll find a drop-down menu of current country requirements and sometimes the country-specific forms.

Not all countries have provided APHIS with information on their requirements, however. Some may have information on their own national government websites, or you will need to call their embassy to inquire. Investigate your airline's requirements as well.

The APHIS website warns, "Since export requirements are determined by each country and can change frequently, every time you plan pet travel you will need to verify the export requirements."

As chapter 1, "The Basics," mentioned, if you're in Canada, the Canadian Food Inspection Agency (CFIA) and Canadian Transportation Agency (CTA) are the chief sources of information. If you go to http://www.inspection.gc.ca and follow the links to "Animals," you'll be taken to the proper pages for information, including downloadable (and country-specific) versions of the Canadian International Pet Health Certificate. The CTA's website is http://otc-cta.gc.ca/eng/service-animals.

## It's Vital to Plan Ahead

Meeting your destination's requirements could be time-consuming. For example, if you are traveling to the rabies-free state of Hawaii, you will need to arrange for your dog's blood to be drawn and sent by the vet to an approved lab at Kansas State University for a $250 blood titer test, technically called a FAVN (Fluorescent Antibody Virus Neutralization), that measures the response of an animal's immune system to the rabies vaccine. And that's just for starters.

The Caribbean island nation St. Kitts and Nevis requires *two* such blood tests, at least thirty days apart.

As another example, if you are going to the Bahamas, even for a stop at one of the "private islands" owned by cruise lines, you must mail an application (found on the APHIS website) for an import permit and allow at least four weeks for it to be returned. You must also carry a stamped import permit into Bahamian waters even if you do not intend to get off the ship with your dog. In the past, Bahamian government officials have allowed travelers to fax documents on short notice, but you can't count on it since their rules change from time to time.

You get the picture. Allow plenty of lead time when you plan to take your dog to a foreign country because you may need it.

It's also possible that when you arrive in many countries, nobody will take notice of you and your dog at all. Still, it's better to be safe than sorry and have that paperwork ready in case you're waylaid by officialdom.

## The Basics

Count on needing *at least* two pieces of paper for international travel and your reentry into the United States: your dog's current rabies certificate and a recent health certificate (Form 7001) issued by a licensed veterinarian, or the equivalent in Canada. The Form 7001 is valid for thirty days after issuance.

The rabies certificate must have the following information according to the Centers for Disease Control and Prevention when you are bringing an animal into the United States:

1. Name and address of owner
2. Breed, sex, age, color, markings, and other identifying information for the dog
3. Date of rabies vaccination and vaccine product information
4. Date the vaccination expires
5. Name, license number, address, and signature of veterinarian who administered the vaccination

If it doesn't have this information, contact your vet and ask for a replacement rabies certificate with it. While you are at it, ask that the vet sign it in blue (not black) ink, since some countries require this.

The full name of APHIS Form 7001 is the "United States Interstate and International Certificate of Health Examination for Small Animals." Look on the APHIS website for a sample of this form, which the vet will give you after examining your dog before your trip.

Note that some countries (Mexico is one example) require a partly bilingual version of the Form 7001. When multiple countries are involved in an itinerary, an APHIS-accredited vet provides and signs all the relevant forms—the English standard form, any country-specific bilingual versions of 7001, and any other required documents.

Form 7001, famous among U.S. service dog partners who want to take their animals abroad, is signed and issued by veterinarians certified by the U.S. Department of Agriculture's Animal and Plant Health Inspection Service. Many foreign countries require that the form also be countersigned by an official APHIS veterinarian. (USDA APHIS)

---

According to the Paperwork Reduction Act of 1995, an agency may not conduct or sponsor, and a person is not required or respond to, a collection of information unless it displays a valid OMB control number. The valid OMB control number for this information collection is 0579-0020 and 0579-0088. The time required to complete this information collection is estimated to average .25 hours per response, including the time for reviewing instructions, searching existing data sources, gathering and maintaining the data needed, and completing and reviewing the collection of information.

UNITED STATES DEPARTMENT OF AGRICULTURE
ANIMAL AND PLANT HEALTH INSPECTION SERVICE

UNITED STATES INTERSTATE AND INTERNATIONAL
CERTIFICATE OF HEALTH EXAMINATION
FOR SMALL ANIMALS

OMB APPROVED
0579-0036
0579-0088

WARNING: Anyone who makes a false, fictitious, or fraudulent statement on this document, or causes such document knowing it to be false, fictitious, or fraudulent may be subject to a fine of not more than $10,000 or imprisonment of not more than 5 years or both (18 U.S.C. 1001).

the dog, cat, nonhuman primate, or additional stock or classes of animals designated by USDA ·I agreiation sh all be del i vered to any intermediate handler or the for transportation in commerce, unless accompanied by a heal th certificate executed and issued by a licensed veterinarian (7 U.S.C. 21.43.9; CFR, Subchapter A, Part 2).

4. TYPE OF ANIMAL SHIPPED (select only one)
☐ Dog  ☐ Cat  ☐ Other
☐ Nonhuman Primate  ☐ Ferret  ☐ Rodent

2. CERTIFICATE NUMBER - OFFICIAL USE ONLY

3. TOTAL NUMBER OF ANIMALS

4. PAGE _____ of _____

5. NAME, ADDRESS, AND TELEPHONE NUMBER OF OWNER (CONSIGNOR)

6. NAME, ADDRESS, AND TELEPHONE NUMBER OF RECIPIENT AT DESTINATION (CONSIGNEE)

USDA Licensee/or Registration Number (if applicable)

7. ANIMAL IDENTIFICATION

| NAME, AND/OR TATTOO NUMBER OR OTHER IDENTIFICATION | BREED – COMMON OR SCIENTIFIC NAME | AGE | SEX | COLOR OR DISTINCTIVE MARKS OR MICROCHIP |
|---|---|---|---|---|
| (1) | | | | |
| (2) | | | | |
| (3) | | | | |
| (4) | | | | |
| (5) | | | | |
| (6) | | | | |

8. PERTINENT VACCINATION, TREATMENT, AND TESTING HISTORY

RABIES VACCINATION
☐ 1 YEAR  ☐ 2 YEARS  ☐ 3 YEARS

| Vaccination Date | Product | OTHER VACCINATIONS, TREATMENT, AND/OR TESTS AND RESULTS | |
|---|---|---|---|
| | | Product Type and/or Results | Date |

9. REMARKS OR ADDITIONAL CERTIFICATION STATEMENTS (WHEN REQUIRED)

VETERINARY CERTIFICATION: I certify that the animals described in box 7 have been examined by me this date, that the information provided in box 8 is true and accurate to the best of my knowledge, and that the following findings have been made ("X" applicable statements).

☐ I have verified the presence of the microchip, if a microchip is listed in box 7.

☐ I certify that the animal(s) described above and on continuation sheet(s), if applicable, have been inspected by me on this date and appear to be free of any infectious or contagious diseases and to the best of my knowledge, exposure thereto, which would endanger the animal or other animals or would endanger public health.

☐ To my knowledge, the animal(s) described above and on continuation sheet(s) if applicable, originated from an area not quarantined for rabies and has/have not been exposed to rabies.

NAME, ADDRESS, AND TELEPHONE NUMBER OF ISSUING VETERINARIAN

LICENSE NUMBER AND STATE

Accredited ☐ Yes  ☐ No
If yes, please complete below
NATIONAL ACCREDITATION NUMBER

ENDORSEMENT FOR INTERNATIONAL EXPORT (IF NEEDED)
PRINTED NAME OF USDA VETERINARIAN

NOTE: International shipments may require certification by an accredited veterinarian.
SIGNATURE OF ISSUING VETERINARIAN

SIGNATURE OF USDA VETERINARIAN    Apply USDA Seal or Stamp here    DATE

DATE

APHIS Form 7001
(NOV 2010)

This certificate is valid for 30 days after issuance

**INTERNATIONAL HEALTH CERTIFICATE FOR DOGS AND CATS**
*CERTIFICAT SANITAIRE INTERNATIONAL POUR CHIENS ET CHATS*

**COUNTRY OF ORIGIN / *PAYS D'ORIGINE*: CANADA**

I.  COUNTRY OF DESTINATION / *PAYS DE DESTINATION*: _____

II.  OWNER / *PROPRIÉTAIRE*: Name / *Nom* _____

Address / *Adresse*: _____

III.  **DESCRIPTION OF ANIMAL / *DESCRIPTION DE L'ANIMAL***

Name / *Nom* : _____  Species / *Espèce* :  Dog/ *Chien* ☐   Cat / *Chat* ☐   Sex / *Sexe*: _____

Date of birth / *Date de naissance* : _____   Breed / *Race* : _____
(yyyy/mm/dd / *aaaa/mm/jj*)

Color / *Couleur*: _____,   Microchip No. / *N° de la micropuce*: _____

Coat type and markings/Distinguishing marks / *Pelage et marques distinctives*: _____

IV.  **VACCINATION (Rabies) / *VACCINATION (Rage)***

I, the undersigned licensed veterinarian, declare that the animal described above has been vaccinated against rabies as shown below:
*Je, soussigné, vétérinaire licencié, affirme que l'animal décrit ci-dessus a été vacciné contre la rage conformément aux renseignements ci-après :*

Date of vaccination / *Date de la vaccination* : _____ (yyyy/mm/dd / *aaaa/mm/dd*)

Vaccination valid until / *Vaccination valide jusqu'à*: _____ (yyyy/mm/dd / *aaaa/mm/dd*)

Name of vaccine / *Nom du vaccin*: _____

Type of vaccine / *Type de vaccin*: _____  Batch number/ *Numéro de lot*:_____

Manufacturer / *Fabricant*:_____

V.  **CLINICAL EXAMINATION / *EXAMEN CLINIQUE***

I, the undersigned licensed veterinarian, declare that the animal described above has been examined before departure on the date indicated below and found clinically healthy and free of external parasites. I believe this animal to be fit to travel.
*Je, soussigné, vétérinaire licencié, affirme que l'animal décrit ci-dessus a été examiné avant son départ à la date indiquée ci-après et qu'il a été jugé cliniquement sain et exempt de parasites externes. Je considère que cet animal est apte à voyager.*

Date of examination / *Date de l'examen*:_____ (yyyy/mm/dd / *aaaa/mm/dd*)

VI.  **OTHER VACCINATIONS/TREATMENTS (if applicable) / *AUTRES VACCINS/TRAITEMENT (le cas échéant)***

I, the undersigned licensed veterinarian, declare that, the animal described above has been vaccinated and/or treated against the following diseases as shown below./ *Je, soussigné, vétérinaire licencié affirme que l'animal décrit ci-dessus a été vacciné ou a reçu un traitement contre les maladies énumérées ci-après :*

| T or/ou V * | Disease Vaccinated for/ Reason for Treatment *Maladie contre laquelle l'animal est vacciné ou traité* | Date | Product Name and Dose (if applicable) *Nom du produit et dose (le cas échéant)* |
|---|---|---|---|
| | | | |
| | | | |
| | | | |
| | | | |

* indicate with a "T" for treatment and a "V" for vaccination/ *"T" signifie traitement et "V" signifie vaccination*

_____     _____
Date (yyyy/mm/dd / *aaaa/mm/jj*)        Signature of Licensed Veterinarian / *Signature du vétérinaire licencié*

Name and address of licensed veterinarian / *Nom et adresse du vétérinaire licencié*:_____
_____

_____     Signature of Official Veterinarian / *Signature du vétérinaire officiel*
Date (yyyy/mm/dd / *aaaa/mm/jj*)        Canadian Food Inspection Agency / *Agence canadienne d'inspection des aliments*
                          Government of Canada / *Gouvernement du Canada*

Official Export Stamp          Name of Official Veterinarian (in block letters) / *Nom du vétérinaire officiel (en lettres moulées)*
*Cachet officiel*

Canada's version of the U.S. Form 7001 is in both English and French, and there is also a trilingual version for Spanish-speaking countries that require it.

# Working with an APHIS-Accredited Vet

We recommend working with an accredited vet for international travel. "Generally, any licensed veterinarian can issue health certificates for pets that do not require APHIS endorsement, including for pets traveling interstate," the APHIS website advises, with this caveat: "When APHIS endorsement of the health certificate is required, the veterinarian that issues the health certificate must be USDA accredited."

Ask if your regular licensed veterinarian is accredited by APHIS (in Canada, the CFIA). If not, your vet may be able to refer you to one nearby who can help when you travel. In either country, you can also find on the websites a regional phone number to call for a list of vets. Provide the accredited vet's office with copies of all your dog's health records including inoculations and microchip information for their files, and give them a copy of your itinerary and travel date.

If you're fortunate, there will be a veterinary practice near your home with one or more APHIS- or CFIA-accredited vets who are experienced and knowledgeable about the requirements and willing to go the extra mile when needed. Unfortunately, that's not always the case. Be sure when you call that the office staff is aware that you need for them to research the country-specific requirements and forms, examine your dog before your departure for a Form 7001 or Canadian International Pet Health Certificate, give the dog any necessary inoculations, tests, or treatments, and prepare and sign all the documents. Your name, home address, and telephone number will be listed as the owner (consignor). In another box, your name will again appear with your destination address (or cruise ship name and ports of call) as the recipient (consignee).

How far in advance should you schedule the examination? Ask the vet's office about that. The Form 7001 is valid for thirty days after issuance (the Canadian version varies by province), but don't have it done too soon—some countries specify that a certificate should be issued "no earlier than" a specified number of days before travel begins. It's a good idea to schedule the exam no later than a week to ten days before leaving home.

# If Your Form 7001 or Canadian Equivalent Must Be Endorsed

*Important:* Many countries require that the 7001 health certificate and other forms be signed by the accredited vet and then endorsed by a "government authority." In the United States, the government authority you'll need is an APHIS Veterinary Medical Officer at a regional APHIS services office, and there are many around the country. All appointments and questions are routed through six primary locations. The APHIS website has a menu of "APHIS Veterinary Services Endorsement Offices," and you can ask your accredited vet to confirm the appropriate location for the state where you reside.

Tip: If endorsement *is* required, ask your vet to print and sign two sets of forms, so you will have a backup set just in case your paperwork gets lost.

If a regional endorsement office is close to your home, make an appointment to have the form endorsed in person while you wait. Otherwise you will need to send it by an overnight delivery service with tracking, such as UPS, and you must include an overnight return envelope. Call the APHIS service center to ask which delivery services they suggest you use. Since time is of the essence, track your package, follow up with the endorsement office if necessary, and ask your vet to get involved if the endorsed certificate is not returned right away.

APHIS does not charge endorsement user fees for service dogs belonging to individuals with disabilities as defined by the Americans with Disabilities Act (ADA), so include a copy of your dog's ID from the training organization and request this waiver.

In Canada, the CFIA web site will give you instructions.

## Can Form 7001 Be Endorsed Electronically?

It depends. Some countries now allow digital signatures on the health forms. The USDA APHIS website indicates, in every country entry, whether they do or do not accept e-signatures. For example, see the site's page for Colombia: https://www.aphis.usda.gov/aphis/pet-travel/by-country/pettravel-colombia.

This means that USDA-accredited vets may be able to e-sign the forms for pets using the Veterinary Export Health Certificate System (VEHCS). The APHIS vets then go into the system, examine the vet's completed forms, and, if the information has been entered correctly, endorse them electronically. The issuing vets then print them out and hand the paper copies to the pet owners.

This system potentially can save service dog handlers time, money, and anxiety, so it's worth investigating with your vet. Many countries, however, won't accept e-signed and e-endorsed forms at all and require conventional paper 7001s signed in original ink. Some countries accept e-signatures from the accredited vets but require ink signatures from APHIS-endorsing veterinary medical officers and an embossed APHIS seal. In those cases, carrying or mailing the forms to an APHIS service center is still necessary.

**Chris:** When you have your original endorsed health certificate, any country-specific paperwork, and an original rabies certificate, your dog is ready to travel. I believe that "more is better" whenever government officials are involved, which means carrying copies of all my dog's official records. This includes her spay certificate, microchip registration form, list of inoculations, and copies of ID cards from both her training program and the International Association of Assistance Dog Partners. I include a one-page summary of all relevant information about my dog—the name and address of her training organization, her APHIS-accredited vet's name, address, phone number, and so on. The extra documentation can't hurt, and having plenty of official paperwork could help smooth the way.

## Nothing Can Go Wrong, Right?

On occasion, while traveling with all the required paperwork that has been correctly issued, you may be pulled out of line before entering a foreign country and taken to a room where your dog will be examined. Service dogs usually handle this easily, since they are accustomed to obeying your "sit" or "down" commands and being touched by strangers. After the examiner reviews your paperwork, the inspection is over, and you can proceed.

However, government officials often have varied levels of knowledge and experience with service dogs, and since they are human beings, sometimes they have a bad day. If you are initially advised that you cannot enter a country, remain calm, point out your documented compliance with the rules, and state your case without getting angry. After answering any further questions, you should be on your way quickly.

## Checking In

Keep an extra set of your paperwork in your luggage as a backup, but hand-carry the originals with your passport and cash. Airline officials may review them at the check-in counter, and you'll need them upon arrival at your destination. (See chapter 5, "Sailing the Seas," for cruise lines' paperwork and check-in procedures.)

## Reentry

When you fly home to the United States from a foreign country or disembark from a cruise ship, remember that you will be "importing" your dog into the United States. You will pass through passport control staffed by U.S. Customs and Border Protection agents. In theory, the CDC requires that pet dogs and cats brought into this country be examined at the first port of entry for evidence of diseases that can be transmitted to humans.

USDA APHIS Veterinary Services also has health requirements related to importing a pet dog to the United States from a foreign country currently affected by specific diseases such as screwworm and foot-and-mouth disease. See the APHIS Pet Travel webpage for more information and talk with your APHIS-accredited vet if you have any questions about the countries you plan to visit.

Your service animal, in our experience, may be examined when you arrive, collect your luggage, and go through passport control. Your airline or ship's officials presumably already have provided the dog's documentation to U.S. officials as part of their clearance procedures, and passport control agents in our experience often do not request it. *But keep your set of the dog's original papers in your hand luggage!*

In Canada, if you're coming in from one of a number of rabies-free countries, there's no requirement. If you're crossing from the United States, bring the dog's rabies certificate. Incidentally, the Canadian government recognizes "Medically Certified Guide Dogs" as "Assistance dogs that are endorsed as a guide, hearing or other service dog" and says they "are not subject to any restrictions for importation when the person importing the dog is the user of the dog and accompanies the dog to Canada."

## About the Dog's Microchip

Vets (and service dog organizations) implant microchips as a permanent way to identify your dog through radio-frequency identification (RFID) technology by a unique combination of letters and numbers that, in theory, can be read with a hand-held scanner by another vet, animal shelter, or government official. You, as the animal's owner, must register the number and your contact information with a recovery database to be reached in case your lost animal is found.

There are several veterinary microchip makers, such as Avid, 24Pet-Watch, Home Again, and others. To complicate matters, different brands (or products within one brand) have digits of varying length, from nine to fifteen, and may have different radio frequencies, because U.S. manufacturers have never agreed upon a uniform standard used elsewhere in the world. Your dog may have been implanted with an ISO fifteen-digit microchip that meets European Union and most other international standards. Not all scanners, including so-called universal scanners, will read all microchips.

The APHIS 7001 and other country-specific forms have a line where the microchip number is recorded, and your APHIS-accredited vet, when examining the dog, verifies the microchip number before signing. A government official, in theory, someday may attempt to scan your dog's microchip as you arrive to verify that your dog matches the paperwork. Perhaps this might happen if you vacation outside the United States and Canada, or stop for the day at a foreign cruise port and attempt to leave the ship. If this concerns you, your options are to borrow, rent, or buy a microchip scanner to take along, after first making sure it works on your dog.

● **Chris:** My dog's microchip has never been scanned by anyone except the vet, including cruise port officials, who apparently are content to trust the APHIS paperwork. But someday I may want to travel with my dog to Europe or other distant locations where entry procedures are potentially stringent. Microchip scanners, new or used, are quite expensive for "just in case" insurance, but I bought a simple, lightweight Halo brand reader online for less than $100 that reads my dog's chip easily. I make sure it is fully charged and carry it in my hand luggage on trips outside the United States.                    ●

## Expect the Unexpected

● **Chris:** A few years ago, we arrived at a New York state park campground in our RV, with the dog, as usual, wagging her tail at the prospect of arrival and trying to get a sniff through the driver's side window of the camp host who was checking us in.

"I'll need to see the dog's rabies certificate," said the man. Gulp!

After a moment of panic, I was able to produce it. We anticipated the possibility of briefly crossing the border into Canada when we visited the U.S. side of Niagara Falls near the campground. The day I packed our passports, I tossed in copies of the dog's papers, too. You never know when it might be important to have a rabies certificate in hand for your dog. I keep a current copy now in the glove box of our RV—and in our car. ●

We strongly recommend that you add travel insurance to your paperwork checklist to help you prepare for the unexpected. Plans vary widely, but a typical comprehensive plan will include medical coverage and emergency evacuation as well as baggage loss, delay, or damage. Trip cancellation and interruption is valuable, as we know from experience, and some plans will allow you to cancel for any reason.

Travel agencies, tour operators, and cruise lines routinely offer such plans, or you can research and purchase them online, perhaps at a lower cost. You may already have some limited coverage as a credit cardholder benefit, but do a side-by-side comparison with other policies. The ones you can buy probably include more extensive coverage and higher reimbursement levels.

Making complicated arrangements and securing all the annoying paperwork that you and your dog will need can be time-consuming and expensive. But it's an investment in your peace of mind as you set out on a travel adventure with your service dog by your side.

Appendix 4 explains in detail import regulations you'll need to follow in order to bring your service animal into countries that make up North and Central America and the Caribbean.

---

## Summing Up

- Find the current animal import requirements for your destination on the APHIS or CFIA websites, but be aware they may change.
- Plan way ahead—even by months. Obtaining documentation could be time-consuming.
- Always carry at least a rabies certificate and APHIS Form 7001 or the Canadian equivalent wherever you go.

- When obtaining documentation, work with an APHIS- or CFIA-accredited veterinarian.
- Go one step further and gather together all your dog's documentation, including training certificates, to carry in your hand luggage. More is always better where foreign country officials are concerned.
- Have your dog microchipped, even if a foreign country may not require it.
- Consider buying travel insurance.

# Appendix 1

# Individual Trains in the United States and Canada

*The following remarks are all by Henry, the rail-buff half of the writing partnership of Henry Kisor and Christine Goodier.*

Trooper and I have traveled on many of the long-distance routes of Amtrak and VIA Rail and have scouted out some of the best places for relief walks. Not every stop is ideal for every dog, especially those who prefer grass, brush, or trees to perform their toilettes. Following are our favorite trains and their stops, taken from the most recent timetables at press time. **The best stations Trooper and I have found for walks are in boldface.**

Be aware that both Amtrak (https://www.amtrak.com) and VIA (http://www.viarail.com) often tweak their schedules. Individual timetables are available online. Download and print one out before you board.

If you are traveling in the directions opposite the ones described below, you can just follow the stops in reverse on the timetable. All times given are times the trains depart the stations.

## Amtrak Routes

### *CAPITOL LIMITED,* CHICAGO–WASHINGTON, D.C.: TRAINS 30 (EASTBOUND) AND 29 (WESTBOUND)

In 2018 Amtrak decided to remove the dining car from the *Capitol Limited*, a highly popular train, and substituted boxed airline-style meals served at coach seats, in sleeper rooms, or at tables in the lounge cars. For many train lovers, including this one, the loss of the diner diminished the experience of rail travel, although the ride otherwise remained the same. One small bright spot is that a service dog team now doesn't have to wonder if going to the dining car is a good idea or not.

On the eastbound *Capitol Limited* (Amtrak 30), before departing from **Chicago Union Station** at **6:40 p.m. Central Time,** visit one of the many roomy raised planters filled with soil, mulch, grass, and bushes behind the station, on the concrete promenade next to the Chicago River just east of the high-rise building over the station concourse. Building security may speak to you sternly if they spot your dog snuffling around in a planter, but often if you say "Service dog! Service dog!" they'll go along with things. Besides, this is where the Amtrak cops relieve their police dogs. Always come equipped with poop bags.

**9:09 p.m. Eastern Time: South Bend, Indiana,** is a five-minute checked baggage stop. Regular passengers aren't allowed to detrain briefly, so prearrange your dog walk with your attendant or conductor—or both. A grassy strip is available right next to the platform. Trooper, who will have peed at home five hours earlier, almost always goes here on his last walk before getting up in the morning.

The stops at Elkhart, Indiana (9:29 p.m.), and Waterloo, Indiana (10:23 p.m.), are quick and should be skipped if possible.

**11:39 to 11:49 p.m.: Toledo, Ohio,** is a ten-minute stop for a change of engineers and conductors. Look for trees, grass, and brush around the parking lot just east of the station building, but be quick. The train might stop on a track requiring passengers to take stairs or an elevator up to an overhead bridge into the station.

Trooper and I have always slept through the other Ohio stops: Sandusky (12:40 a.m.), Elyria (1:15 a.m.), Cleveland (1:45 to 1:54 a.m.), and Alliance (3:05 a.m.)—and so has our attendant, unless passengers are detraining or boarding our car at those stops.

**5:05 to 5:20 a.m.: Pittsburgh, Pennsylvania.** We are always awake for this fifteen-minute crew change stop, though no grassy areas are available. Attendants have suggested that Trooper try the (unfortunately rather dirty) concrete between the rails of an adjacent track or a post between tracks forward and right across from the locomotives.

That last is Trooper's favorite, and we are always careful to look both ways. Once, however, our attendant shouted, "Don't cross the tracks!" when he saw us there, and upbraided us gently when we returned to the train. Safety rules, he said. We didn't argue. Different attendants, different rules. Railroaders are individualists. When they see a perceived offense, some get their undies in a bunch, and others just smile and carry on if the infraction is more technical than not—especially the dog people among them. They *understand*.

After the *Capitol Limited* leaves Pittsburgh, Trooper, Debby, and I stay aboard through Connellsville, Pennsylvania (6:59 a.m.), while we take our breakfasts between 6:30 and 7:30 a.m. so that we can get off the train at Cumberland for Trooper's midmorning pee.

**9:20 to 9:32 a.m.: Cumberland, Maryland.** Twelve minutes are normally allotted for a change of engineers, less if the train's running behind (as happened to us on one trip). Normally the train makes two stops at the station's short platform, one for the sleepers up front and the second for the coaches in the rear. There's a grassy incline just across the station driveway. If you're in a sleeper and people are boarding, sometimes there's time to pee your dog and scramble back aboard before the train moves forward to spot a coach. Otherwise you then get back aboard at the coach and walk through the train to get back to your sleeper. This is the last good dog relief stop before the train arrives in Washington.

We'll pass up the quick stops at Martinsburg (11:01 a.m.) and Harpers Ferry (11:31 a.m.) in West Virginia and Rockville (12:21 p.m.) in Maryland before arrival at **Washington Union Station** at **1:05 p.m.** At Washington there is lots of greensward on Columbus Circle outside Union Station, but it's advisable to go south across Massachusetts Avenue to the next park. Sadly, homeless people, some of whom are drug addicts, abound in Columbus Circle during the summer, and syringe needles may lie unseen in the grass. So may unidentifiable scraps of food—not good for dogs apt to scavenge.

### SOUTHWEST CHIEF, CHICAGO–LOS ANGELES: TRAINS 3 AND 4

Amtrak's *Southwest Chief* through Illinois, Iowa, Missouri, Kansas, Colorado, New Mexico, Arizona, and Southern California follows the pretty desert-and-mountains route that the storied Santa Fe *Super Chief,* the favorite train of Hollywood stars of old, took between Chicago and Los Angeles. For a service dog team who must have grass and trees for relief stops, this isn't the best long-distance train to take, simply because it goes largely through the arid Southwest—but with careful planning it's doable.

The westbound *Southwest Chief* leaves Chicago at 3:00 p.m. Central Time. Here are the likeliest relief stops for that train:

**5:26 p.m.: Galesburg, Illinois.** This is a checked baggage stop, but *Southwest Chief* passengers generally are not permitted to get off to take the air or have a smoke. If you think you may need to walk your service dog, tell the attendant well ahead of time—upon boarding in Chicago, for instance—so that he or she can open the car door for you. You'll find plenty of grass along the platform. Otherwise you could wait a bit more than an hour for:

**6:30 p.m.: Fort Madison, Iowa,** a long baggage and fresh air stop (and crew change point). If your dog is choosy about where it goes, be warned that there are no grassy spots or trees here—just concrete, asphalt, and crushed rock.

**7:39 p.m.: La Plata, Missouri,** always has been a choice relief spot for us— there is a planter of tall grass on the eastern edge of the station building—but you will need to arrange this with your attendant, because it's not a fresh air stop.

If we've walked Trooper at Chicago, La Plata will be just six hours later, an ideal span of time for him.

La Plata, by the way, is a two-stage stop because the platform is very short. The sleepers are first "spotted" in front of the station. After passengers for those cars are detrained and boarded, the train then pulls forward to spot the coaches. Often Trooper and I get off from the sleepers, do our business, and then reboard the train at the coaches, walking forward through the cars until we reach our sleeper. The conductors will make sure we get back on.

We generally go to bed after that.

**10:00 to 10:42 p.m.: Kansas City, Missouri.** This is a nice long urban service and crew change stop for dogs happy to use hard surfaces, but there are no natural areas at all.

**11:49 p.m.:** Lawrence, Kansas. A quick stop, but if your dog needs greenery, there's lots just northwest of the station building.

**12:29 a.m.:** Topeka, Kansas. Checked baggage stop. Grass is located north of the station building.

**2:45 a.m.:** Newton, Kansas. Baggage stop. A bit of grass can be found behind the station.

**3:20 a.m.:** Hutchinson, Kansas. Nothing but hard surfaces here.

**5:19 a.m.: Dodge City, Kansas.** There's plenty of greenery along the platform. Trooper likes this ten-minute crew change stop for his early-morning relief.

On one occasion Dodge City didn't work out for us. Our attendant said he wouldn't be available at that hour, but that he'd ask a conductor to let us off. Unfortunately there was no conductor at the door when the train stopped, and none showed up. We think the busy crew change must have caused the conductor to forget us. Or maybe the attendant forgot. Stuff happens, and be ready for it.

Fortunately the next stop was less than an hour later, at **6:10 a.m.: Garden City, Kansas.** Trooper was able to hold his water until he saw the grass and bushes along the platform on both sides of the station. There's a fence, but it's an easy walk around it to the greenery.

**6:38 a.m. Mountain Time: Lamar, Colorado.** Plenty of grass and bushes surround the station building. Central Time changes to Mountain Time here, the beginning of the arid desert Southwest.

**7:49 to 8:04 a.m.: La Junta, Colorado.** This is a baggage and crew change stop that sometimes takes half an hour. There's not a blade of grass to be seen, or a scrubby tree either. It was here that Trooper finally learned that sometimes he didn't have a choice.

**9:24 a.m.:** Trinidad, Colorado. Nothing but concrete and asphalt.

**10:30 a.m.: Raton, New Mexico.** Only asphalt and gravel used to be found at this five-minute fresh air stop, but in 2016 the city fathers built a huge courtyard just east of the station—one full of luxuriant turf. All it needs to be the perfect relief stop for all service dogs is a few bushes and a tree.

**12:12 p.m.:** Las Vegas, New Mexico. Some trees lie north of the station building.

**1:58 p.m.: Lamy, New Mexico.** There's a large patch of grass and scrub northwest of the station, making this a good relief area for Trooper, but we have to ask the attendant to get the conductors to hold the train long enough.

**3:29 to 4:19 p.m.: Albuquerque, New Mexico.** There's no convenient grass at this long, long stop, but Trooper quickly took to the scrubby dirt courtyard just west of the combined bus and rail station building. Even if your dog wants lush vegetation, the lengthy station dwell will encourage him to use what's available.

The area around the combined train and bus depot tends to be trash-strewn, so try to keep your dog from scavenging. A grassy area is visible in back of the station building, but avoid it, for it's a favorite shooting-up gallery for local junkies and is full of dangerous needles.

**6:46 p.m.:** Gallup, New Mexico. Grass and trees abound in back of the station building, but this tends to be a quick stop. Still, it's usable if you ask the attendant in plenty of time.

**Note: Arizona is always on Mountain Standard Time, so if you're traveling in the seasons when everyone else in the Mountain Time area is on Daylight Saving Time, timekeeping is tricky. Trains may arrive and depart an hour ahead of the time on your watch. Not important if you're just passing through, but the Navajo Nation in the northeast part of Arizona observes Daylight Saving Time. Not, however, the Hopi Nation, surrounded entirely by the Navajo Nation. Go figure.**

**7:30 p.m.:** Winslow, Arizona. There's a lush garden behind the low wall separating the famed La Posada Hotel from the platform. Enter through the gateway, but be quick—the train does not stop here long, and if it's running late, the conductors and attendants will try to persuade you to wait just an hour until the next stop.

Debby, Trooper and I have detrained at Winslow to stay overnight in this historic hotel and visit the nearby Painted Desert/Petrified Forest National Park. We have found all the public venues here not only tolerant of but also welcoming to service dog teams.

**8:32 to 8:38 p.m.: Flagstaff, Arizona,** is a checked baggage and fresh air stop. This is the jumping-off point for the Grand Canyon, so lots of passengers usually are going and coming. There's a patch of grass and trees around a fence at the west end of the platform, perfect for service dog teams in sleepers.

**11:28 p.m.** Kingman, Arizona. A crew change stop, but not much greenery here. Stay in bed.

**12:31 a.m.:** Needles, California. Pacific Time starts here. There's a tree adjoining the station building on the west and a little brush in back of the station, if your dog must go.

**3:45 a.m.:** Barstow, California. There are trees and grass near the platform on both sides of the station building.

**4:24 a.m.: Victorville, California.** A quick stop, but with trees and brush just off the eastern platform, and this is a decent opportunity for early risers or when the train is not running late.

**5:42 a.m.:** San Bernardino, California. Nothing but concrete.

**6:03 a.m.:** Riverside, California. Another beautiful testament to the concrete industry.

**6:54 a.m.:** Fullerton, California. There's grass, but the conductors want to keep the stop as short as possible. It doesn't matter, for the end of the line is only half an hour away.

**8:00 a.m.**, but the train often arrives an hour early, thanks to schedule padding: **Los Angeles.** Green spots abound in front of Los Angeles Union Station and in its courtyards.

### CALIFORNIA ZEPHYR, CHICAGO–SAN FRANCISCO: TRAINS 5 AND 6

The *California Zephyr* arguably owns Amtrak's best scenery and is worth taking just for the ride all the way from Chicago to San Francisco Bay. It's a long, long trip, fifty-two hours, and stops should be planned carefully.

The westbound *Zephyr* leaves Chicago at **2:00 p.m. Central Time** and speeds through quick stops at Naperville, Illinois (2:34 p.m.) and Princeton, Illinois (3:44 p.m.). The first dog-walking opportunity for us is the checked baggage and fresh air stop at busy **Galesburg, Illinois,** at **4:38 p.m.** (Trains 3 and 4 don't allow passengers to disembark for a smoke here, but Trains 5 and 6 do.) There's lots of grass by the platform, and although a low fence separates the two, you can either go around the fence or through the entry to the station.

It was in Galesburg that in early 2015, before Trooper and I were partnered, I met a woman from Denver who was walking a huge Great Dane. I had seen the dog in the sleeper lounge at Chicago Union Station, complete with red service dog vest, but dismissed it as a fake. No, the woman said when we got back on the train. Her 145-pound dog, she said, had been trained first to alert her to an oncoming epileptic seizure and bring her meds. If a seizure should arrive, the Dane would lie atop her, paws over her shoulders, to keep her from injuring herself.

That sounded persuasive to me. We had a nice chat in our sleeper room with the dog sitting athwart my feet (a Great Dane is both large and heavy). The woman said that she had informed Amtrak that they were coming, and in mutual agreement with the railroad they had dinner in their room the night before because Danes are just too big to fit under a diner table.

The next morning, however, the woman popped her head into our room and asked us to watch the dog (so large he had his own sleeper bedroom) while she and her daughter went to breakfast.

While they were gone, the dog nosed aside the heavy door to the room and stalked out into the corridor looking for his partner. In a panic he bounded down the stairs to the vestibule, then bounded back up, running up and down the corridor to the consternation of other passengers heading for the dining car.

Debby and I wrestled him into our bedroom and managed to get him settled down, although he kept whimpering for his partner, who after a while came back and collected him with thanks.

Now that I'm part of a service dog team myself, I have my doubts about that Dane—at least, his partner. I doubt that a genuine service dog handler would leave her frightened animal alone like that.

Amtrak crew have told me that the most common story told to justify the presence of a fraudulent animal is that it's a "seizure dog." There's no way to tell if it really is—unless the handler has a genuine seizure, and that apparently has yet to happen to someone with a dog aboard a train.

I'll never know about that Dane. But the episode brought home the sad truth that telling a genuine service dog team from a fake one may not be easy.

This may be the underlying reason for an unpleasant encounter Trooper and I had on the *Zephyr*. One afternoon a conductor stopped at the door to our bedroom and fixed a baleful gaze at the dog lying quietly on the floor. A long stare often makes dogs uncomfortable, and Trooper reacted with a low whine.

"That dog is grouchy!" declared the conductor, who clearly was not a dog person. "It can't go to the dining car! You'll have to eat in your room!"

And then she added: "People don't like dogs in the dining car."

That remark was clearly against ADA public access rules, but I was not going to argue with an official who had full authority to eject us from the train. "Yes, ma'am," I said. "You're the boss."

Our sleeping car attendant, who had observed the entire exchange, was appalled. "Trooper did absolutely nothing wrong," she said later, after a crew change in which new conductors came aboard. For the rest of the trip I took Trooper to the dining car, where the entire crew warmly welcomed us.

After Galesburg, the *Zephyr* calls briefly at Burlington, Iowa (5:25 p.m.), and Mount Pleasant, Iowa (5:59 p.m.).

**6:53 p.m.:** A ten-minute crew change stop is scheduled for **Ottumwa, Iowa.** As at Galesburg, a grassy strip is separated by a fence from the platform, but it's easy to go around or through the station access.

The train then stops briefly at Osceola, Iowa (8:09 p.m.), and Creston, Iowa (8:41 p.m.).

**10:55 to 11:05 p.m.: Omaha, Nebraska.** A ten-minute "fresh air" stop—with grass in the parking lot behind the station. Be quick.

**12:05 a.m. to 12:14 p.m.:** Lincoln, Nebraska. Night owls might prefer to walk their dogs on the platform at this crew change spot—but there's no grass.

Let your attendant sleep through the Nebraska stops at Hastings (1:47 a.m.), Holdrege (2:34 a.m.), and McCook (3:43 a.m.). Fort Morgan, Colorado (5:05 a.m. Mountain Time), is usable if your dog needs to go, but there's not much grass.

**7:15 a.m. to 8:05 a.m.: Denver, Colorado.** This is the longest stop on the *Zephyr*'s route. Denver Union Station is surrounded by asphalt and concrete, but even if the train is late you might hurry through the station building and take a sharp left out the front door. To the east you'll spot a row of trees set in steel grates—and a slightly raised bed of mulch and bushes. Don't forget poop bags!

**10:07 a.m.:** Fraser, Colorado. In the winter this is a lengthy stop while skis are taken off the train for nearby Winter Park, but in the summer things move quickly. Gravelly areas run along the platform, and there's a tiny bit of greenery just south of the station building.

At 10:37 a.m. the *Zephyr* stops briefly at Granby, Colorado, gateway to the Rocky Mountain National Park.

**1:53 p.m.: Glenwood Springs, Colorado.** This is almost always a five- to ten-minute checked baggage and fresh air stop in all seasons, thanks to the resorts nearby. Go up the stairs west of the station to find grassy and brushy spots, or walk the platform east of the station for the same.

**4:10 p.m.: Grand Junction, Colorado.** This is usually a five-minute fresh air stop for smokers. There are trees and grass northwest of the station building. For service dogs, this is the best relief stop before Salt Lake City.

The next stops are short ones in Utah at Green River (5:58 p.m.), Helper (7:20 p.m.) and Provo (9:26 p.m.).

**11:05 p.m. to 11:30 p.m.: Salt Lake City, Utah.** This service stop is lengthy enough for you to take your dog to a concrete park just north of the station that features lots of trees in raised planters.

The *Zephyr* then speeds across the night desert into Nevada, calling briefly at Elko (3:03 a.m. Pacific Time) and Winnemucca (5:40 a.m.) The latter is a crew change and smoking stop with a little scrub brush and plenty of light poles.

**8:36 a.m.: Reno, Nevada.** This is a service stop, but if the train's much behind time, it will be short. There's not much for a dog here—the platform is in a long concrete channel cut into the earth, and the station is up at ground level. No grass anywhere around.

**9:37 a.m.:** Truckee, California. There are a couple of trees set into grassy planters in front of the station, but the rest is just concrete and asphalt.

After that, the train stops briefly at Colfax, California (11:48 a.m.), and Roseville, California (12:57 p.m.).

**2:13 p.m.:** Sacramento, California. The platforms are a long walk through an underpass to the station, and there's only dirt where the underpass emerges from the ground. The train will be here for at least five minutes for a baggage stop, but in my experience it's best to see if the dog will go against a post on the platform. Otherwise wait for the next stop.

**2:44 p.m.: Davis, California.** Another baggage stop, with many trees, bushes, and grass along the platform.

**3:26 p.m.:** Martinez, California. This baggage stop features trees, grassy spots, and brush along the platform.

There's a short stop at Richmond, California, at 3:59 p.m.

**4:10 p.m.: Emeryville, California.** The *Zephyr's* western terminus features plenty of trees and planters around the station. Shortly after the train arrives, an Amtrak bus takes San Francisco–bound passengers over the Bay Bridge to several stops in the city.

### *EMPIRE BUILDER*, CHICAGO–SEATTLE/PORTLAND: TRAINS 7 AND 8, 27 AND 28

This storied two-night train along the "High Line," as railroaders call the route following the northern border of the United States to the West Coast, is really two trains in one. At Spokane, Washington, 1,819 miles from Chicago, the *Builder* splits into two. Train 7 goes to Seattle, Washington, and Train 27 to Portland, Oregon.

The combined trains depart Chicago at **2:15 p.m. Central Time**, and we've found the following stations given in bold face are the best relief stops for service dogs:

The first stop, at Glenview, Illinois (2:39 p.m.) is just to pick up passengers.

**3:52 p.m.:** Milwaukee, Wisconsin, a baggage stop. There's no greenery in this station, entirely under a roof, and service dog teams who need grass are advised to wait until Columbus.

**5:02 p.m.: Columbus, Wisconsin.** There's grass along the platform west of the station building at this baggage stop.

Portage, Wisconsin, at 5:31 p.m. is almost always just a quick hello from the conductor before the train resumes its journey.

**5:49 p.m.: Wisconsin Dells, Wisconsin.** This popular resort town is a short stop in the winter, but during the summer, crowds of arriving and departing vacationers give plenty of time for a service dog to get off and do its business. The platform is lined with grass.

The train stops briefly at Tomah, Wisconsin, at 6:27 p.m.

**7:47 p.m.: Winona, Minnesota.**, a ten-minute crew change stop. There's plenty of grass and greenery in front of the station building.

Red Wing, Minnesota (8:49 p.m.) is a short station call.

**10:03 p.m. to 10:20 p.m.: St. Paul–Minneapolis, Minnesota.** Near the end of the long concrete platform farthest from the station, there's a three-foot-by-eight-foot area made up of six trays of artificial turf, complete with a fireplug, intended for service dogs—and probably the only such facility at a U.S. train station. Trooper took to it quickly, despite his preference for greenery. If your dog must have the real stuff, there's grass in front of the station building, but it's a longish walk over a ramp and through the station, so hustle.

Your attendants will want to catch some sleep in the small hours, so pass up the quick Minnesota stops at St. Cloud (12:24 a.m.), Staples (1:26 a.m.), and Detroit

Lakes (2:22 a.m.) Consult with the attendants or conductors well beforehand if you want to take your dog off at the next two stops, where the train may not dwell for long.

**3:24 a.m.:** Fargo, North Dakota, a baggage stop, features a courtyard of grass west of the old station building. That's convenient for passengers in the front of the train, less so for riders in the rear.

**4:41 a.m.: Grand Forks, North Dakota,** is also a baggage stop and has lots of grass along the platform. This is a good spot for early risers.

But mind the two-foot gap between train and platform. Big dogs can handle that easily, but I had to hand Trooper through the door to Debby on the platform.

**6:02 a.m.:** Devils Lake, North Dakota, has a lawn across the street from the station, but this is almost always a one-minute stop.

**6:56 a.m.: Rugby, North Dakota,** is also a very brief stop, but the conductor held the train three minutes for one anxious service dog to do its business. There's no grass, but there's a handy telephone pole with plenty of previous calling cards to entice a dog to reply.

**8:29 a.m. to 9:06 a.m.: Minot, North Dakota.** This long service stop offers plenty of time and plenty of grass behind the station building across the parking lot.

There is a swift midmorning stop at Stanley, North Dakota (9:57 a.m.).

**11:07 a.m.:** Williston, North Dakota. A baggage stop, but it's usually a quick one, and the greenery is a longish walk away behind the station. It's usable if the train arrives ahead of time. Talk to your attendant.

**11:41 a.m. Mountain Time:** Wolf Point, Montana. At the eastern end of the parking lot at this quick stop lies grass that's close to the coaches on the westbound train, but the sleepers are a little too far away. Travelers with dogs had best wait for the next stop.

**12:26 p.m.:** Glasgow, Montana. There's a little grassy patch at the western end of the parking lot, convenient to the sleeping cars on the westbound *Builder* but not the coaches at this quick stop.

Pass up the quick stop at Malta, Montana (1:25 p.m.).

**2:39 p.m. to 3:04 p.m.: Havre, Montana.** There's apparently no grass when one gets off the train at this long service stop, but don't worry—there's a tiny green square of turf just behind the preserved steam locomotive next to the platform and plenty of time to get to it and back to the train. Don't dawdle.

**5:17 p.m. to 5:22 p.m.:** Shelby, Montana, is a crew change stop. No grass at all for dogs who must have it, but there's a little gravel and dirt for dogs OK with that.

The next two Montana stops are Cut Bank (5:51 p.m.) and Browning (time not specified on most recent timetable) instead of East Glacier, which closes for the winter in October.

**6:45 p.m.: East Glacier, Montana,** is the gateway to Glacier National Park, and in the summer the train stops there for quite a while to unload and load scores of passengers. You'll find plenty of grass along the platform.

At 7:41 p.m. the train stops at Essex, Montana, for passengers to and from the famed Izaak Walton Inn, but the platform is very short and not good for relieving service dogs.

**8:56 p.m. to 9:16 p.m.: Whitefish, Montana.** This is the favorite before-bedtime stop for Trooper and me. There's a nice large lawn with trees east of the depot building. During the long winter, snow covers everything.

If you relieved your dog at Whitefish, there is no need to get off the train at Libby, Montana (10:59 p.m.), or Sandpoint, Idaho (11:49 p.m. Pacific Time), both quick stops.

**1:40 a.m. to 2:15 a.m. (Train 7**, to Seattle, Washington) or **2:45 a.m. (Train 27**, to Portland, Oregon): The train splits shortly after arrival at **Spokane, Washington.** The front half of the train, ending at the dining car, goes on to Seattle. The rear half, beginning with the lounge car, is cut off, picks up an engine, and heads for Portland half an hour later. There is a broad lawn with trees out front of the station building, reachable from the platform by stairs, escalator, and elevator. If you want to get off here, speak to your attendant and conductor well before arrival. You don't want to get back on the wrong train.

Trooper and I always slept through this one, but the last time we were there the eastbound *Builder* was eight hours late, so we made use of the stop by daylight.

For **Train 7**, here are the best stops (in bold face) on the way from Spokane to Seattle.

It is advisable to skip the wee-hours stop at Ephrata, Washington (4:22 a.m.), and wait for:

**5:35 a.m.: Wenatchee, Washington.** This is a crew change point, and the train will stop here for at least seven minutes. You'll find grass and brush along the parking lot southeast of the station shack.

Leavenworth, Washington, at 6:08 a.m. can be ignored. The following stops are more suitable:

**8:38 a.m.:** Everett, Washington. Baggage stop. Some spots of greenery along platform.

**9:10 a.m.:** Edmonds, Washington. A little grass and trees northeast of the station building.

**10:25 a.m.: Seattle, Washington.** End of the line for Train 7. No grass lies at the station, but there's a small green park next to the sports stadium a long block south of the station building. Turn left as you go out the door to the taxi stand.

For **Train 27,** here are the best stops on the route from Spokane to Portland:

**5:35 a.m.: Pasco, Washington.** This is a long baggage and fresh air stop. Inform your attendant the night before so that he or she or a conductor will open the door if you want to get off here to use the plentiful grass in front of and around the station.

It's best to stay on the train and have breakfast during the short stops at Wishram, Washington (7:30 a.m.), and Bingen-White Salmon, Washington (8:04 a.m.), and wait for:

**9:18 a.m.: Vancouver, Washington.** There's plenty of greenery around the station building at this baggage stop.

**10:10 a.m.: Portland, Oregon.** Train 27 ends here. Go through the station building and out the front door to the left to find a broad lawn with plantings in front of a restaurant.

## COAST STARLIGHT, LOS ANGELES–SEATTLE: TRAINS 11 AND 14

Passengers on the *Coast Starlight* get terrific views of both Pacific beaches and Northwest peaks as the overnight train knits together many of the bigger cities in California, Oregon, and Washington. The train uses double-decker Superliner equipment with excellent sight lines from the upper level.

**An important warning:** After Emeryville, California, on the northbound *Starlight*, Train 14, there's little opportunity to find grass or trees for fourteen hours until the train stops the next day at Eugene-Springfield, Oregon. This run is best for dogs comfortable with transacting their business on pavement and light poles.

Before Train 14 departs **Los Angeles, California,** at **10:10 a.m. Pacific Time,** the area in front of Los Angeles Union Station offers plenty of greenery, and it's worth walking your dog there just to admire the station's majestic Spanish Art Deco architecture.

Pass up the very quick California stops at Burbank/Bob Hope Airport at 10:29 a.m., Van Nuys at 10:40 a.m., and Simi Valley at 11:11 a.m., and consider the pretty Oxnard, with grass and ivy ground cover all around the station, only in a pinch at 11:44 a.m. because this stop is also brief.

**12:33 p.m. to 12:40 p.m., Santa Barbara, California.** This is a busy stop for baggage and fresh air. There's plenty of grass just east of and behind the station building.

**3:22 p.m. to 3:35 p.m.: San Luis Obispo, California.** The operating crews change here, giving plenty of time for a quick walk amid trees on both sides of the station.

Paso Robles at 4:37 p.m. offers a little scrubby brush. Salinas at 6:28 p.m. features a lonely bush at one eastern corner of the station. Pass them up—use them only in an emergency.

**8:11 p.m. to 8:23 p.m.: San Jose, California.** There's enough time to take your dog out to the lawns out of sight behind the station building, but make sure attendants and conductors know where you are. Diridon Station and environs are full of homeless people, and while most of them will politely leave you alone, a few are disturbed and noisily scary. Some have dogs of their own that are not always on leash, including inside the station building. Keep a weather eye out for those. Although I've never had to use it, I carry a pepper spray canister just in case a loose dog is vicious.

**9:24 to 9:39 pm.: Oakland, California,** is also a crew change stop with saplings and a few convenient planters holding bushes and ground cover at the north side of the station. Trooper likes this one for his bedtime pee.

**9:54 p.m. to 10:04 p.m.: Emeryville, California,** is a ten-minute dwell for baggage and passengers. There's plenty of grass and trees around the station. This spot is more convenient for *Coast Starlight* coach passengers with service dogs than it is for those in sleepers, because it's a long walk down the very narrow platform from the sleeping car to the station building past last-gasp smokers and passengers with clumsy piles of luggage.

**11:59 p.m.:** Sacramento, California. This short baggage stop isn't the greatest station for dogs that need dirt or grass, since the nearest natural spot is a long, long walk away.

Chico (**1:47 a.m.,** trees), Redding (**3:06 a.m.,** trees and planters), and Dunsmuir (**4:56 a.m.,** trees and grass) are all quick stops that could serve in emergencies, but attendants need their sleep, so be judicious with your requests and make them well ahead of time before the attendants turn in.

**8:17 a.m.: Klamath Falls, Oregon,** is carded as a ten-minute crew change stop, but there's no grass or trees to speak of anywhere near the station. Trooper, however, has found that the local light posts hold plenty of pee-mail for him to acknowledge. The train can arrive as many as forty-four minutes early, affording lots of time for persnickety pooches to adapt to the conditions.

**9:32 a.m.:** Chemult, Oregon, has no grass but some dirt.

**12:36 p.m.: Eugene-Springfield, Oregon.** There are a few grassy and brushy clumps around the parking lot at this baggage stop. Trooper has made good use of them.

**1:22 p.m.:** Albany, Oregon. Another baggage stop, this one with a brushy area southwest of the station building.

**1:55 p.m.:** Salem, Oregon. There are trees along the platform and grass in the parking lot behind the station building.

**3:32 p.m. to 3:56 p.m.: Portland, Oregon.** There's a grassy courtyard next to a restaurant to the left outside the station's front door, and if the train's on time there will be ample opportunity for a relief walk. But if the train is late, Amtrak will try to get it out of town as soon as possible, so make sure your attendant and conductor know that you'll be out of sight for a while. This really ought to be your last relief stop before Seattle four hours later. If not, there are several additional stops:

4:16 p.m.: Vancouver, Washington. A checked baggage stop.

4:51 p.m.: Kelso-Longview, Washington.

5:36 p.m.: Centralia, Washington.

6:01 p.m.: Olympia-Lacey, Washington.

**6:50 p.m.: Tacoma, Washington.** Plenty of grass and trees lie along the platform.

**7:56 p.m.: Seattle, Washington.** There's a park two blocks south of the station building.

### *CRESCENT*, NEW YORK CITY–NEW ORLEANS: TRAINS 19 AND 20

No. 19, the daily train on the historic route between New York and New Orleans, leaves **Manhattan's Penn Station at 2:15 p.m. Eastern Time.** It's a popular train, but service dog teams must understand that it's not the best idea to request relief stops during the first three hours of the 1,377-mile run. That's because Newark, New Jersey (2:37 p.m.), Trenton, New Jersey (3:18 p.m.), Philadelphia, Pennsylvania (3:55 p.m.), Wilmington, Delaware (4:19 p.m.), and Baltimore, Maryland (5:12 p.m.) are all *receive-only* stops, where passengers climb aboard but do not detrain. This means the stops will be short and sweet, and the conductors will shout "All aboard!" before you know it.

Still, in an emergency the conductors will hold the train while your dog does its business. Be assured of that.

The first possible stop with grass is Washington, D.C., at 6:30 p.m. This is about a twenty-minute layover while the electric locomotive that pulled the train from New York is replaced by a diesel engine. You *might* have time to get your dog up the escalator and out of the station to the grassy circle in the front plaza if you hustle and know where you're going—and also know how to get back through the gates to your train. But *ask the conductor first.*

The engine change may be done rapidly, and since the eastbound *Crescent* does not take on new passengers in Washington, the train may leave before the scheduled time. Trooper and I prefer not to risk it, and instead wait until the next stop.

**6:49 p.m.: Alexandria, Virginia.** Grass and scrub is handy to the platform for *southbound Crescents* at this busy checked baggage stop, but not *northbound* trains, for the grassy side of the station must be accessed via underground ramp from the northbound platform. Consulting with the conductor may give northbound passengers enough time to run under the ramp to the grass by the station.

7:22 p.m.: Manassas, Virginia, and 7:55 p.m.: Culpeper, Virginia, are quick station stops usable chiefly in emergencies.

**8:47 p.m. to 8:52 p.m.: Charlottesville, Virginia,** is a five-minute baggage stop with convenient grassy spots right in front of the station building.

**10:00 p.m. to 10:06 p.m.: Lynchburg, Virginia.** A large patch of grass lies south of the station building at this baggage stop. If your car is near the front of the westbound train, that will be easy to reach, but passengers in the rear might be too far away to make it to the patch quickly. There's a strip of green across the parking lot at the north end. If you're far away, be sure to consult with the attendant or conductor before stepping off.

11:14 p.m.: Danville, Virginia, is a quick stop best passed up unless your dog really needs to go.

**12:15 a.m. to 12:22 a.m.: Greensboro, North Carolina,** is a seven-minute crew-change station, but passengers must take a longish walk through an underground ramp from platform to station, where grass is available outside. Again, speak with the attendant or conductor—and hustle.

If you can, let your attendant sleep through High Point, North Carolina, at 12:39 a.m. and Salisbury, North Carolina, at 1:17 a.m., but there's a good chance all the crew will be awake for the twenty-five-minute service stop from **2:20 a.m. to 2:45 a.m. at Charlotte, North Carolina.** There's scrubby grass from southwest to northeast along the platform and in front of the station.

Skip Gastonia, North Carolina, at 3:12 a.m. and Spartanburg, South Carolina, at 4:14 a.m. If you're up early, **Greenville, South Carolina, from 4:54 a.m. to 5:01 a.m.** is long enough for you to find grass and trees across the station's parking lot, and there's a handy patch of greenery at the building's southeast corner. Ask if your attendant will be awake at that hour; if not, the conductor will either open your car's door or ask you to walk through the train to another car whose door will be open at that stop.

In emergencies, Clemson, South Carolina, at 5:39 a.m., Toccoa, Georgia, at 6:15 a.m., and Gainesville, Georgia, at 6:58 a.m. are usable.

There's a normally long (thirty-minute) stop at **Atlanta, Georgia, from 8:13 a.m. to 8:38 a.m.** To find grass and bushes at this long crew change and service stop, you must take your dog up a long and steep flight of stairs or use an elevator to get into the station building and turn right, where there's a small grassy courtyard.

Before we could find the elevator, Trooper discovered a sprig of grass poking up from a crack in the asphalt just around the foot of the stairway—and drowned it. That was that.

Anniston, Alabama, comes along at 10:00 a.m. Central Time. There's a lawn around the station building next to the platform, but this is usually a quick stop.

**Birmingham, Alabama, from 11:50 a.m. to 12:08 p.m.** is carded as an eighteen-minute stop. The platform is raised above ground level, and you have to go down stairs or use an elevator to get into the station. Right across the street from the building is a parking lot with scrubby grass and gravel. Make sure your attendant knows where you've gone, because you'll be out of sight. Trooper passed up a chance to go here, presumably because of the trash and debris strewn around the place.

"Don't worry," our sleeper attendant (one of the best we have ever had) said. "I'll get the conductors to OK letting you off at Tuscaloosa. It's just an hour away, and it's got grass and a tree."

At **1:07 p.m.** the train calls at **Tuscaloosa, Alabama,** a baggage stop. A patch of trees and grass is almost out of sight from the platform around the southwest corner of the station building, but our attendant pointed to an almost hidden spot of greenery right across from the sleeping car—and Trooper performed.

From **2:58 to 3:04 p.m. Meridian, Mississippi,** a long baggage stop, features plenty of greenery and trees easily reachable west and east of the station building.

The conductors will thank you not to get off at Laurel, Mississippi (4:01 p.m.), Hattiesburg, Mississippi (4:36 p.m.), Picayune, Mississippi (5:42 p.m.), and Slidell, Louisiana (6:07 p.m.). All but Hattiesburg are flag stops, meaning the train will just blow through without stopping if no one is on the platform to board or is scheduled to detrain.

The *Crescent* arrives at its final destination, **New Orleans, Louisiana, at 7:32 p.m.** Upon detraining, you can find a large green courtyard in front of New Orleans Union Station.

### *CITY OF NEW ORLEANS*, CHICAGO–NEW ORLEANS: TRAINS 58 AND 59

The southbound leg (Amtrak 59) of this song-celebrated train departs Chicago at **8:05 p.m. Central Time**.

If you have relieved your dog at Chicago, there's no need to do so at the brief stops of Homewood, Illinois (8:54 p.m.), and Kankakee, Illinois (9:23 p.m.).

**10:34 p.m.:** The first good relief stop is **Champaign-Urbana, Illinois.** There's plenty of grass along the platform of this baggage stop. Trooper always gets off here before bedtime.

The next three Illinois stations, at Mattoon (11:13 p.m.), Effingham (11:37 p.m.), and Centralia (12:25 a.m.) are flag stops, meaning the train won't halt there if there are no passengers to board or detrain. It's advisable not to ask the conductors to allow you to relieve your dog there and delay the train.

**1:21 to 1:26 a.m.: Carbondale, Illinois.** Night owls might go for the five-minute baggage stop and crew change at Carbondale, where grass abuts the length of the platform

Two flag stops follow, one at Fulton, Kentucky, at 3:14 a.m. and the other at Newbern-Dyersberg, Tennessee, at 3:56 a.m. Stay aboard and let the train sleep.

**6:27 to 6:40 a.m.: Memphis, Tennessee,** is a long service and crew change stop, and there'll be plenty of time to find the grassy, tree-shaded spots in and along the parking lot just south of the station. This is a favorite place for Trooper and me to stretch our legs before breakfast.

Pass up the flag stop at Marks, Mississippi (8:01 a.m.), but consider Greenwood, Mississippi (9:00 a.m.), if you need to—and your dog doesn't mind concrete, asphalt, or gravel. Yazoo City, Mississippi (9:51 a.m.), is another flag stop to ignore.

**11:11 to 11:20 a.m.:** Jackson, Mississippi. This is a baggage stop, but there's only a platform at this stop, raised a story above ground level. No grass, gravel, or dirt. If your dog needs grass, wait a bit longer.

The train will pass through the Mississippi flag stops of Hazlehurst (11:55 a.m.), Brookhaven (12:16 p.m.), and McComb (12:40 p.m.). In an emergency, you could ask the conductor to stop at Brookhaven, because lots of greenery abuts the platform.

**1:28 p.m.: Hammond, Louisiana,** is a baggage stop where you'll find grass along the walkway between platform and station.

**3:32 p.m.: New Orleans, Louisiana.** There's a large grassy courtyard across the street from the station.

### SILVER METEOR, NEW YORK–MIAMI: TRAINS 97 AND 98

Of the two New York–to–Miami *Silver Service* trains, Trooper and I prefer the *Silver Meteor* because it has a dining car, and the *Silver Star* (Trains 91 and 92) doesn't. The latter stops at some of the same stations as the former but from time to time follows a different route. The following remarks apply to the *Meteor*.

The southbound train (Amtrak 97) departs New York City at **3:15 p.m. Eastern Time** and then receives passengers only at the New Jersey stops of Newark (3:38 p.m.) and Trenton (4:18 p.m.), then Philadelphia, Pennsylvania (4:54 p.m.), Wilmington, Delaware (5:18 p.m.), Baltimore, Maryland (6:12 p.m.), and Washington, D.C. (7:25 p.m.). Avoid asking to take your dog off the train at these quick stops, and wait until:

**7:44 p.m.: Alexandria, Virginia.** Southbound passengers can find grass north of the station, but northbound passengers must hustle through an underground passage. Be sure to inform your conductor if you're taking your dog off to find greenery.

There is a quick stop at Fredericksburg, Virginia, at 8:33 p.m., but it's best to wait until:

**9:34 p.m. to 9:44 p.m.: Richmond Staples Mill, Virginia.** Here boarding passengers are kept behind a barrier until detraining passengers have passed through to the station, giving a service dog team plenty of time for relief at a grassy patch right in front of the station building by the barrier. When we've taken the *Meteor*, this has always been the last outside stop for the night for Trooper and me.

The train stops briefly at Petersburg, Virginia (10:18 p.m.), then two North Carolina stations at Rocky Mount (11:50 p.m.) and Fayetteville (1:22 a.m.) There is grass at Petersburg and at Rocky Mount, but not at Fayetteville.

**3:05 a.m. to 3:13 a.m.:** Florence, South Carolina. Grass can be found around the station and in the parking lot at this crew change stop.

We recommend sleeping through the South Carolina stops of Kingstree (3:51 a.m.), Charleston (4:51 a.m.), and Yemassee (5:43 a.m.), although grass is available close by all three stations.

**6:34 a.m. to 6:40 a.m.: Savannah, Georgia.** Trooper makes use of the grass in front of the station, and we have breakfast in our room upon leaving.

A quick stop follows at Jesup, Georgia (7:35 a.m.), which features gravel only.

**9:09 a.m. to 9:34 a.m.: Jacksonville, Florida.** We like to stretch our legs at the grassy spots in front of and northwest of the station building.

Palatka, Florida, is a quick stop at 10:40 a.m., with scrubby grass. DeLand, Florida, follows at 11:38 a.m., with grass on each side of the station. Same at Winter Park, Florida, at 12:26 p.m.

**12:49 p.m. to 1:04 p.m.: Orlando, Florida.** There's enough time to go into the station and out the back door to find a grassy spot with bushes.

Kissimmee, Florida (with a few patches of grass), comes along at 1:26 p.m., then Winter Haven, Florida (also a few clumps of grass), at 2:13 p.m. Sebring, Florida, follows at 2:54 p.m., but there is no grass near the platform. All are carded as baggage stops.

We recommend skipping West Palm Beach (4:47 p.m.), Delray Beach (5:11 p.m.), and Deerfield Beach (5:25 p.m.), although all feature some grass.

**5:43 p.m.: Fort Lauderdale, Florida.** The train will be here for a baggage stop, but it's a good idea to ask the conductor to hold the train while your dog makes use of the grass around the station building. Trooper and I have detrained here for the cruise ships in Fort Lauderdale harbor.

The train makes a baggage stop at Hollywood, Florida, at 5:59 p.m., but it's better to wait forty minutes until:

**6:39 p.m.** The train ties up at **Miami, Florida.** Service dog teams will find plenty of grass and trees on the other side of the station building.

# VIA Rail Routes

### THE *CANADIAN*, TORONTO, ONTARIO–VANCOUVER, BRITISH COLUMBIA: TRAINS 1 AND 2

VIA Train No. 1, the *Canadian*, from Toronto to Vancouver (VIA No. 2 in reverse) is a bucket-list trip world famous for both its luxury and its breathtaking High Plains and Rocky Mountain scenery. Much of the charm lies in the 1950s-era rolling stock, much-refurbished but sturdy museum pieces in remarkably good condition. The *Canadian* is considerably pricier than Amtrak from Chicago to the West Coast, but you do get the quality of service you pay for—especially in the dining car, whose cuisine is unmatched elsewhere on North American rails.

What's more, the crews aboard all Canadian trains seem to adore service dogs. On a recent trip Trooper and I took aboard two flagship Canadian trains—the

*Ocean* and the *Canadian*—attendants and waiters frequently dropped by our compartment for a quick hello and ear ruffling.

The *Canadian* is a leisurely four-night adventure, and arrival in Vancouver is sometimes many hours late, so it's a sensible idea not to book connecting travel on the same day. (Trooper and I always overnight in a hotel and resume travel the next day—in the United States as well as in Canada.)

As with Amtrak, it's best to work with the VIA crew on the best places to relieve your dog, employing scheduled longer station dwells—crew change and passenger smoke stops—of twenty minutes or more.

In recent summers the *Canadian* often was six to twenty-four hours late arriving at its terminals. The dictum "a late train always gets later" applied—in spades. The problem was that the freight trains of the Canadian National, the railroad over which the *Canadian* mostly runs, had grown too long for the sidings. The shorter passenger trains often needed to "go into the hole" and stop to allow up to 150 freight cars to pass. A timetable change in 2018 added half a day to the schedule of the Canadian and vastly improved on-time performance.

Because of uncertain timekeeping, VIA Rail's official list of scheduled stops seven to ten hours apart for servicing your dog may not work. You may need to request that the train halt at a "flag stop," a small, unattended station in the great green outback. At such a stop, a traveler without a reservation can flag down the train to board it, but that rarely happens. The flag stop must be booked well ahead of time if the train is to halt there to discharge passengers.

In case of delay, or in an emergency, you can ask your attendant or the train manager to call the engineers to stop at one of these flag stations to accommodate your dog's needs. (The *Canadian* does not have conductors; car attendants and train managers do those jobs instead and communicate via radio with the engineers.)

Before a recent trip, it took several tries before I was able to get a more or less firm answer from VIA Rail's customer service people in this matter: "VIA will accommodate when feasible however it may not be possible to accommodate in all circumstances. For example, the train might be delayed in an area such that it cannot stop at a station where a dog can safely disembark."

For this reason it might be a good idea to minimize your dog's water and food intake, both before departure and during the trip, to lengthen the time it can hold between relief stops—unless the dog has been trained to use a pee pad.

The *Canadian* departs **Toronto at 09:30 hours Eastern Time** (that's 9:30 a.m. in the United States). Before departure, you can relieve your dog in planters along Front St. just northwest of the station or on York St. on the east edge of the station. If there's time, you also can walk two blocks west to a grassy park adjoining the Steam Whistle Brewery in an old locomotive roundhouse between the CN Tower and the waterfront.

For the next seven and a half hours the *Canadian* will breeze through the Ontario flag-stop towns of Washago (12:10 hours), Parry Sound (14:12), and Sudbury Junction (16:42).

All stations listed below in bold face are official stops for service dogs. Most of those in light face are flag stops.

**17:07 to 17:37: Capreol, Ontario,** is a half-hour crew change and smoke stop and the logical place for your dog's late afternoon relief on this first day of the run. There are trees and grass just west of the station building for dogs requiring greenery. On a recent November trip, Trooper found some greenery along the fence right in front of our sleeping car.

Unless there are reservations for boarding or deboarding, No. 1 may roar without stopping through the small Ontario flag-stop towns of Laforest (18:33), McKee's Camp (18:46), Felix (19:06), Ruel (19:13), Westree (19:30), Gogama (20:03), Foleyet (22:29), Elsas (23:23), and Oba (01.23). In an emergency you could ask the train manager to arrange for a relief stop at one of these towns, but it would be better to ask the attendant to awaken you at:

**02:14 to 02:54: Hornepayne, Ontario.** Trooper and I found lots of grass around the station building—if it isn't covered by snow. It's a good idea to get off to relieve your dog here, because it'll be eight hours until the next lengthy crew change and smoke stop.

During that time the train will stop only by reservation at the little Ontario towns of Hillsport (03:50), Caramat (04:40), Longlac (05:19), Nakina (05:58), Auden (07:04), Ferland (07:41), Mud River (07:50), Armstrong (09:02), Collins (09:30 Eastern Time), Allanwater Bridge (09:11 Central Time), Flindt Landing (09:27), and Savant Lake (09:44). A request for a relief stop at one of these towns might be honored if safety conditions permit it.

**11:10 to 11:40: Sioux Lookout, Ontario.** As at Hornepayne, there is plenty of grass around the station, but on our trip Trooper had to go in the snow. This is the last official smoke (and pee) stop for nine hours, so try to use it for your dog.

In an emergency, any of these Ontario flag stops might be used: Richan (12:50), Red Lake Road (13:26), Canyon (13:55), Farlane (14:32), Redditt (15:08), Minaki (15:29), Ottermere (15:46), Malachi (15:52), Copelands Landing (15:54), Rice Lake (15:57), and the Manitoba towns of Winnitoba, (16:11), Ophir (16:16), Brereton Lake (16:34), and Elma (16:55).

**19:30 to 21:30: Winnipeg, Manitoba.** This two-hour layover is a good one for you to exercise your service dog—and yourself. There's plenty of grass, bushes, and trees on either side of the station, and a beautiful riverside park lies just a block south.

When Trooper and I rolled in on the *Canadian* one November, temperatures were approaching zero degrees Fahrenheit (minus eighteen degrees Celsius), and the wind was picking up. I wished I had had the foresight to bring along booties and a warm cape for Trooper. The icy sidewalks hurt his feet.

Next come the Manitoba flag stops at Portage la Prairie (23:04) and Rivers (01:31), followed by a locomotive crew change at **Melville, Saskatchewan (06:04)**, whose trees and grass are a good place to relieve your dog, but be sure to arrange matters with your attendant. The province of Saskatchewan is always on Central Standard Time, so if you're riding in the summer, keep that in mind.

Watrous, Saskatchewan, (08:54) comes next.

**10:50 to 11:50: Saskatoon, Saskatchewan.** This hour-long dwell is your dog's logical last official pee stop for the morning. Long strips of grass and trees lie just east of the station building. During our November visit there, the temperature had dropped well below zero degrees Fahrenheit in a biting wind, blowing around foot-deep snow. Instead of immediately decorating a light post upon stepping down from the train, Trooper whirled, whined, and pulled on his leash to get back aboard.

Maybe, I asked the attendant, we could get off for a pee at one of the two next Saskatchewan flag stops: Biggar (13:39) or Unity (14:44), or maybe two similar stops in Alberta: Wainwright (16:33 at the Mountain Time change) and Viking (17:26)?

Afraid not, said the attendant. Safety issue. Unshoveled platforms full of ice and snow. In our sleeper cabin he laid a pile of towels atop a large plastic bag for an impromptu pee pad in case Trooper needed to go. He did not get the picture and instead used the towels as a bed.

The train was at this time running seven hours late, and not until we reached Edmonton, eighteen hours after his last relief in Melville, was Trooper—by now visibly uncomfortable—able to let go at last on snow-covered grass beside the station building in slightly warmer weather.

I vowed never to put Trooper through that ordeal again. Probably not even a bulky full-length cape and booties would have persuaded him to perform at Saskatoon. Winter can blow in early and with a vengeance on the High Plains of Western Canada.

I would strongly caution against riding the *Canadian* in winter with a service dog who either has not been trained to use a pee pad or is unaccustomed to arctic conditions.

**20:50 to 00:01: Edmonton, Alberta.** In better weather this long and late station dwell affords plenty of time to walk your dog on the broad expanses of grass on either side of the station building.

Three more Alberta flag stops follow: Evansburg (01:29), Edson (02:52), and Hinton (03:58).

**06:30 to 09:30: Jasper, Alberta.** Three hours are allotted for this stop at a pretty resort town deep in the Rocky Mountains. Spots of grass and trees abound around the station building, and there is a large park across the street a few steps north.

After Valemount, British Columbia (10:50 at the Pacific Time change), there is a conditional stop, timekeeping permitting, at **Blue River, British Columbia**

**(13:36)**, where you can get off to relieve your dog if you make arrangements with the attendant—and if there are no safety issues.

Clearwater, British Columbia, follows (15:45).

**18:28 to 19:03: Kamloops North, British Columbia.** There's a little scrubby grass along the track behind the tiny station building at this thirty-five-minute stop, the last lengthy one until the train arrives at its destination ten hours later.

There are flag stops at the British Columbia towns of Ashcroft (20:49), Boston Bar (00:06), Hope (02:01), Chilliwack (06:40), and Abbotsford (03:56). Those last two are usable in emergencies if your dog can't make it to the end of the line at **Vancouver, British Columbia (08:00),** eleven hours from Kamloops.

At Vancouver there's a big city park with lots of trees and grass right across from the front door of Pacific Central Station—the roomiest you'll find on the route.

At the time of publication, the westbound Canadian (VIA No. 1) was running two days of the week in winter (Wednesday and Saturday) from Toronto to Vancouver. No. 2, the return trip, was running Monday and Friday. During the high season, VIA runs three *Canadians* weekly each way between Toronto and Vancouver. However, because of extensive track work on the line during the summer of 2019, the third train (VIA No. 3) was to run only from Edmonton, Alberta, to Vancouver (No. 4 returning). At the time of this book's publication, if the track work had been completed VIA planned to restore the full three-times-weekly schedule between Toronto and Vancouver during the summer of 2020 while keeping winter departures to twice a week. Always be sure to check the latest timetable on the VIA Rail website for station times and days of operation.

### THE *OCEAN*, MONTREAL, QUEBEC–HALIFAX, NOVA SCOTIA: TRAINS 14 AND 15

This popular 836-mile-long overnight train to the Maritime Provinces runs three times a week (Wednesday, Friday, and Sunday) between Montreal and Halifax.

The *Ocean* offers a slightly threadbare but still modern European–style charm with coaches and sleeper cars originally built in the mid-1990s for the overnight service under the English Channel from the coast of Britain to Paris. That project never saw the light of day, so VIA Rail bought the cars for a song and put them on the *Ocean*. They are shorter, narrower, and sleeker than North American rolling stock.

During the summer, sleeper passengers can enjoy the much larger North American–style Park car, one of several luxurious, dome-topped, round-ended observation cars built in the 1950s and named for Canadian national parks. Newspapers, coffee, and munchies are provided all day, and sleeper passengers can eat gratis in the dining car, whose meals are excellent examples of the French-style precision-cooking, quick-freezing, and reheating process called *sous-vide*.

VIA No. 14 leaves **Montreal at 19:00 Eastern Time** (7 p.m. to Americans). Before departure, service dogs can be walked along the grassy, tree-shaded Boulevard Robert Bourassa at the northeast corner of Gare Centrale (Central Station) or in the gardens of the opulent Mary Queen of the World Basilica just to the southwest.

In Quebec, Saint-Lambert (19:25), Saint-Hyacinthe (19:58), and Drummondville (20:47) are flag stops that the train usually passes by.

**22:34 to 22:49: Sainte-Foy, Quebec**, is a fifteen-minute call suitable for the last pee stop of the day before you and your dog go to bed. There's plenty of grass along the platform and a copse of trees behind the station building.

During the night the *Ocean* slips past the Quebec flag stops of Montmagny (23:40), La Pocatiere (00:28), Riviere-du-Loup (01:13), Trois-Pistoles (01:55), Rimouski (03:01), Mont-Joli (03:39), Sayabec (04:40), Amqui (05:03), Causapscal (05:23), and Matapedia (06:10). In an emergency you can ask your attendant about stopping at any of these stations, but if your dog has successfully performed his toilette at Sainte-Foy, that probably will not be necessary.

**07:48 Atlantic Time: Campbellton, New Brunswick,** should be the logical early-morning stop for your dog, but don't dawdle, for the station dwell is brief. The wisps of grass around a light pole satisfied Trooper when we rode the train.

The *Ocean* continues past the New Brunswick flag stops of Charlo (08:23), Jacquet River (08:47), Petit Rocher (09:10), Bathurst (09:37), Miramichi (11:23), and Rogersville (12:15).

**13:23 to 13:38: Moncton, New Brunswick,** is a fifteen-minute stop with scrubby grass along the platform fence, enough to entice a dog.

One more New Brunswick flag stop passes by at Sackville (14:26), followed by three in Nova Scotia at Amherst (14:42), Springhill Junction (15:03), and Truro (16:22).

**17:51: Halifax, Nova Scotia,** the end of the line, features plenty of grass outside the station, including a large park across the street.

# Appendix 2

# On the Road: Evacuating in an Emergency

When Hurricane Irma churned toward the state of Florida on September 8, 2017, Governor Rick Scott held a press conference and warned that "all Floridians should be prepared to evacuate soon." A goodly number of the state's twenty million residents packed and departed in an exodus that headlines referred to as the largest evacuation in history. Other brave souls sheltered in place, while thousands checked into public shelters.

Obviously, Floridians are not alone in needing an exit strategy since few places in the United States are immune from natural disasters. Coming up with a plan and a list ahead of time can help keep panic from setting in if and when you have to evacuate with your service dog. The Federal Emergency Management Agency (FEMA) has suggested lists for people and dogs (you'll find them on https://www.ready.gov).

If you and your service dog travel together frequently for business or pleasure, you're ahead of the game. You already have a set of key documents assembled, and you keep your dog's microchip enrollment contact information up-to-date whenever you change your phone number or address. You're accustomed to assembling a travel bag with the dog's paperwork, food, medications, bowls, harness, leashes, microfiber towel, first aid kit, poop bags, and other essentials.

Those things form the basis of a "go-bag" for emergencies. Add a toy and some bedding with the familiar scent of home, a roll of paper towels, and trash bags. Put the paperwork and a photo of your dog in a plastic bag or box along with your family's other important documents.

Be sure your supply of food and drinking water is adequate for both yourself and your dog. It's a good habit to routinely order extra dog food and medications long before you run out, rather than waiting until the supply runs low.

You may decide to leave your home and stay in a shelter. After Hurricane Katrina, when many residents refused to leave their pets behind and some people died as a result, President George W. Bush signed the Pets Evacuation and Transportation Standards Act (PETS). The law now requires that state and local emergency management officials address the needs of individuals with pets and service animals in a disaster or emergency.

National television coverage of Hurricane Harvey in 2017 indeed showed rescuers leading people and their animals to safety as Houston, Texas, flooded. Each state should have its own written policies on how such animals will be housed and cared for. Only a few specified shelters in a given locale might be designated as pet-friendly, however, so some might not have supplies and a plan in place to accommodate service dogs' needs. Be prepared to present a copy of your dog's rabies certificate when you check in.

If you stay in your boarded-up home during a lengthy storm, dangerous wind gusts may make it a bad idea to try taking the dog outside to pee or poop. Have a plan in mind for how your dog could relieve itself at an indoor station you can create in a bathroom or attached garage. Use puppy pads, shredded newspapers, or, for larger dogs, a mulch-filled box or child's wading pool. It will help if your dog has learned commands such as "Do your business" and has received praise or training treat rewards for responding.

# Appendix 3

# Cruise Line
# Service Dog Policies

Following are the service dog policies of the cruise lines that operate in United States waters and therefore are subject to most provisions of Title III of the Americans with Disabilities Act, which prohibits discrimination against people with disabilities. Note that when ruling on a class action suit on this subject in 2005 (*Spector v. Norwegian Cruise Line Ltd.*), the Supreme Court held that Title III did not apply to foreign cruise lines' internal affairs, and that permanent and significant structural modifications to foreign flag cruise ships were not required. For this reason, ledges and other barriers still exist on some ships, presenting a challenge to wheelchair users, including those with service animals.

The policies are roughly similar to one another, but some lines emphasize particular regulations or conditions, some lines' policies are bare-bones, and some lines apparently have had little or no experience with service animals. All policies are quoted verbatim from the lines' websites, edited as appropriate to eliminate non–North American requirements. Because no cruise line allows emotional support animals aboard, statements about prohibiting those animals have been eliminated.

Many cruise lines that call at Canadian ports extend the same policies to Canadians and their service dogs but may ask for documentation that is not required of U.S. citizens. Always call the cruise line and inquire.

If a cruise line is not listed, it either does not call at U.S. ports or declined to respond to requests for information.

## AMERICAN CRUISE LINES
### (WWW.AMERICANCRUISELINES.COM)

The only animals American Cruise Lines permits on board our ships are working service dogs, which are legally defined and individually trained to meet disability-related needs by performing tasks like guiding a blind person, alerting a deaf person, pulling wheelchairs, alerting and protecting a person who is having a seizure, or performing other special tasks. Working service dogs are not pets.

**Service dogs in training are not allowed aboard.**

Service dogs are permitted to accompany the person with a disability in all public areas, including dining venues. While in public areas, service dogs must be on a leash, harness or other restraining device. Due to health and safety concerns, service dogs are not permitted to eat off of the tables in the dining room or sit on dining room chairs or tables.

Care and supervision of the service dog is the sole responsibility of the owner. The ships are not required to provide food or care for the dog. Note that the ship's staff is not required to care for the dog, nor can the dog be left in the stateroom unattended. American Cruise Lines will provide a potty box if ordered prior to the cruises departure.

ACL must have documents 21 days before the cruise departs.

The following documents are required: ID Card; Service Certificate; Rabies Certificate; Vaccination Records.

## AMERICAN QUEEN STEAMBOAT COMPANY
### (WWW.AMERICANQUEENSTEAMBOATCOMPANY.COM)

Only designated service animals are permitted onboard. You are required to notify American Queen Steamboat Company in advance of departure if you plan to bring along a service animal. The deck department creates a dog relief area out on deck for the service animals, when we are sailing. When docked the animals can be taken ashore to use the grassy areas if available.

## AZAMARA CLUB
### (WWW.AZAMARACLUBCRUISES.COM)

Azamara Club Cruises welcomes service dogs on all ships. Please note we do not accept pets.

A service dog is defined as "any dog that is individually trained to do work or perform tasks for the benefit of a person with a disability." Service dogs are not considered pets.

Evidence that a dog is a service dog is helpful but not required (such as identification cards, other written documentation, presence of harnesses and/or tags or the credible verbal assurance of the person with a disability using the dog).

We provide 4 feet by 4 feet relief areas with cypress mulch to accommodate service dogs. Sod for sailings from the U.S. can be provided if ordered in advance and is available. Relief areas are provided on a shared basis with other service dogs onboard.

Please notify our Access Department at time of booking but no later than 30 days prior to sailing if a service dog relief area is needed.

Service dogs are permitted to accompany the person with a disability in all public areas, including dining venues. While in public areas, service dogs must be on a leash, harness or other restraining device. Due to health regulations, service dogs are not permitted in pools, whirlpools or spas.

Care and supervision of the service dog is the sole responsibility of the owner. The ships are not required to provide food or care for the dog.

Guests may bring a reasonable quantity of food and bowls for the dog onboard the ship at no additional charge. If refrigerated space is needed, notify our Access Department at time of booking but no later than 30 days prior to sailing.

Guests are responsible for obtaining all required permits for service dogs to depart the ship in ports of call and at final destination. For document requirements, visit:

- U.S. Department of Agriculture website [https://www.aphis.usda .gov/aphis/pet-travel]
- Hawaii Department of Agriculture website [https://hdoa.hawaii.gov/ ai/aqs/guide-service-dogs/]

[The line also lists the websites for the United Kingdom and Australia, which are not germane to this book.]

A copy of these permits must be carried on the ship, and a copy left with Guest Relations Desk upon boarding the ship. All documentation and immunization requirements are established by government authorities and not Azamara Club Cruises. Please note requirements are subject to change without notice.

If the guest chooses to disembark the ship at a port at which the service dog must remain onboard, the guest must make arrangements to ensure that the dog is cared for. Note that the ship's staff is not required to care for the dog, nor can the dog be left in the stateroom unattended.

Guests are responsible for the behavior or damage caused by their service dog. A cleaning fee may be charged to the guest's shipboard account.

If the service dog's behavior creates a fundamental alteration or a direct threat to safety, the dog may be denied boarding or removed from the ship along with the owner at the guest's expense. Examples include: growling, barking excessively, initiating unsolicited contact, biting other guests and/or crewmembers, failure to use designated relief areas, sitting on furniture, eating from the table, etc.

If you have an animal that does not meet the definition of a service animal (i.e. a dog trained to perform a task) but must accompany you in order to assist you with your disability, please contact our Access Department at least 60 days prior to sailing.

## CARNIVAL (WWW.CARNIVAL.COM)

The only dogs Carnival permits aboard our ships are working service dogs, which are legally defined and individually trained to meet disability-related needs by performing tasks like guiding a blind person, alerting a deaf person, pulling wheelchairs, alerting and protecting a person who is having a seizure, or performing other special tasks. Working service dogs are not pets.

Pets, or service dogs in training, are not allowed aboard. Emotional support dogs, which are not recognized by the Department of Justice, are also not permitted on Carnival ships.

If you are traveling with a working service dog that meets the requirements described above, please review the following policies and procedures:

Many of our ports of call have established strict entry requirements for animals. Therefore, guests traveling with working service dogs must visit the Department of Agriculture web site [https://www.aphis.usda.gov/aphis/pet-travel], or their service animal's veterinarian, to determine each destination country's policy regarding admission of working service dogs.

Note that many of the ports you may visit will only accept annual rabies vaccinations and do not recognize three-year rabies vaccination.

Mexican ports require service dogs to have received an ecto-parasite and endo-parasite treatment no more than 15 days prior to arrival to port and this information should be included in the dog's health certificate. If you have any questions, please consult with your veterinarian. [*Authors' note:* Actually, Mexico requires dogs to have the ecto- and endo-parasite treatments within six months of entering the country. Mexico requires dogs to have had rabies immunizations at least fifteen days before entering the country.]

You must hand-carry (not packed in your baggage) all required documents, along with your working service dog's current vaccination records. You will be asked to submit these records once aboard.

So that we may provide you with the additional information you will need in order to sail with your working service dog, please contact our Guest Access Department at specialneeds@carnival.com, or 1.800.438.6744 ext. 70025.

## CELEBRITY (WWW.CELEBRITYCRUISES.COM)

Celebrity welcomes service dogs on all ships. Please note that pets are not accepted onboard any Celebrity ship. A service dog is defined as "any dog that is individually trained to do work or perform tasks for the benefit of a person with a disability." Service dogs are not considered pets. Evidence that a dog is a service dog is helpful, but not required (such as identification cards, other written documentation, presence of harnesses and/or tags or the credible verbal assurance of the person with a disability using the animal).

A 4 feet by 4 feet relief area with cypress mulch is provided to accommodate service dogs. Sod for sailings from the U.S. can be provided if it is requested in advance and is available. Relief areas are provided on a shared basis with other service dogs onboard. Please note that The Lawn Club on Solstice class ships is not designated as a relief area. Please notify us at time of booking but no later than 30 days prior to sailing if a service dog relief area is needed.

Service dogs are permitted to accompany the person with a disability in all public areas, including dining venues. While in public areas, service dogs must be on a leash, harness, or other restraining device. Due to health regulations, service dogs are not permitted in pools, whirlpools or spas. Care and supervision of the service animal is the sole responsibility of the owner. The ships are not required to provide food or care for the animal.

Guests may bring a reasonable quantity of food and bowls for the dog onboard the ship at no additional charge. If refrigerated space is needed, notify our Access Department at time of booking, but no later than 30 days prior to sailing.

Guests are responsible for obtaining all required permits for service dogs to depart the ship in ports of call and at the final destination. Guest must carry a copy with them on the ship, and leave a copy with the Guest Relations Desk after boarding the ship.

If the guest chooses to disembark the ship at a port at which the service dog must remain onboard, the guest must make arrangements to ensure that the dog is cared for. Note that the ship's staff is not required to care for the dog, nor can the dog be left in the stateroom unattended.

Guests are responsible for the behavior or damage caused by their service dog. A cleaning fee may be charged to the guest's shipboard account. If the service dog's behavior creates a fundamental alteration or a direct threat to safety, the dog may be denied boarding or removed from the ship along with the owner at the guest's expense. Examples include: growling, barking excessively, initiating unsolicited contact, biting other guests and/or crewmembers, failure to use designated relief areas, sitting on furniture, eating from the table, etc.

## CRYSTAL CRUISES (WWW.CRYSTALCRUISES.COM)

While we do accommodate requests for service animals to join guests onboard, due to the rarity of these requests we do not have any formal printed materials that we provide on this topic prior to boarding. Typically, upon request to bring a service animal aboard we build a potty crate to accommodate the dog's size. Should a guest want to request to have a service animal onboard they simply contact our On Board Guest Services department prior to their cruise to arrange.

## CUNARD (WWW.CUNARD.COM)

[The following has been edited to remove material relevant only to transatlantic crossings.]

Cunard accepts registered assistance dogs on board that have been specifically trained to assist a person with a disability and has been certified by an organisation that is a full member of Assistance Dogs International (ADI) or International Guide Dog Federation (IGDF), the accrediting bodies for assistance dog organisations worldwide.

All assistance dogs are carried free of charge.

Cunard Line welcome registered assistance dogs on all their vessels.

We would advise all owners to carry their dog's identification card, or similar, with them at all times in case local authorities require proof. . . .

Travelling alone: Guests with an assistance dog are not required to travel with a companion provided they are able to undertake day to day tasks independently.

Our crew members cannot assist with any day to day personal care tasks. Should it become apparent that during the voyage that you are not managing independently you will be required to discuss this with a member of the ships company. We reserve the right to refuse future travel unaccompanied.

Harness/Leash: Your dog must wear its harness, or vest, at all times when not in the stateroom. Due to the nature of cruising we are unable to provide a safe off leash area for assistance dogs.

We carry small and large canine life jackets on each of our vessels. The relevant life jacket will be placed in your stateroom alongside your own.

Disembarkation in ports of call: It is the responsibility of the owner to research each county's individual regulations . . . in order to go ashore with their assistance dog. . . .

You will be required to send in copies of the relevant pages from the PETS Passport or Official Veterinary Health Certificate, once your booking has been made. Cunard Line will not issue your assistance dog permission to travel until this paperwork has been produced and verified. . . .

Food & Bedding: Please ensure that you bring a suitable supply of all dry dog food, food and water bowls plus any applicable blankets/bedding. Dogs can only be fed in the stateroom and under no circumstance should your dog be fed "tit-bits" in any public areas.

We do allow assistance dogs into our buffet restaurants, however your dog must remain at the table. Should you be travelling alone our crew will be happy to assist you with food selection and carry your tray back to the table.

Dog toileting: The vessel will provide a wooden 4ft x 4ft box that will be filled with mulch. Your stateroom location will determine exactly where the litter box will be placed and we will endeavour to ensure that this is as close to your stateroom as possible without compromising safety.

On your arrival your cabin steward will show you to the location of the relief box, please note litter boxes cannot be placed on stateroom balconies or inside the stateroom itself.

We would ask owners to clean up after their dog and our staff will advise you once you are on board where to dispose of your dog's waste. The box will be emptied and replenished by the staff on board every day.

Accessible areas of the ship: Assistance dogs are welcome in all areas of the ship apart from:

- Designated children's areas
- Swimming pools or the "beach" area surrounding the pool where water may flow freely in and out of the pool
- Jacuzzis
- Crew areas
- Galley visits

Vet on board: We currently do not offer the service of a vet on board any of our ships and the ship's doctors are unable to assist should your dog be taken ill on board. Therefore, it is imperative that you consult your vet prior to your voyage for advice to ensure your dog is fit to travel. It may be a good idea to talk to your vet regarding motion sickness.

### DISNEY (DISNEYCRUISE.DISNEY.GO.COM)

Trained service animals are welcome in most locations onboard Disney Cruise ships. All service animals must remain on a leash and under your control, or that of someone in your travel party, at all times. Further, you will be responsible for the care and feeding of your animal.

Service animals are not permitted in the pools or wet play areas onboard our ships and may not be left unattended inside a stateroom. Disney Cruise Line Crew Members are not permitted to take control of a service animal.

Due to the nature of some Port Adventures excursions, service animals may not be permitted.

Important note: You are responsible for obtaining the import permits from all countries that require those special documents and must have those original documents available at all times. Please be aware that obtaining those permits can take weeks or months, and some countries may not allow animals to enter at all.

Copies of completed permits for each port of call must be sent to Disney Cruise Lines Special Services (SpecialServices@disneycruise.com) prior to the sail date.

We strongly encourage Guests traveling with a service animal to contact Disney Cruise Line Special Services as soon as possible to discuss required documentation, the set-up of a relief area and the availability of Port Adventures.

## FRED. OLSEN (WWW.FREDOLSENCRUISES.COM)

Fred. Olsen Cruise Lines does accept service dogs on board all of our vessels, however, the acceptance is dependent on the cruise itinerary.

We do not require a written agreement regarding access areas for the assistance dog. The guest and the assistance dog can use all the public areas on board. No guests are allowed in crew/restricted areas and we do not ask for written agreement of this from any guest.

We can provide any specification of toileting materials that the assistance dogs require and is used to and trained to use at home. We ask our guest what is needed, whether it be a litter tray, faux grass or any other material. We make sure that whatever is required is purchased and on board for the arrival of the guest and assistance dog.

The location of the toileting area is in a different place on each ship. The guest is escorted with the assistance dog on arrival and can be escorted as many times as required until confident of locating the area alone. The area is outside and under cover.

We feel it is best that the guest provide the dog food the dog is used to at home.

At the booking stage any guest asking to bring an assistance dog on board would be advised of the documentation required.

## HOLLAND AMERICA (WWW.HOLLANDAMERICA.COM)

Holland America Line only permits service animals on board, defined as those animals that are individually trained to provide assistance to an individual with a disability. We do not permit our guests to bring pets, therapy/companion animals, and other animals that do not meet the definition of service animals. If you have any questions about whether the animal you wish to bring on board is, in fact, a service animal, you may contact our Access & Compliance Department.

Your itinerary may include ports of call that have very specific and strict requirements that need to be met prior to your service animal being allowed off of the ship. Please be sure you understand the requirements for a service animal to disembark in each port of call. The best places to obtain specific information on required documentation and immunizations for your service animal are the U.S. Department of Agriculture's website, local customs offices in the specific ports, and from your service animal's veterinarian. All documentation and immunization requirements are established by government authorities and not by Holland America Line. Should you need assistance in locating this information, please contact our Access & Compliance Department.

To board the ship, your service animal must have current vaccinations. Records confirming the vaccination status should be provided to our Access & Compliance Department prior to your departure. We also recommend that you carry the immunization records with you in case they are required at any port of call.

If you do not have the proper documentation and proof of vaccinations for your service animal required at a port of call, or if there are local quarantine requirements, your service animal will be denied the right to leave the ship. If your service animal is denied the right to leave the ship in a specific port of call, the staff and crew will work with you to determine what actions may be possible to allow you to visit the port without your service animal. Please note that in your absence, you will need to provide for the care and supervision of your service animal. Except in those circumstances where your service animal has been denied disembarkation, you may not leave your service animal unattended on the vessel or in your stateroom at any time.

## LINDBLAD CRUISES (WWW.LINDBLADCRUISES.COM)

We do not have documents that we provide to guests who travel with service dogs. Dogs recognized as service animals under ADA are ones who have been specifically trained to do work or perform tasks for persons with a disability. When a person with a service animal books with us, we typically review the layout of the cabin in detail so they can envision where the dog will sleep and where the pee pads can be placed. We use leak-proof plastic lined pads with a super absorbent cotton base. These are better as they can be disposed of after use. We also review the itinerary in detail so the guest is aware of the number of times they will disembark the ship in a given day.

All of the service animals that we have had the pleasure of working with have been true professionals and they have not required any instruction on our part.

## MSC CRUISES (WWW.MSCCRUISESUSA.COM)

Properly trained and certified guide dogs are allowed on board, provided they are in good health and have all documents required for entering the countries visited during the cruise. The guest will be informed in advance about the kind of accommodation provided for the dog, any facilities provided and the procedure for embarking and disembarking. Guests are personally responsible for the custody, feeding and general care of the animal.

## NORWEGIAN (WWW.NCL.COM)

Norwegian Cruise Line accepts service dogs that are trained to perform a specific task. A service dog may be needed for many different conditions, which would be acceptable under the American with Disabilities Act (ADA) guidelines. . . .

Guests must provide copies of the dog's current vaccination records that show all shots are up-to-date (including Rabies), as well as a USDA or International Health certificate.

Guests are responsible for checking with all ports of call for any special requirements they may have. Guests are responsible for bringing all food, medication and life jacket for the dog.

A sand box will be provided.

All guests traveling with service animals must book at least two weeks in advance to allow sufficient time to check with each port of call and provide Norwegian Cruise Line with all required documentation.

For additional information, call (866) 584-9756 (voice), fax (305) 468-2171, or send an e-mail to accessdesk@ncl.com, or have your travel agent contact us.

### OCEANIA (WWW.OCEANIACRUISES.COM)

Service animal requests are reviewed on a case by case basis and must be in compliance with ADA requirements.

### P&O CRUISES (WWW.POCRUISES.COM)

P&O cruises accepts registered assistance dogs on board that have been specifically trained to assist a person with a disability and has been certified by an organisation that is a full member of Assistance Dogs International (ADI) or International Guide Dog Federation (IGDF), the accrediting bodies for assistance dog organisations worldwide. . . .

Due to national regulations in certain ports, guests with assistance dogs may be required to remain on board.

If you intend to travel with an assistance dog, please notify us in advance and at least 48 hours prior to departure.

We can only accept assistance dogs that are fully trained and we are unable to allow emotional support dogs or any other animal to travel. All assistance dogs are carried free of charge.

We would advise all owners to carry their dog's identification card, or similar, with them at all times in case local authorities require proof. Once your booking has been made confirmation of this will need to be submitted.

Once your booking has been made and your paperwork has been checked . . . and you have completed and signed P&O Cruises terms and conditions, we will send you a confirmation letter. This letter confirms your Assistance Dog has been given permission to travel and must be produced at check-in. Failure to produce this letter may result in your Assistance Dog being denied boarding.

If we do not receive a completed and signed copy of P&O Cruises terms and conditions we regret we are unable to allow your dog to travel.

### PONANT (US.PONANT.COM)

Ponant does not allow any pets, including service dogs, on any of its vessels. This is due to special regulations in the different destination countries.

### PRINCESS (WWW.PRINCESS.COM)

Before we can approve the service animal to sail, we will first need an email describing the specific tasks and/or services the dog provides the guest. Princess abides by the Americans with Disabilities Act, a federal law. The work or task a dog has been trained to provide must be directly related to the person's disability.

Once we have this information, and the animal is approved to sail, we will send you the necessary information for boarding.

Please note, our guests are responsible for verifying the port requirements and providing the necessary documentation for their animal to travel, we only require the animal have all its current vaccinations. Even if not required by any of the ports of call, Princess recommends obtaining an International Health Certificate, as in the event of an emergency we may call and/or disembark in an unscheduled port. Guests may obtain the port requirements by contacting the Department of Agriculture, local customs offices in the specific ports and from your service animal's veterinarian. We will need copies of the animal's current vaccinations and all other paperwork sent to our office within two weeks of sailing.

We are unable to blanket approve an animal without a booking with a set itinerary.

We cannot predict how a given country may enforce service animal regulations. Noncompliance may result in the need to make arrangements to put your pet into quarantine at your expense, return your pet to the country of origin, or other remedies. We suggest that you minimize the disruptions that may occur by following the rules of the country you are visiting.

## REGENT SEVEN SEAS (WWW.RSSC.COM)

We do not have an official written policy as we comply with all applicable state and/or Federal laws.

## ROYAL CARIBBEAN (WWW.ROYALCARIBBEAN.COM)

Royal Caribbean International welcomes service dogs on all ships. Please note we do not accept pets.

A service dog is defined as "any dog that is individually trained to do work or perform tasks for the benefit of a person with a disability." Service dogs are not considered pets.

Evidence that a dog is a service dog is helpful but not required (such as identification cards, other written documentation, presence of harnesses and/or tags or the credible verbal assurance of the person with a disability using the dog).

We provide 4 feet by 4 feet relief areas with cypress mulch to accommodate service dogs. Sod for sailings from the U.S. can be provided if ordered in advance and is available. Relief areas are provided on a shared basis with other service dogs onboard. Please note that *Central Park* on Oasis class ships is not designated as a relief area.

Please notify our Access Department at time of booking but no later than 30 days prior to sailing if a service dog relief area is needed.

Service dogs are permitted to accompany the person with a disability in all public areas, including dining venues. While in public areas, service dogs must be on a leash, harness or other restraining device. Due to health regulations, service dogs are not permitted in pools, whirlpools or spas.

Care and supervision of the service dog is the sole responsibility of the owner. The ships are not required to provide food or care for the dog.

Guests may bring a reasonable quantity of food and bowls for the dog onboard the ship at no additional charge. If refrigerated space is needed, notify our Access Department at time of booking but no later than 30 days prior to sailing.

If the guest chooses to disembark the ship at a port at which the service dog must remain onboard, the guest must make arrangements to ensure that the dog is cared for. Note that the ship's staff is not required to care for the dog, nor can the dog be left in the stateroom unattended.

Guests are responsible for obtaining all required documents for the animal to depart the ship in ports of call and at final destination. For document requirements, visit:

- U.S. Department of Agriculture website at http://awic.nal.usda.gov/companion-animals/travel-and-transport
- Hawaii Department of Agriculture website at http://hdoa.hawaii.gov/ai/aqs/guide-service-dogs/

A copy of these permits must be carried on the ship, and a copy left with Guest Relations Desk upon boarding the ship.

Please note all documentation and immunization requirements are established by government authorities and not Royal Caribbean International. Please note requirements are subject to change without notice.

Guests are responsible for the behavior or damage caused by their service dog. A cleaning fee may be charged to the guest's shipboard account.

If the service dog's behavior creates a fundamental alteration or a direct threat to safety, the dog may be denied boarding or removed from the ship along with the owner at the guest's expense. Examples include: growling, barking excessively, initiating unsolicited contact, biting other guests and/or crewmembers, failure to use designated relief areas, sitting on furniture, eating from the table, etc.

If you have an animal that does not meet the definition of a service animal (i.e. a dog trained to perform a task) but must accompany you in order to assist you with your disability, please contact our Access Department at least 60 days prior to sailing.

## SEABOURN (WWW.SEABOURN.COM)

Seabourn only permits service animals on board, defined as those animals that are individually trained to provide assistance to an individual with a disability. We do not permit our guests to bring pets, therapy/companion animals, and other animals that do not meet the definition of service animals. If you have any questions about whether the animal you wish to bring on board is, in fact, a service animal, you may contact our Access & Compliance Department.

Your itinerary may include ports of call that have very specific and strict requirements that need to be met prior to your service animal being allowed off of the ship. Please be sure you understand the requirements for a service animal to disembark in each port of call. The best places to obtain specific information on required documentation and immunizations for your service animal are the U.S. Department of Agriculture's website, local customs offices in the specific ports, and from your service animal's veterinarian. All documentation and immunization requirements are established by government authorities and not by Seabourn. Should you need assistance in locating this information, please contact our Access & Compliance Department.

To board the ship, your service animal must have current vaccinations. Records confirming the vaccination status should be provided to our Access & Compliance Department prior to your departure. We also recommend that you carry the immunization records with you in case they are required at any port of call. If you do not have the proper documentation and proof of vaccinations for your service animal required at a port of call, or if there are local quarantine requirements, your service animal will be denied the right to leave the ship. If your service animal is denied the right to leave the ship in a specific port of call, the staff and crew will work with you to determine what actions may be possible to allow you to visit the port without your service animal. Please note that in your absence, you will need to provide for the care and supervision of your service animal. Except in those circumstances where your service animal has been denied disembarkation, you may not leave your service animal unattended on the vessel or in your suite at any time.

### SILVERSEA CRUISES (WWW.SILVERSEA.COM)

Silversea does not have a written policy concerning service dogs, but service animals are allowed on all cruises beginning or ending in a United States port consistent with all applicable laws, regulations, bulletins and other directives.

### UNCRUISE ADVENTURES (WWW.UNCRUISES.COM)

We accept service animals on our vessels. The safety of our guests and the service animal is very important, and we have several questions that need to be addressed before we can confirm and make arrangements. Please provide answers to the following questions so we can work with our Operations team for approval and to make the necessary arrangements.

How does the animal help you?

Can the animal defecate/urinate on command?

How long can they hold before relief?

Can they go on a steel deck or special pad that the owner will provide? Please understand there will be many times where the animal cannot be brought ashore to relieve itself.

Will the owner be responsible for handling relief materials on or off the boat?

Has the animal been on a small boat? Ideally the service animal will have some experience on small inflatable skiffs as this is our only method to get ashore mid-week.

Is the animal permitted to participate in on-shore hikes, etc.? If so, they must be leashed at all times.

Where will the animal eat? Are you prepared to bring all food items necessary for the service animal (7 days plus transit time)?

Are other people allowed to interact with the service animal? If not, what is your plan for communicating this need to other passengers?"

### VICTORY CRUISES (WWW.VICTORYCRUISELINES.COM)

We don't have a policy in place (or print yet) for service animals however they are certainly welcome onboard—we would handle each request to travel with service dogs in cooperation with all US laws and regulations. We ask for guests that need to travel with working service dogs to contact us via email at info@victorycruiselines.com so we can garner all information and assist with the handling of this request.

### VIKING OCEAN CRUISES (VIKINGCRUISES.COM)

All animals which would be permitted aboard must be registered as service animals. Once a booking is made, please be sure to submit all forms of certification for approval. Please call us directly [1-866-984-5464] and or your agent for further details.

### WINDSTAR CRUISES (WWW.WINDSTARCRUISES.COM)

You must notify your travel professional at time of booking if you intend to board with a Service Dog.

**What is a Service Dog?** At Windstar Cruises, a Service Dog is defined as a dog that is personally trained to do work or perform tasks for the benefit of a guest with a disability. There are many different acceptable conditions for using a service dog such as guiding a blind person, pulling a wheelchair, or alerting and protecting a person who is having a seizure, and other special tasks as defined in Title III of the Americans with Disabilities Act (ADA). *A Service Dog is not a pet. . . .*

### What do guests need to do to meet the requirements to bring a Service Dog on board a Windstar yacht?

1. Allow at least a year of planning in order to get a Service Dog certified, especially if the guest is visiting more than one country.
2. Contact the embassy or consulate of the country(ies) they will be visiting for information on the policies and requirements of the country.
3. Contact the Department or Ministry of Agriculture in their destination country (including U.S. travel) as many ports of call have strict entry requirements for animals.
4. Obtain health and rabies certificates from their veterinarian. Have these documents notarized and certified by the U.S. Department of Agriculture or similar authority in residing country.
5. Obtain a good health letter from their veterinarian on letterhead stating their Service Dog is in good health and current on all vaccines.
6. Obtain a letter from their personal physician also on letterhead, stating that they require the assistance of a Service Dog and for what reason(s).
7. Outfit their Service Dog with recognizable gear as a way to let people know that their dog is an official Service Dog. For example, a jacket or vest or guide dog-type harness with words on the side like Service Dog or Guide Dog.
8. Make sure they hand carry all these documents, not pack them in their luggage. They will be asked to submit these records prior to boarding.
9. All guests traveling with service animals must book at least 60 days in advance to allow time for Windstar Cruises to review documents and approve the Service Dog request in writing.

### What additional information do guests need to know?

1. Only one Service Dog can be accommodated per (suite/stateroom) or (person).
2. The dog's breed and the size restrictions of our yachts may limit the Service Dogs we can accept.
3. A sand/ relief box will be provided.
4. Windstar Cruises will do our best to assist guests and they should contact our Reservation Department at 1-877-203-5279 to make sure both they and Windstar Cruises have all the additional information needed.

### What happens on board?

1. Service Dogs are permitted to accompany guests with a disability in all public areas, including dining venues.

2. Service Dogs must be on a leash, harness or other restraining device in public areas.
3. Service Dogs are not permitted in pools, whirlpools or spas.
4. The care and supervision of Service Dogs is the sole responsibility of the owner. Yachts are not required nor do they have the capacity to provide food or care for Service Dogs.
5. Owners may bring a reasonable quantity of food and bowls for their Service Dog at no additional charge.
6. If a guest wishes to disembark at a port that does not allow their Service Dog, the guest must make arrangements for the dog on board to ensure the dog is cared for. The ship's staff is not able to care for the dog and the Service Dog may not be left unattended in the guest's suite/stateroom.
7. Owners of Service Dogs are responsible for the behavior or damage caused by their Service Dog. A cleaning fee may be assessed if necessary.
8. If a Service Dog's behavior creates a distraction, such as growling, barking excessively, initiating unsolicited contact, biting, failing to use the designated relief area, sitting on furniture, eating from the table, etc., the dog may be denied boarding or removed from the yacht along with the owner, at the owner's expense.

## Local and Coastal Ferries

Coastal and municipal ferries in the United States and Canada follow service dog laws and will take aboard such animals as well as pets. So do overnight ferries, such as those that travel along the west coast of Alaska and British Columbia or in Atlantic Canada. The quality of accommodations, however, tends to be much less convenient than those aboard cruise ships. There are no wooden relief boxes, just bare decks (often so smelly that passengers and crew call them "poo decks"), and service dog partners are expected to clean up after their animals. Many travelers recommend bringing along small squares of artificial turf to encourage bashful dogs. Here is how three popular North American ferry systems handle the matter:

**Alaska Marine Highway** transports service dogs for free and allows them in passenger areas, but it requires prior approval and a health certificate that attests to the dog's rabies immunization. Paper towels and trash receptacles are provided in an area on the steel car deck that can be so busy it has been described by one passenger as "being like a dog park without any grass." Even on overnight routes, service dogs are expected to do their business on the deck during port calls or can get off the ship at terminals to be walked. On long sea stretches between ports, special car deck calls are made while en route. (https://www.dot.state.ak.us/amhs/)

**BC Ferries'** smaller vessels provide tight enclosures (mainly for pets but also service dogs) with lockable kennels. There are no relief boxes, just a wooden platform, poop bags, and a water hose for sluicing waste off designated areas of the vehicle deck. Many passengers liken the small pet area to a jail cell. For shorter voyages of a few hours or less, the Pacific Northwest line recommends relieving your dog and restraining food and water before boarding. As in most of Canada's transportation facilities, documentation from an accredited training organization and proof of rabies inoculation is required for service dogs, who, unlike pets, have the run of the passenger decks. Service dogs ride free. (https://www.bcferries .com).

**Marine Atlantic** operates a car ferry year-round across the Cabot Strait from North Sydney, Nova Scotia, to Port aux Basque, Newfoundland, a trip of 96 nautical miles (110 statute miles, or 177 kilometers) with a crossing time of approximately seven hours. From June to September, the company adds overnight ferry service between North Sydney, Nova Scotia, and Argentia, Newfoundland, a trip of 280 nautical miles (322 miles, or 519 kilometers) lasting approximately sixteen hours.

Service dogs are allowed in passenger areas. (Pets must be confined to their handlers' automobiles on decks not accessible to passengers or taken to a kennel stowage area in owner-provided pet travel carriers.) Marine Atlantic requests that you advise them at least forty-eight hours prior to sailing that you will be traveling with a service dog, and that you present your dog's documentation at check-in. "You may be asked to provide supporting documents including photo ID and the certification papers verifying the training the service animal has received," according to the Marine Atlantic website.

"While traveling with your service animal onboard our vessels you will have full use of the pet relief station located in the pet stowage area," advises Marine Atlantic's Customer Relations Department. "Depending on which vessel you travel on the pet relieving area is filled with either sand or gravel and has a drainage system for sanitation. This area is cleaned after each sailing. This area is fully enclosed and is not exposed to any elements. While waiting to board the ferries our terminals offer grassy areas for dogs to use. This area is equipped with pet waste bags." (https://www.marineatlantic.ca)

# Appendix 4

# Animal Import Regulations

Here is a digest of the current regulations a service dog partner might encounter in traveling to countries located in North America. Individual travelers are responsible for obtaining their dog's necessary documentation prior to a trip. Do not expect that a travel agency, airline, tour operator, or cruise line will perform this task.

**Be aware that in many nations, animal health and importation rules can and do change from time to time. Always check for the most up-to-date regulations** with the U.S. Department of Agriculture's Animal and Plant Health Inspection Service (APHIS) on their website (https://www.aphis.usda.gov).

In Canada, the equivalent offices are the Canadian Food Inspection Agency, or CFIA (http://www.inspection.gc.ca/). The Canadian Transportation Agency, or CTA (https://otc-cta.gc.ca/eng/service-animals), is another source of information.

You should also check with the embassies or consulates of the countries to which you want to take your service dog. Regulations change frequently, so sometimes the APHIS and Canadian CFIA people haven't been informed yet of the changes.

We recommend that you work with an APHIS-accredited veterinarian when you are planning international travel. Verify the regulations with your veterinarian, who will examine your dog and issue an APHIS Form 7001 Health Certificate. U.S. veterinarians who practice in locales where their customers are frequent foreign travelers might be more au courant with changing regulations abroad than the APHIS regional people are. Allow extra lead time if the form also must be endorsed by an APHIS Veterinary Medical Officer at an APHIS regional office.

"A few countries may allow health certificates to be submitted via APHIS' electronic certification system, called VEHCS," according to the APHIS website. "When available, this option will be clearly noted on the APHIS Pet Travel Website. In these cases, the issuing veterinarian's signature will be securely applied within the system and electronically submitted to APHIS for endorsement."

When you see references to a "blood titer test" requirement by Hawaii and certain Caribbean countries, that means that you will need to arrange for your dog's blood to be drawn and sent by the vet to the approved Veterinary Diagnostic Laboratory at Kansas State University for the $250 blood test. It is technically called a FAVN (Fluorescent Antibody Virus Neutralization) and measures the response of your animal's immune system to the rabies vaccine. Check the website for more information about the FAVN test (https://www.ksvdl.org/rabies-laboratory/favn-test/).

As you research the current regulations, take note of requirements that might affect you. Aruba's policy, for example, is that the dog must have been in the United States continuously for the six months preceding the date of export.

**In the following pages, whenever the APHIS Form 7001 is mentioned, the Canadian International Pet Health Certificate is that country's equivalent.**

## Canada

Taking a dog, whether service animal or pet, from the United States into Canada is simple: just carry a valid and current rabies certificate. (Be aware that Ontario bans pit bulls and other "bully" breeds, and you will be turned back at Immigration and Customs if an agent thinks your dog is one of them.)

As explained earlier in this book, if your animal is a service dog, Canadian airlines and railroads may want to see a health certificate signed by your veterinarian as well as documentary proof of the dog's training and your disability before issuing tickets and allowing it aboard. Many provincial governments allow public venues such as restaurants and sports stadiums to ask for such documents as well.

## United States . . . and Particularly Hawaii

If you're coming in to the U.S. mainland or Alaska from Canada or Mexico, or anywhere else, your dog needs a valid rabies immunization certificate, even if it's from a rabies-free country. (The U.S. federal government doesn't require rabies vaccinations for dogs from rabies-free countries, but all states do.) Your dog must be in good health.

But be aware that Hawaii, a rabies-free state, requires a blood titer test as well as certain other mandatory items before it'll let the dog in. In fact, Hawaii is exceptionally tough, even with service dogs. It's never had a case of rabies and wants to keep it that way.

Normally Hawaii requires pet dogs to be quarantined for up to 120 days after arriving, but makes an exception for guide and service dogs. Nonetheless, the dog must meet the following requirements:

- Be microchipped.
- Have a current rabies vaccination, with the documents including product name, lot or serial number, and expiration date of the lot.
- Have passed one blood titer test after twelve months of age, "with a level of 0.5 I.U. rabies antibody or greater . . . A passing test result is valid for three years."
- Have a valid health certificate (APHIS Form 7001) issued not more than thirty days prior to arrival in Hawaii, attesting that the dog was treated within fourteen days of arrival with Fipronil or equivalent product labeled to kill ticks.
- The tasks the animal has been trained to perform must be disclosed.
- The dog must be traveling with the disabled handler on arrival in Hawaii.

Hawaii's Rabies Quarantine office strongly suggests that all required documents be sent to it well ahead of your arrival date. It must be notified at least twenty-four hours in advance of your arrival and must be informed where the dog will be staying. On arrival at Honolulu International Airport, the dog must be brought to the Airport Animal Quarantine Holding Facility for examination of the paperwork and a check for external parasites.

Or you could request inspection in the terminal rather than the holding facility between 8 a.m. and 4 p.m.—but you must make the request to the Rabies Quarantine Office sat least seven days ahead of time. Your airline must be notified of this as well.

If you are arriving in Hawaii via a cruise ship, things become more complex. "Please contact us directly as the service varies depending on where the ship first docks and whether staff is available on the island," the Rabies Quarantine office says. "There are so many variables that we handle these on a case-by-case basis." The office may need to make arrangements with a local veterinarian to inspect your dog, and you will be responsible for the fee.

For a cruise in late 2017, in addition to the requirements listed above, a service dog handler we know was required to include her itinerary (name of the ship and ports with the dates and times of arrival). She also needed a notarized State of Hawaii Department of Agriculture Dog & Cat Import Form AQS 278 (found on the website shown below) and a record of her dog's current Bordetella and leptospirosis immunizations. She was asked to provide all of the paperwork thirty days prior to arrival on the first island. When planning a cruise with your service dog, always contact the Rabies Quarantine Office, as they suggest, to review current requirements well in advance.

Current information about the Rabies Quarantine Program can be found on the website (http://hdoa.hawaii.gov/ai/aqs/aqs-info). That page, its FAQs, and its links will give you all the information you need. There's a lot of it, updated in 2018. The email address is RabiesFree@Hawaii.gov, and the fax number is 808-483-7161.

## Mexico and Central America

South of the U.S. border, service dogs mostly enjoy no special recognition in law. The political histories and economic conditions of most Latin American countries have kept disability rights from getting much of a foothold. When they manage to get enacted, as they have in Mexico, carrying out the law has lagged behind good intentions.

As a result, expect your service dog to be regarded legally as no more than a pet, and follow the pet import regulations to the letter. They can vary widely among countries.

Also expect your service dog and its papers to be carefully examined at ports of entry—and don't be surprised if you are asked to pay unanticipated "fees" to animal officials.

Happily, many tourist venues will grant access to service dogs, especially popular resorts and restaurants that cater to U.S. citizens and Canadians. When booking a resort suite, hotel room, or restaurant meal, ask.

Central American ports and back-country areas are full of feral dogs. They might take exception to the presence of your service dog—and attack. In *some* countries you can bring a pepper spray canister or other repellent and keep it handy for instant deployment. Check the regulations before going. If you do carry pepper spray, be careful, however, for other dogs may belong to nearby families.

What you can basically expect are three things: (1) A health certificate, either the APHIS Form 7001 or a country-specific one, is required, as is a valid rabies immunization certificate. (2) Implanted microchips are not required in some countries, but don't let that stop you from microchipping your dog. (3) In Central America, titer blood tests for rabies are not required, as they are on some Caribbean islands.

Some countries require immunizations for leptospirosis and other diseases not common in most of the United States and Canada. A few countries require import permits, even for brief visits from cruise ships. **Again, don't expect the following information to be absolutely accurate and up-to-date. We checked everything just before going to press, but south of the border, regulations change fast and frequently.**

## MEXICO

Since 2015 Mexico City has had a municipal ordinance allowing service dogs full access to public spaces in the capital with city-issued ID cards, but reports are that the law is spottily enforced.

If you take a service dog into Mexico, be careful with the paperwork. For instance, Mexican officials will reject an international health certificate filled in by hand, or if the vet employs common abbreviations such as "Jan." for "January," "AZ" for "Arizona," or "mos." or "yrs." instead of "months" or "years." Ask your vet to spell out everything and fill in the form on a computer, then print it out.

For documentation, Option A is a partly bilingual version of Form 7001 that must be signed by an APHIS-accredited veterinarian within ten days prior to export and then endorsed and sealed by an APHIS regional Veterinary Service Center. It expires after thirty days.

Travelers coming from the United States have Option B, a bilingual health certificate imprinted on an APHIS-accredited vet's letterhead, with template language as provided by Mexico with no changes. Option B does not require endorsement. The certificate is good for six months.

Whether it's a 7001, the Canadian equivalent, or a vet's health certificate, the document must be in both English and Spanish and must have a rabies vaccination and expiration date and a statement that the animal was examined and found healthy. The vet must attest that the animal was treated against ectoparasites and endoparasites in a period not longer than six months prior to export.

When crossing the border, your dog and its documents will be inspected by Mexican officials.

## BELIZE

*An import permit is required for all animals,* and a fee of $50 BZD (about $25 USD) applies for the application process. Telephone: 011-501-824-4872/99; fax: 011-501-824-4889; email: animalhealthbz@gmail.com.

Visit the Belize Agricultural Health Authority, or BAHA (baha.org.bz/ departments/animal-health/entry-requirements/) for more information to down-load the import permit application form. A veterinary certificate (Form 7001) issued by an APHIS-accredited vet in the United States must attest that the dog is "clinically healthy, free of signs of infectious and contagious disease, is free of ticks and has no fresh wound or wound in the process of healing." A current vaccination against rabies is required, and the date of vaccination and the trade name of the vaccine must be indicated on the certificate. The 7001, signed by an APHIS-accredited veterinarian, does not need to be endorsed by an APHIS official. Finally, Belize "strongly recommends" that the dog be vaccinated against distemper, hepatitis, leptospirosis, and parvovirus, and that pets be treated against endo-parasites and ectoparasites within thirty days of exportation. All incoming dogs will be inspected at the port of entry by a BAHA official.

## COSTA RICA

Costa Rica requires a bilingual Veterinary Health Certificate for the Export of Cats and Dogs from the United States to Costa Rica, available online from the APHIS website. The certificate must show vaccination against rabies, *moquillo* (distemper), hepatitis, leptospirosis, and parvovirus. The vet must attest that the animal was treated within the fifteen days prior to exportation with approved products for endo- and ectoparasites, ensuring that animals are free of ticks and other external and internal parasites. The health certificate must be filled out by a USDA-accredited veterinarian and endorsed by APHIS. If you are shipping your dog separately, you also need an import permit, and the person receiving the dog at the port needs a customs clearance authorization form. The Costa Rican government recommends hiring a local customs broker to help with this matter.

The APHIS Pet Travel website advises for Costa Rica that "health certificates may be issued electronically by the USDA Accredited Veterinarian and endorsed by the APHIS Veterinary Medical Officer through the online Veterinary Export Health Certification System (VEHCS). The APHIS embossed seal is not required. Note: a printed paper copy of the completed health certificate must accompany each shipment."

## EL SALVADOR

El Salvador requires its own health certificate in duplicate (available online from the APHIS website), a rabies vaccination certificate, and a pet import permit issued by the General Direction of Plant and Animal Health, Ministry of Agriculture and Livestock of El Salvador. The permit can be obtained either before travel or when you arrive at the port of entry. If you want to get it ahead of time, call the nearest El Salvador consulate. The health certificate does not need to be endorsed by APHIS.

## GUATEMALA

You will need to have a bilingual Guatemala-specific version of Form 7001 found on the APHIS website (or Canada's equivalent) filled in, signed by a registered veterinarian, and endorsed by a government official for travel from the United States or Canada.

The APHIS Pet Travel website advises for Guatemala that "health certificates may be issued electronically by the USDA Accredited Veterinarian and endorsed by the APHIS Veterinary Medical Officer through the online Veterinary Export Health Certification System (VEHCS). The APHIS embossed seal is not required.

Note: a printed paper copy of the completed health certificate must accompany each shipment."

## HONDURAS

The APHIS site states that the requirements for pet travel to this country are not known, but it recommends that you travel with a Form 7001 issued by a USDA-accredited veterinarian and endorsed by APHIS. According to a tourism website, an international health certificate filled out by your veterinarian no more than ten days before departure is required. A query to Mahogany Bay Cruise Center in the port of Roatan brought this answer: "For Honduras the following vaccines are required: 1. Leptospirosis 2. Hepatitis 3. Parainfluenza 4. Parvo Virus 5. Canine Distemper 6. Rabies. Once the vaccines are confirmed, an inspection is required at inward clearance. The inspection fees are USD$23.00. If the guest does not intend to go ashore, NO inspection is required." At press time the government website (www .honduras.com/requirements-for-traveling-to-honduras-with-a-pet) was not up.

## NICARAGUA

The Nicaraguans require an International Health Certificate for Dogs from the United States to Nicaragua, available online from APHIS. It should be made out at least in duplicate but does not need to be signed by a notary or stamped by a Nicaraguan consul. A dog accompanying you on an airplane or a ship does not need an import permit, but a quarantine permit must be obtained at Nicaraguan ports of entry upon arrival. A rabies vaccination certificate should accompany the health documents.

## PANAMA

This country requires an international health form signed by your vet and endorsed by APHIS or CFIA, then stamped by a Panamanian consul or embassy *before* travel. If you live in a state without a Panamanian diplomatic office, the certificate can be stamped by the U.S. State Department's Office of Authentications, Bureau of Consular Affairs, in Washington, D.C. See the website for further information (https://travel.state.gov/content/travel/en/legal-considerations/judicial/authentication-of-documents/apostille-requirements.html). All this has to be done within ten days of travel, so be prepared to pay for an overnight envelope containing two prepaid envelopes, one to the Panamanian consulate or embassy and one back to you. Finally, you must notify Panama at least three days before arriving by completing a Home Quarantine Request, downloadable from http://www .minsa.gob.pa, and emailing it to cam@minsa.glob.pa. In the email you must provide a scanned copy of the health certificate as well as information related to your dog's date of arrival, time, flight number, and airline (or cruise ship). And, oh yes, in addition to the valid document of rabies vaccination, the dog must have current vaccinations for distemper, parvovirus, and leptospirosis.

# The Caribbean, Bahamas, and Bermuda

### ANGUILLA

USDA APHIS reports, as of early January 2019, that it has no information on requirements for Anguilla. However, the Anguilla government website (http://www.gov.ai/pets.php) offers simple pet import requirements: A dog must be accompanied by a vet-signed Form 7001, or the Canadian equivalent, and must have a rabies vaccination between thirty days and one year before entering. To obtain an import permit, call the Anguilla Agriculture Department (264-497-2615 or fax 264-497-0040).

### ANTIGUA AND BARBUDA

USDA APHIS says, as of early January 2019, it has no official information about this country's requirements but recommends traveling with a 7001 endorsed by APHIS as well as proof of a current rabies vaccination. Antigua's published rules are stiff and can be found at http://www.antigua-barbuda.org/Import%20 Requirements%20for%20importing%20pets.pdf. An animal import permit is required, as is a microchip; a titer test must be performed, and the dog must have a rabies immunization within one year before arrival. (No two- or three-year vaccinations.) The dog must be tested for Ehrlichia and Lyme disease and the results provided. The Form 7001 or Canadian equivalent must have been issued no more than seven days before arrival. And no pitbulls. To obtain an import application, contact the Veterinary and Livestock Division, P.O. Box 1282, Friars Hill Road, St. John's, Antigua. Fax or phone: 268-460-1759 or 462-6104; email: vld@ab.gov.ag.

### ARUBA

Aruba's Veterinary Health Certificate for Export of Dogs and Cats from the United States of America to Aruba (found on the APHIS website) must be issued within fourteen days of arrival into Aruba by an APHIS-accredited veterinarian and endorsed by an APHIS Veterinary Service Center. You must bring a valid certificate of rabies inoculation, and your dog must have an Avid brand or ISO compatible microchip. (For another type of microchip, you can bring your own microchip scanner capable of reading it.)

The dog must have been in the United States continuously for the six months preceding the date of export. If the dog or cat is younger than six months, it must have been born and lived continuously in the United States at the date of export. Written exemption from these requirements must be obtained from the head of the Veterinary Service of Aruba. Telephone: +297-5850400; fax: +297-5851828; or email: vetservice@aruba.gov.aw.

## BAHAMAS

An animal import permit is required for all dogs entering Bahamian waters, as is a health certificate provided by the Bahamas and filled out by your vet, and proof of rabies immunization, *even if your dog stays aboard a ship docked in port or anchored offshore*. To apply for the permit, fill out the form found on the APHIS website and send it by overnight mail with US$10 in cash or money order—no checks—(plus US$5 if you want the signed permit faxed back to you) to the Director of Agriculture, Department of Agriculture, Levy Building, East Bay Street, P.O. Box N-3704, Nassau, Bahamas. Telephone: 242-325-7502 or 242-325-7509; fax: 242-325-3960. Apply at least four weeks in advance. Include proof that your dog is a service animal (copies of your training organization card, IAADP card, and the like) with a note if you wish to request a waiver of the $10 fee. You might ask your vet to fax the application under his or her letterhead; that may result in a much quicker response. Note that the Bahamas requires examination of the dog by a veterinarian for internal and external parasites no more than forty-eight hours before ship departure or flight time.

## BARBADOS

Getting a dog into this country is quite complex, and the requirements for bringing one by air and bringing one on a cruise ship are different. See the APHIS website for full details. The Barbados government link to obtain an import permit was down as of early January 2019. To get that permit as well as all details, we recommend writing or phoning the Barbados Veterinary Services Department, The Pine, St. Michael BB11091, Barbados, 246-535-0221 or 246-535-0226. The dog will also need an APHIS-endorsed Form 7001, a microchip, certain immunizations besides rabies, and *maybe* a blood titer test.

The APHIS Pet Travel website advises for Barbados that "USDA Accredited Veterinarians may issue health certificates electronically through the online Veterinary Export Health Certification System (VEHCS). *Health certificates must then be printed and require the APHIS Veterinary Medical Officer's original signature with the application of the APHIS embossed seal.* NOTE: A printed paper copy of the completed health certificate must accompany each shipment."

## BERMUDA

The Veterinary Health Certificate for Export of Dogs and Cats from the United States of America to Bermuda form is available on the APHIS website. The procedure is to visit your accredited veterinarian to obtain a microchip (if your dog doesn't have one), international health certificate, and the Bermuda-required veterinary statements within ten days of your arrival in that country. Then fax the veterinary documents to 441-232-0046. A response with an import permit will be by fax, usually within one business day. Be sure that your fax number is shown on the application form. The fax import permit and the original veterinary certificates must accompany the animal on arrival in Bermuda. For more information see the government website (https://www.gov.bm/importing-animals-bermuda). The dog will need to have had anti-tick and, of course, rabies immunizations. Certain breeds are restricted or prohibited entirely. A customs officer examining your dog may ask for a refundable deposit before allowing the animal into the country. There are no laws specific to service dogs. Period. You'll have to inquire well ahead if hotels and restaurants will allow your dog.

## BONAIRE, SINT EUSTATIUS, AND SABA

APHIS says, as of early January 2019, it has not been officially informed about the requirements of these Netherlands outpost islands but recommends a Form 7001 issued by a USDA-accredited veterinarian and endorsed by an APHIS official, a rabies certificate, and a microchip. The dog should be vaccinated against canine distemper. The Bonaire Information Site (https://www.infobonaire.com/getting-to-bonaire/visiting-bonaire-with-your-pet) recommends that your vet complete and sign the Bonaire Veterinary Certificate available on the site.

## BRITISH VIRGIN ISLANDS

The British Virgin Islands have stiff requirements for bringing a dog. Your animal must be microchipped and must have an import permit, a government-endorsed health certificate, a rabies blood titer test under specific conditions, and the usual parvovirus/distemper/hepatitis-adenovirus, parainfluenza, leptospirosis, and Lyme disease vaccinations. The APHIS website has downloadable copies of the import application and links to the conditions of import—the required immunizations and the details of bringing the dog into Tortola airport or a cruise ship port. Fortunately, the fee for the permit is only US$10. Further information is available from the Department of Agriculture, Paraquita Bay, Tortola, phone: 284-495-2532; airport office: 284-494-3701, ext. 6449; fax: 284-495-1269; email: agriculture@bvigovernment.org.

## CAYMAN ISLANDS

This country's requirements are complex but not confusing. Besides a country-specific international health certificate available at USDA APHIS, the usual immunizations are required, plus microchipping and a blood titer test, and an import permit that you must obtain. Pit bulls and other fighting dog breeds are forbidden. The APHIS site has a helpful list that will direct you to the relevant documents on the Cayman Islands government website. That site warns you to start the process no fewer than six months ahead of entry.

### CUBA

This country has no service dog laws, so you are on your own finding accommodations that will accept your dog. USDA APHIS has no official information, but other sources say that bringing a dog into the country is fairly easy. No microchip or blood titer test is required, nor is an import permit. Proof of rabies immunization and an APHIS-endorsed Form 7001 are all that is needed.

### CURAÇAO

A country-specific international health certificate prepared by an APHIS-accredited veterinarian and endorsed by USDA APHIS (available at APHIS for download), a valid rabies certificate, and an ISO microchip are required for entry. Also, the dog must be treated for ectoparasites forty-eight hours before departure and endoparasites fourteen days before departure. No pit bulls.

### DOMINICA

USDA APHIS has no official information about this country, but other sources say an import permit must be obtained, and to get it the dog owner must have a blood titer test for rabies done and must obtain the usual Form 7001 and rabies certificate. The dog must be certified parasite-free as well as heartworm-free by a U.S. veterinarian. Further information may be available by writing divisionofagriculture@dominica.gov.dm, or calling the Dominica embassy in Washington, D.C. (202-364-6781).

### DOMINICAN REPUBLIC

It's comparatively easy to get a dog onto this island. According to USDA APHIS, a rabies immunization and a country-specific international health form prepared by an APHIS-accredited veterinarian and endorsed by APHIS are all you need. APHIS has the health form online, and it is valid for ten days after issuance.

### GRENADA

As of January 2019, USDA APHIS has no official information for this country. However, the Grenada government website does offer instructions for the importation of dogs and cats (https://www.grenadaembassyusa.org/wp-content/uploads/2017/02/Instructions-for-Pet-Permit-Feb-2017.pdf). To obtain an import permit, write or call Veterinary Department, Ministry of Agriculture Ministerial Complex, Botanical Gardens, Tanteen St. George's, Grenada W. I. Telephone: 473-440-2708; fax: 473-440-4191, or email livestock@gov.gd or grenadalivestock@gmail.com. The permit needs to be filled out and faxed to the island's veterinary department with a return fax number for reply. The fee is US$15. In addition, other sources say Grenada recommends obtaining an international health form endorsed by APHIS or CFIA and that the country does not recognize the three-year vaccination.

## GUADELOUPE

APHIS says the requirements for exporting a pet to France should be followed: the dog must be microchipped, vaccinated against rabies at least twenty-one days before entering the country, and have a European Union health certificate signed by an accredited veterinarian and endorsed by APHIS.

## HAITI

APHIS says it hasn't been officially informed about the requirements of pet travel to Haiti, but other sources suggest that all you need for that country is an APHIS-endorsed Form 7001 (it is good for fourteen days in Haiti), plus proof of rabies immunization.

## JAMAICA

Getting a dog into this country is extremely involved. First, a rabies vaccination and then implantation of a microchip are required, followed by a rabies antibody test given not less than three months and not more than twelve months after the blood is drawn. Examinations of feces and for external parasites must be performed. Other vaccinations must be given. All these health reports must be submitted to the proper ministry before an import permit is issued. A fourteen-day quarantine upon arrival may be required. APHIS has a link to the Jamaican website containing the guidelines for importation (https://www.aphis.usda .gov/pet-travel/health-certificates/non-eu/jamaica-pet-guidance.pdf). For further information contact the Permit Unit of Veterinary Services Division at vsdpermits@gmail.com or 876-927-0594; 876-977-2489/92. Pit bulls and other fighting breeds are banned.

## MARTINIQUE

A Form 7001 signed by your veterinarian plus a valid rabies vaccination thirty days before travel is all that is required. According to the APHIS Pet Travel website, an APHIS endorsed International Health Certificate is not required.

## MONTSERRAT

USDA APHIS offers no information about pet travel to this island, but other sources say a rabies vaccination, a Form 7001 completed within seventy-two hours prior to entry, and an animal import permit are required. In some cases *a four-month house quarantine may be imposed.* For details and to apply for an import permit, contact the Montserrat Department of Agriculture, P.O. Box 272, Brades, Montserrat. Telephone: 660-491-2546/2075; email: malhe@gov.ms.

## PUERTO RICO AND THE U.S. VIRGIN ISLANDS (ST. THOMAS, ST. CROIX, AND ST. JOHN)

Look on the APHIS Pet Travel website's "Travel with your pet state to state" drop-down menu for full details. Since Puerto Rico is a self-governing Commonwealth in association with the United States and the U.S. Virgin Islands are U.S. territories, the ADA applies. By law, public accommodations must accept service dogs (but now and then, as in the mainland United States, you may encounter folks who are unfamiliar with the ADA). A Form 7001 health certificate with proof of rabies immunization is required. In both locales, microchips are not required but are recommended. Puerto Rico, however, forbids entry of "bully breeds" such as pit bulls, Staffordshire terriers, and mixes of those breeds.

### SINT MAARTEN/ST. MARTIN

A special veterinary health certificate, issued by an APHIS-accredited veterinarian and endorsed by APHIS, for Sint Maarten (site of the airport for both Dutch and French sides of the island) is required, as is an animal import permit. Links to both are available from the APHIS website. Your dog must be immunized against rabies, distemper, hepatitis, parvovirus, leptospirosis, and adenovirus, it must carry a microchip, and it must be declared free of internal and external parasites. No pit bulls are allowed.

### ST. KITTS AND NEVIS

This country is exceptionally hard-nosed about dogs brought into it. Your dog must have not one but *two* rabies titer tests. A microchip, a valid rabies immunization certificate, an APHIS-endorsed Form 7001 with evidence of internal and external parasite treatment, and an import permit (form available at APHIS) are also required. No pit bulls, American bulldogs, Staffordshire terriers, Dogos Argentinos, Presa Canarios, Fila Brasileiras, or Japanese Tosas allowed. All dogs must be home quarantined for thirty days upon entry. Euthanasia or deportation is threatened if all requirements are not met.

### ST. LUCIA

This is also one of the tougher countries to get a dog into. It requires a blood titer test for rabies no less than six months before entering the island, a St. Lucia–specific health certificate endorsed by APHIS, and specific vaccinations as well as microchipping. APHIS has the various forms online, and so does the St. Lucia government website. The particular requirements for dogs are on the latter website (http://www.govt.lc/services/veterinary-import-permit). Pit bulls and similar dogs are prohibited.

## ST. VINCENT AND THE GRENADINES

This country requires ISO microchipping and a blood titer test as well as vaccinations against rabies, canine distemper, parvovirus, leptospirosis, hepatitis, and parainfluenza not less than seven days prior to import. A heartworm test and treatment for external and internal parasites are also needed. Full information about requirements can be found on the APHIS link to the country-specific international health certificate (https://www.aphis.usda.gov/pet-travel/health-certificates/non-eu/st-vincent-grenadines-dog-cat.pdf). The health certificate must be endorsed by APHIS.

## TRINIDAD AND TOBAGO

These islands' requirements are both rigorous and complex, and the best way to meet them is to obtain an application for an import permit from the Veterinary Officer, Havelock Street, Curepe, Trinidad, West Indies. Telephone: 768-662-5986 or 868-642-0063/4, or at the USDA APHIS link to the import permit application. A health certificate, ISO-compatible microchip, proof of rabies vaccination, blood titer test, and either a thirty-day or six-month quarantine may be required; quarantine space must be applied for at least three months before entry. Quarantine fees also apply. Special conditions apply for service dogs; to obtain them, write the Head Office, Animal Production and Health Division, Ministry of Food Production, Trinidad and Tobago, 80 Abercromby St., Port-of-Spain, Trinidad and Tobago. Telephone: 868-625-5997/1473; email: aphmalmr@gmail.com or aphmalmr@tstt.net.t.

## TURKS AND CAICOS

The requirements are complicated and lengthy, so read them carefully on the APHIS website and talk to your APHIS-accredited vet well in advance of your proposed travel date. An APHIS-endorsed, country-specific health certificate must be issued no more than ten days before travel, and it must be completed, signed, and endorsed in a color other than black. (The form also has a section to be signed by the dog's owner, who must accompany the dog.) The dog must have a rabies certificate and proof of a blood titer test. It must also have a microchip or tattoo and must be vaccinated against canine parvovirus, distemper, hepatitis, adenovirus, parainfluenza, leptospirosis, and Lyme disease. The vet must attest on the form that the animal has been spayed/neutered and was treated against internal parasites (including tapeworms) and external parasites (including ticks) within fourteen days of the scheduled date of entry. The country's import permit must be obtained (the application is available for download at APHIS). Six breeds, including pit bulls and Staffordshire terriers, are prohibited, and seventeen others are restricted. Port or airport officials must be given forty-eight hours' advance notice before arrival so that the dog can be inspected. If these regulations are not followed, the animal will be returned to the country of origin. For full details, email agriculture@gov.tc.

# South America

Although this book is primarily for travelers from and in North America, many Caribbean cruises stop at two countries on the South American geological plate that borders the Caribbean Sea.

### COLOMBIA

This country's requirements call for a country-specific health certificate endorsed by APHIS within ten days of travel (available on the APHIS website) and a valid rabies certificate. The dog also must be vaccinated against distemper, hepatitis, leptospirosis, and parvovirus. A microchip is not required but is recommended, and so is a flea and tick program. Travel with at least one photocopy of the original health certificate. Almost always, Colombian officials will inspect your dog and its paperwork at the port of entry. The APHIS Pet Travel website advises for Colombia that "health certificates may be issued electronically by the USDA Accredited Veterinarian and endorsed by the APHIS Veterinary Medical Officer through the online Veterinary Export Health Certification System (VEHCS). The APHIS embossed seal is not required. Note: a printed paper copy of the completed health certificate must accompany each shipment."

### VENEZUELA, INCLUDING MARGARITA ISLAND

An APHIS-endorsed country-specific health certificate within two weeks of travel is required, in duplicate. The dog must have a valid rabies certificate and be vaccinated for distemper, hepatitis, leptospirosis, parvovirus, and parainfluenza virus.

# Appendix 5

# Useful Organizations and Links

## Government Services

### CANADIAN FOOD INSPECTION AGENCY (WWW.INSPECTION.GC.CA/)

This federal department issues health certificates for animals traveling abroad.

### CANADIAN TRANSPORTATION AGENCY

The CTA's page "Travelling with a Service Animal" (https://otc-cta.gc.ca/eng/service-animals) is another source of health certificate information for Canadians with service dogs who want to travel inside and outside the country. The site also has a link to the Canadian Food Inspection Agency's animal health certificates.

### U.S. ARMY MEDICAL COMMAND

The U.S. Army Medical Command's "Guidance on Service Animals" (https://www.army.mil/article/81195/the_united_states_army_medical_commands_guidance_on_service_animals) is a short outline of the army's commitment to service dogs for needful soldiers.

### U.S. CENTERS FOR DISEASE CONTROL AND PREVENTION

The CDC, the nation's health protection agency, aims to protect people from potential threats to health, safety, and security. "Traveling with Pets" (https://www.cdc.gov/features/travelwithpets/index.html) provides travel information and requirements for animals entering the United States.

### USDA ANIMAL AND PLANT HEALTH
### INSPECTION SERVICE (APHIS)

"APHIS Pet Travel" (https://www.aphis.usda.gov/aphis/pet-travel) provides U.S. service dog partners with essential health information on foreign travel as well as the Form 7001 international health certificate and other country-specific health certificates.

### U.S. DEPARTMENT OF JUSTICE, CIVIL RIGHTS DIVISION

The Department of Justice's "Frequently Asked Questions about Service Animals and the ADA (https://www.ada.gov/regs2010/service_animal_qa.html) is the clearest, most useful explanation of the rights of service dog handlers as well as those of venues they might visit.

### U.S. DEPARTMENT OF LABOR

The Department of Labor's "Disability Resources" (https://www.dol.gov/odep/topics/disability.htm) contains useful listings of disability-specific organizations and links to them.

### U.S. DEPARTMENT OF VETERANS AFFAIRS

The VA's "PTSD: National Center for PTSD" (https://www.ptsd.va.gov/gethelp/dogs_ptsd.asp) is a useful information page on acquiring PTSD service dogs and explains the VA's evolving stance on their efficacy.

### U.S. TRANSPORT SECURITY ADMINISTRATION

The TSA's "Disabilities and Medical Conditions" (https://www.tsa.gov/travel/special-procedures) explains how people with disabilities will be examined at airport security gates. Scroll down to "Please choose a situation to see more information" and click on "Service Dogs and Animals."

## Service Dog and Dog Training
## Umbrella Organizations

### ASSISTANCE DOGS INTERNATIONAL

Assistance Dogs International
P.O. Box 276
Maumee, OH 43537
419-350-5788                          www.assistancedogsinternational.org

This is the number one go-to source for information about service dogs the world over, especially if you're an interested person with a disability. A coalition of nonprofit training groups, it doesn't train dogs itself but accredits facilities that pass its tests for rigorous training and behavior standards. It not only offers useful FAQs but also pages on how to find training programs in every U.S. state and Canadian province. There are also pages for many European and Asian countries.

## ASSOCIATION OF PROFESSIONAL DOG TRAINERS

2635 Harrodsburg Road A325
Lexington, KY 40504                                                    www.apdt.com

An excellent source for finding general trainers to help a service dog partner maintain and improve the animal's skills.

## CANADA'S GUIDE TO DOGS

www.canadasguidetodogs.com

Here's a comprehensive website of all things canine north of the border, including breed information and, most important, a lengthy section devoted to service dog entities across the provinces (https://canadasguidetodogs.com/working-dogs/service-dogs/).

## INTERNATIONAL GUIDE DOG FEDERATION

Hillfields, Burghfield Common
Reading, UK RG7 3YG                                                    igdf.org.uk

This group is roughly similar to Assistance Dogs International, but it is devoted to guide dogs for persons who are blind or sight-impaired. Based in the United Kingdom, it offers programs for assessment and accreditation of dogs and their training facilities.

## CERTIFICATION COUNCIL FOR PROFESSIONAL DOG TRAINERS

Professional Testing Corporation
1350 Broadway, 17th floor
New York, N.Y. 10018                                                   www.ccpdt.org

An independent certifying organization for maintaining professional standards, and a good place to check out the bona fides of a dog trainer.

## GOLDEN STATE GUIDE DOG HANDLERS

1271 Washington Avenue, #144
San Leandro, CA 94577
510-846-4080

A relatively new (founded 2017) group serving California guide dog partners.

## GUIDE DOG USERS OF CANADA

214 Rose Street
Barrie, ON L4M 2V1
Canada                                    gduc.ca/gduc/member/about.asp

Publishes a newsletter for its members as well as a comprehensive list of guide dog schools and organizations.

## GUIDE DOG USERS, INC.

3603 Morgan Way
Imperial, MO 63052                        guidedogusersinc.org

A leading consumer-driven international organization of guide dog handlers that advocates for the rights of guide dog users everywhere. The website contains helpful resources and an Internet "chat list" open to all with an interest in guide dogs.

## INTERNATIONAL ASSOCIATION
## OF ASSISTANCE DOG PARTNERS (IAADP)

P.O. Box 638
Sterling Heights, MI 48311                www.iaadp.org

A nonprofit, cross-disability organization for people already partnered with service dogs of all kinds. It advocates, educates, and provides a host of useful links such as Who's Who in the Assistance Dog Field and Assistance Dog Laws and Legal Resources. The authors of this book believe that everyone with a service dog should be a member.

## MY ASSISTANCE DOG, INC.

Address unlisted
Clovis, CA                                www.myassistancedoginc.org

Contains an excellent resource directory of dog providers, financial aid for acquiring a dog and paying vet bills, care and health, laws, and organizations.

## NATIONAL ASSOCIATION OF GUIDE DOG USERS

Jernigan Institute, 200 East Wells Street
Baltimore, MD 21230                       www.nagdu.org

A division of the National Federation of the Blind, this advocacy group provides useful information about legal rights as well as details about sound training practices.

## PSYCHIATRIC SERVICE DOG PARTNERS

1651 Sandpiper Drive
Rock Hill, SC 29732                                    www.psychdogpartners.org

The organization's stated purpose "is to promote the mental health of people using service dogs for psychiatric disabilities by educating, advocating, providing expertise, facilitating peer support, and promoting responsible service dog training and handling."

## SERVICE DOG CENTRAL

www.servicedogcentral.org

This is an excellent online information resource for U.S. service dog partners and people interested in the issue. It offers a useful community forum on a range of topics and a clear and understandable FAQ list. One of the questions answered is how to spot people fraudulently trying to pass a pet off as a service dog. Finding a trainer is also a well-researched topic.

## U.S. COUNCIL OF GUIDE DOG SCHOOLS

625 West Town Street
Columbus, OH 43215                                          No website

A consortium of schools that train guide dogs for the blind to high standards and work on safety and access issues. They meet once a year to review new materials and training methods.

# Service Dog Training Organizations
# Cited in This Book

*(Needless to say, many other excellent programs exist in the United States and Canada)*

## CANINE COMPANIONS FOR INDEPENDENCE (CCI)

P.O. Box 446
Santa Rosa, CA 95402-0446                                    www.cci.org

## DIAMOND DOGZ OF ARIZONA

P.O. Box 13163
Scottsdale, AZ 85267                                    www.diamonddogzaz.org

## DOGS FOR BETTER LIVES (FORMERLY DOGS FOR THE DEAF)

10175 Wheeler Road
Central Point, OR 97502                    www.dogsforbetterlives.org

## GUIDE DOGS FOR THE BLIND (GDB)

P.O. Box 151200
San Rafael, CA 94915                        www.guidedogs.com

## INTERNATIONAL HEARING DOG, INC.

5901 E. 89th Avenue Henderson, CO 80640
303-287-EARS                               www.hearingdog.org

## MIRA FOUNDATION INC.

1820 Rang Nord-Ouest
Sainte-Madeline, QC J0H 1S0
Canada                                      www.mira.ca

## MIRA FOUNDATION USA

77 Cherokee Rd.
Pinehurst, NC 28374                         www.mirausa.org

## NEADS WORLD CLASS SERVICE DOGS

P.O. Box 1100
Princeton, MA 01541                         www.neads.org

## PALMETTO ASSISTED ANIMAL LIFE SERVICES (PAALS)

221 N. Grampian Hills Road
Columbia, SC 29223                          www.paals.org

## PAWS WITH A CAUSE

4646 S. Division St.
Wayland, MI 49348                           www.pawswithacause.org

## PSY'CHIEN

Marie-Ange Saintagne
16 rue du Père Brottier
Meudon, 92190
France                                      www.psychien.org

## PSY'CHIEN INTERNATIONAL

675 rue de Cadillac
Montreal, QC H1N 2T2
Canada                                    www.psychien.org

## SERVICE DOGS, INC.

4925 Bell Springs Rd.
Dripping Springs, TX 78620                www.servicedogs.org

## SOUTHEASTERN GUIDE DOGS

4210 77th Street East
Palmetto, FL 34221                        www.GuideDogs.org

## THAMES CENTRE SERVICE DOGS

23698 Sutherland Rd.
Mount Brydges, ON N0L 1W0
Canada                          www.thamescentreservicedogs.com

# Miniature Service Horse Organizations

## GUIDE HORSE FOUNDATION

1775 West Williams Street, PMB 120
Apex, NC 27523                            www.guidehorse.com

# Disability Organizations Serving Communities That Use Service Dogs

## ALEXANDER GRAHAM BELL ASSOCIATION
## FOR THE DEAF AND HARD OF HEARING

3417 Volta Place NW
Washington, DC 20007                      www.agbell.org

## AMERICAN ASSOCIATION OF PEOPLE
## WITH DISABILITIES (AAPD)

2013 H Street N.W., 5th Floor             www.aapd.com
Washington, DC 20006             communications@aapd.com

### AMERICAN COUNCIL OF THE BLIND

1703 Beauregard St., Suite 420
Alexandria, VA 22311　　　　　　　　　www.acb.org

### AMERICAN FOUNDATION FOR THE BLIND (AFB)

2 Penn Plaza, Suite 1102
New York, N.Y. 10121　　　　　　　　　www.afb.org

### AMERICAN DIABETES ASSOCIATION

2451 Crystal Drive, Suite 900
Arlington, VA 22202　　　　　　　　　www.diabetes.org

### AMPUTEE COALITION OF AMERICA

9303 Center Street, Suite 100
Manassas, VA 20110　　　　　　　www.amputee-coalition.org

### ASSOCIATION OF LATE DEAFENED ADULTS (ALDA)

8038 Macintosh Lane, Suite 2
Rockford, IL 61107　　　　　　　　　www.alda.org

### AUTISM SOCIETY

4340 East-West Highway, Suite 350
Bethesda, Md. 28014　　　　　　　　www.autism-society.org

### AUTISM SPECTRUM DISORDER FOUNDATION (ASDF)

228 W. Lincoln Highway, Suite 301
Schererville, IN 46375　　　　　　　　www.myasdf.org

### CANADIAN COUNCIL ON REHABILITATION AND WORK (CCRW)

477 Mount Pleasant Road, Suite 105
Toronto, ON M4S L29
Canada　　　　　　　　　　　　www.ccrw.org

### CANADIAN NATIONAL INSTITUTE FOR THE BLIND (CNIB)

1929 Bayview Avenue
East York, ON M4G 0A1
Canada　　　　　　　　　　　　www.cnib.ca

## APPENDIX 5

### DIABETES CANADA

1400-522 University Avenue
Toronto, ON MSG 2R5
Canada                                    www.diabetes.ca

### DISABLED AMERICAN VETERANS (DAV)

3275 Alexandria Pike
Cold Spring, KY 41076                     www.dav.org

### EASTER SEALS

141 W. Jackson Blvd., Suite 1400A
Chicago, IL 60604                         www.easterseals.com

### EPILEPSY FOUNDATION

8301 Professional Place East, Suite 200
Landover, MD 20785
www.epilepsy.com/learn/seizure-first-aid-and-safety/staying-safe/seizure-dogs

### HEARING LOSS ASSOCIATION OF AMERICA (HLAA)

7910 Woodmont Avenue, Suite 1200
Bethesda, MD 20814                        www.hearingloss.org

### NATIONAL ASSOCIATION OF THE DEAF (NAD)

8630 Fenton Street, Suite 820
Silver Spring, MD 20910                   www.nad.org

### NATIONAL AUTISM ASSOCIATION (NAA)

One Park Avenue, Suite 1
Portsmouth, RI 02871              www.nationalautismassociation.org

### NATIONAL DISABILITY RIGHTS NETWORK (NDRN)

820 1st Street NE, Suite 740
Washington, DC 2002                       www.ndrn.org

### NATIONAL FEDERATION OF THE BLIND

200 East Wells Street at Jernigan Place
Baltimore, MD 21230                       www.nfb.org

### NATIONAL ORGANIZATION ON DISABILITY

77 Water Street, Suite 204
New York, N.Y. 10005                                    www.nod.org

### PARALYZED VETERANS OF AMERICA

801 Eighteenth Street NW
Washington, D.C. 2006-3517                              www.pva.org

### TASH (FORMERLY THE ASSOCIATION OF PERSONS WITH SEVERE HANDICAPS)

1875 Eye Street NW, Suite 582
Washington, DC 2006                                    www.tash.org

### UNITED CEREBRAL PALSY (UCP)

1825 K Street NW, Suite 600
Washington, DC 20006                                   www.ucp.org

### UNITED SPINAL ASSOCIATION

120-34 Queens Boulevard #320
Kew Gardens, NY 11415                          info@unitedspinal.org

### WORLD INSTITUTE ON DISABILITY (WID)

3075 Adeline Street, Suite 155
Berkeley, CA 94703                                     www.wid.org

# Checklists

## The Basics

○ Take trial runs to give your dog a little experience before an ambitious trip.

○ Mind your dog's relief habits; keep to a schedule and train the dog to use a relief box.

○ Prepare a "go bag" of food and meds suitable for the trip you're taking.

○ Be wise about where you take your dog.

○ Know the law and be ready to defend your presence.

○ Call ahead to hotels, restaurants, airlines, and so forth, and let them know you are bringing a service dog.

○ Carry a current rabies certificate and, if traveling outside the United States or Canada, at least an APHIS Form 7001 International Health Certificate or the Canadian International Health Certificate for Dogs and Cats.

○ Carry ID cards, if your dog's training organization has issued them, and dress your dog in an identifying vest.

○ Make sure your dog obeys all accepted service animal behavioral standards—and be ready to retrain him if he slips.

**NOTES**

# Air Travel

○ Before going through airport security with your dog, familiarize yourself with TSA service animal rules.

○ If you have metal in your body, give your dog a few "dry runs" with the help of a friend willing to simulate a TSA pat-down.

○ For a smoother trip through security, enroll in TSA PreCheck or Global Entry.

○ Consider limiting your dog's food and water before a flight.

○ Ask the airline for a bulkhead seat, if you wish, or a coach seat with extra room.

○ Arrange for special assistance in advance and at the check-in counter if you have a mobility disability.

○ Locate airport animal relief facilities online, both outside and inside the security-sanitized zone.

○ Go online to check the service animal policy of the airline you are flying.

○ When flying outside the United States or Canada, investigate animal import rules and documentation for your destination.

**NOTES**

# Rail Travel

○ When planning a train ride, consider your dog's relief needs.

○ Pack sufficient food and treats for your dog.

○ Let the conductors and attendants know <u>your</u> needs as well as your dog's.

○ Always make sure the conductors and your car attendant know when and where you get off the train to relieve your dog, and always stay within their sight.

○ You have three choices of accommodations: inexpensive and roomy coach seats, quieter business class on some trains, or more costly roomettes or full bedrooms on overnight trains.

○ You can take your dog to the dining car, but you may prefer to remain at your coach seat or in your sleeper room, where attendants will bring your meals. (Be sure to tip.)

○ Be careful when moving between cars, especially on Amtrak, where the sharp footplates are dangerous.

○ It is a good idea to call ahead with Amtrak so that crews are ready for you. In Canada, providing documentation is essential for VIA Rail rides.

**NOTES**

# Road Travel

○ If you don't have access to a car, use a taxicab or a ride-sharing service such as Uber for short trips, or book a bus for longer journeys with your dog.

○ Protect your dog while traveling in your car with a harness or other restraint system.

○ Pace yourself on long road trips for your dog's well-being and your own enjoyment.

○ Notify tour operators in advance that extra space will be needed in vehicles for your service dog.

○ Travel with your dog's complete medical records and carry a first aid kit for emergencies.

○ Be vigilant in unfamiliar locations for potential hazards to your dog's health, including other dogs with bad intentions.

**NOTES**

# Cruises

- ○ Always check with a cruise line (or have your travel agent do so) about the line's service dog policy before booking a cruise.
- ○ Fill out the cruise line's special needs forms and advise them of your expectations, especially what you want for the dog's relief box.
- ○ Pack enough food and meds for the entire cruise plus a few days' extra.
- ○ Pay particular attention to required documentation for foreign ports, including proof of rabies vaccination, international health certificates, and dog import permits.
- ○ When arriving at the cruise terminal, have copies of all your dog's documentation ready to give the ship's personnel.
- ○ Upon boarding ship, make sure the relief box's location and filling meets your dog's needs.
- ○ Next, consult the dining room maître d' to reconfirm your request for a suitable table for the duration of the voyage.
- ○ Survey the ship for protected places to sit, such as in the theater, where your dog won't be stepped on.
- ○ Be ready to fend off friendly fellow passengers who want to interact with your dog.
- ○ Never leave your dog unattended aboard ship, even in your stateroom.
- ○ Tip well for exceptional personal service.
- ○ When booking foreign shore day trips, ask the cruise line's excursions department to obtain advance permissions to bring your dog with you.
- ○ For reentry into the United States or Canada, keep your dog's original documents in your hand luggage in case officials request it.

**NOTES**

# Paperwork

○ Find the current animal import requirements for your destination on the APHIS or CFIA websites, but be aware they may change.

○ Plan way ahead—even by months. Obtaining documentation could be time-consuming.

○ Always carry at least a rabies certificate and APHIS Form 7001 or the Canadian equivalent wherever you go.

○ When obtaining documentation, work with an APHIS- or CFIA-accredited veterinarian.

○ Go one step further and gather together all your dog's documentation, including training certificates, to carry in your hand luggage. More is always better where foreign country officials are concerned.

○ Have your dog microchipped, even if a foreign country may not require it.

○ Consider buying travel insurance.

**NOTES**

# Acknowledgments

First among equals who have helped us with this book are Henry's wife, Deborah Abbott, and Chris's husband, Robert Goodier. They have been not only patient but also encouraging, and have offered excellent counsel as well as companionship on our travels.

In the travel industry, we owe much to John Busbee and Marc Magliari of Amtrak; Jessica Correa Hernandez and Bernest Castro Arrieta of the National Aviary of Colombia; Johannes Urbanski of VIA Rail Canada, and Michael McCarthy of the Transport Security Administration.

The USDA APHIS Veterinary Trade Services staff answered our questions about the Online Veterinary Health Certification System.

Toni Eames, president of the International Association of Assistance Dog Partners, Ruth Lando of Southeastern Guide Dogs, and Deborah Guy of the School of Social Work, Marywood University, provided valuable information.

We particularly appreciate the insights of fellow service dog partners Vince F., Jean M. and her husband Tom, Najawarie, Eric W. and his mother Sarah, David Caras, Mary Seamon, Rosalyn Silberschein, Dianne Urhausen, Amy Bosworth, Flo Kiewel, Diane Munro, Gayle Crabtree,

Steve White, Suzy Wilburn, Morgan W., Jen, and Melanie, as well as an early peer reviewer of the manuscript who prefers to remain anonymous.

At the University of Illinois Press, we owe a great deal to our acquisitions editor James Engelhardt, whose counsel made this book better than it might have been, and to Paul Arroyo, Margo Chaney, Jennifer Comeau, Kevin Cunningham, Jane Curran, Kirsten Dennison, Jennifer Fisher, Heather Gernenz, Katherine O'Neill, Michael Roux, Roberta Sparenberg, and Alison Syring. We thank Sheila Bodell for her expert indexing.

We owe much to customer support departments everywhere for trying their best, even if their best at first wasn't always helpful.

And, of course, Raylene and Trooper, graduates of Dogs for Better Lives, to which this book is dedicated.

Thank you all.

# Index

# About the Authors

**Henry Kisor** is the author of nine previous books. Three are nonfiction—*What's That Pig Outdoors? A Memoir of Deafness*, *Zephyr: Tracking a Dream across America*, and *Flight of the Gin Fizz: Midlife at 4,500 Feet*. Six are mystery novels set in the Upper Peninsula of Michigan: *Season's Revenge*, *A Venture into Murder*, *Cache of Corpses*, *Hang Fire*, *Tracking the Beast*, and *The Riddle of Billy Gibbs*.

He was the book review editor and critic for the *Chicago Daily News* and *Chicago Sun-Times* from 1973 to his retirement in 2006. In 1981 he was a finalist for the Pulitzer Prize in Criticism and is a member of the Chicago Journalism Hall of Fame.

His service dog, Trooper, is an eighteen-pound "schnoodle"—a miniature schnauzer/miniature poodle cross. Trooper came to him in 2015 from Dogs for the Deaf (now Dogs for Better Lives), a training facility in Central Point, Oregon. Trooper alerts Henry to sounds of all kinds: fire and smoke alarms, doorbells and knocks, alarm clocks, oven timers, Instant Pots, telephone rings, the call of his name—and small boys speeding by on bicycles.

Henry Kisor and his hearing dog, Trooper, an eighteen-pound schnoodle, during a photo excursion to the Chicago Botanic Garden in Glencoe, Illinois. (Photograph by Deborah Abbott)

Together Henry and Trooper have traveled North America from coast to coast as well as much of the Caribbean, Colombia, Panama, Guatemala, and the west coast of Central America.

**Christine Goodier** is a Florida-based freelance writer who learned the nuts and bolts of travel during twenty-eight years of marketing work for international airlines, cruise lines, cultural attractions, and resorts. Her career path also led to the John F. Kennedy Center for the Performing Arts in Washington, DC, where she was an event planner and fundraiser.

After moving to St. Croix, U.S. Virgin Islands, in 1999, Chris began writing for in-flight magazines, hotel websites, and tourist guides. She was managing editor of *St. Croix This Week* from 2003 to 2005 and editor

Christine Goodier and her hearing dog, Raylene, a seventy-pound Labrador, enjoy sunset from the deck railing of a cruise ship as it departs St. Thomas. (Photograph by Robert Goodier)

of *All at Sea,* a monthly magazine distributed to Caribbean boaters, from 2006 to 2010.

Upon returning to the continental United States, Chris and her husband Bob acquired a small recreational vehicle van and set out to see America in it. Since 2011, she has written more than twenty travel articles for *MotorHome,* a magazine for RV enthusiasts.

At last count, Chris has visited sixty-four countries, eight Canadian provinces, and all fifty of the United States. She has been accompanied since 2014 by her hearing dog, Raylene, a seventy-pound black Labrador. Raised by Guide Dogs for the Blind, Raylene unfortunately failed her vision test due to a tiny cataract but made a serendipitous career change with the help of Dogs for the Deaf.

The University of Illinois Press
is a founding member of the
Association of University Presses.

---

University of Illinois Press
1325 South Oak Street
Champaign, IL 61820-6903
www.press.uillinois.edu